T0333628

# TEXANS
## AT
# ANTIETAM

# Reviews for *Texans at Antietam*

This encyclopedic compilation of primary sources on the renowned Texas Brigade at Antietam belongs in every Civil War enthusiast's library.
- John Michael Priest, author of *Before Antietam: The Battle For South Mountain and Antietam: The Soldiers Battle.*


Joe Owen, Phil McBride and Joe Allport's, *Texans at Antietam* is a remarkable accounting of the fabled Hood's Texas Brigade at Antietam. Volumes have been written regarding the actual combat that bloody September 17th. However, the authors have performed a remarkable task transcribing the heroic exploits of Hood's Texas Brigade that fateful day. This spellbinding narrative is not accomplished through a scholarly discussion of the strategy involved in those breathtaking hours whereupon the Texas Brigade held the left against overwhelming odds, but through the accounts of individual soldier-participants on the ground. The narrative is coupled with commentary of mainly local newspapers attempting to make sense of the carnage that befell their citizen-soldiers so far from home, as well as the reports of those in command of the units involved.

While a profusion of accounts exists on that battle *per se*, as well as Hood's Texas Brigade's involvement therein, nothing thus far brings home the actual fighting experienced by the common soldier that day as well as the authors' superb narrative. I highly recommend this work to anyone who has an interest in the involvement of Hood's Texas Brigade and its fateful, yet glorious encounter at Antietam, where it enhanced its fame as "Lee's Grenadier Guard." My sincere congratulations to the authors on a riveting and extremely well-presented work.
- John F. Schmutz, author of *"The Bloody Fifth": The 5th Texas Infantry Regiment, Hood's Texas Brigade, Army of Northern Virginia: Vol.1: Secession to the Suffolk Campaign.*


"Such havoc is awful," wrote a Texas newsman about the horrific losses of the 1st Texas at Sharpsburg while awaiting further information from the far-off battlefield. Over the course of the next few decades, recollections of the savage fighting near Antietam Creek poured in to Lone Star papers. Authors Joe Owen, Phil McBride, and Joe Allport have compiled many of these old accounts as a testament and enduring record of the Texans who fought so hard during America's "Bloodiest Day." - Scott L. Mingus, Sr., co-author of *The Second Day at Gettysburg: The Attack and Defense of Cemetery Ridge, July 2, 1863.*


At Gaines Mill, Sharpsburg, Gettysburg, Chickamauga, and the Wilderness, Hood's Texas Brigade earned, with their sacrifice and blood, the nickname of Gen. Robert E. Lee's "Grenadier Guards." Joe Owen, Philip A. McBride, and Joe Allport have written fascinating selected biographies of the soldiers, and collected an amazing array of reports, letters, memoirs, and newspaper articles detailing the privations and heroics of the Texan's fight near the Dunker Church and Miller's cornfield. Highly recommended!
- Zack C. Waters, co-author of *A Small but Spartan Band: The Florida Brigade in Lee's Army of Northern Virginia*

# TEXANS AT ANTIETAM

## A TERRIBLE CLASH OF ARMS, SEPTEMBER 16–17, 1862

### JOE OWEN, PHILIP MCBRIDE AND JOE ALLPORT

FONTHILL

*Front cover:* 'Heart of Texas' by Mark Maritato. (*www.maritato.com*)

*Back Cover:* "Bloody but Unbeaten." The Battle for Dunkard Church, Antietam, September 17, 1862. (*Chris Collinwood. collingwoodhistoricart.com*)

Fonthill Media Language Policy

Fonthill Media publishes in the international English language market. One language edition is published worldwide. As there are minor differences in spelling and presentation, especially with regard to American English and British English, a policy is necessary to define which form of English to use. The Fonthill Policy is to use the form of English native to the author. Joe Owen, Philip McBride and Joe Allport were born and educated in the United States; therefore American English has been adopted in this publication.

Fonthill Media Limited
Fonthill Media LLC
www.fonthill.media
books@fonthill.media

First published in the United Kingdom and the United States of America 2017
Reprinted 2024

British Library Cataloguing in Publication Data:
A catalogue record for this book is available from the British Library

Copyright © Joe Owen, Philip McBride and Joe Allport 2017, 2024

ISBN 978-1-62545-022-7

The right of Joe Owen, Philip McBride and Joe Allport to be identified as the authors of this work has been asserted by them in accordance with the Copyright, Designs and Patents Act 1988.

All rights reserved. No part of this publication may be reproduced, stored in a retrieval system or transmitted in any form or by any means, electronic, mechanical, photocopying, recording or otherwise, without prior permission in writing from Fonthill Media Limited

Typeset in 10pt on 13pt Sabon
Printed and bound in England

*To the soldiers of Hood's Texas Brigade, who fought and died on September 17, 1862 during the bloody battle of Antietam (Sharpsburg).*

*Yea, though I walk through
the valley of the shadow of death,
I will fear no evil: for thou art with me;
thy rod and thy staff they comfort me.*

Psalm 23, Verse 4 (KJV)

*From this day to the ending of the world,
But we in it shall be remembered—
We few, we happy few, we band of brothers;
For he today that sheds his blood with me
Shall be my brother.*

Shakespeare, *Henry V*

Corporal Howard E. Perry, 1st Texas Infantry, killed at the Battle of Antietam, September 17, 1862. (*Texas Heritage Museum–Historical Research Center*)

# Foreword

The columns dressed in gray and butternut wound their way through the swift current of the Potomac River. Private John W. Stevens of the 5th Texas recalled that day in early September, 1862. As the bands played airs such as 'Dixie' and 'Maryland My Maryland', Stevens recalled:

> All the men are apparently jolly. I, at least did not feel very jolly … I could not for the life of me suppress a feeling of sadness as I beheld this vast concourse of humanity wading the river, so full of music and apparently never once thinking that their feet (many of them) would never press the soil on the south side of the Potomac again.

This Confederate Army had been fighting all that summer, defending the capital of Richmond and repelling General George B. McClellan and his Army of the Potomac from the Virginia Peninsula; they then marched to northern Virginia to defeat the Union Army of Virginia under General John Pope at Second Manassas.

The Army of Northern Virginia, dubbed with that title by its commander, General Robert E. Lee, entered Maryland in high spirits. Yet a closer look at the soldiers of this army reveals many troubling signs. Thirty years of examining letters, diaries, and reminiscences of the soldiers reveal a number of common denominators. For one, these men were tired: they had fought the battles around Richmond, marched about 100 miles, and fought the battles of the Second Manassas Campaign. Now these mighty warriors were entering Maryland, and maybe Pennsylvania, for more campaigning.

Food was another issue: these men were hungry. Often, they were reduced to eating green corn. Many Confederates wrote home telling of their great fatigue and hunger. This in turn caused sickness. Indeed, many were too sick to go on. Studies show that thousands stayed on the south side of the river. Not because of objections to invading the north, as has sometimes been erroneously stated in some histories, but rather they were too sick to go on. The Texans were no exception. Except for a half ration of beef and green corn, the Lone Star soldiers had gone for three days without food prior to arriving at Sharpsburg.

Lee's army represented a cross section of the American South. Nearly 25 percent were from Virginia. Another 21 percent hailed from Georgia. All other deep South states were represented. The Texas Brigade entered Maryland as one of the smallest commands in the Army of Northern Virginia. This was in no small part to the casualties incurred at Second Manassas, where the 5th Texas earned the dubious sobriquet "the Bloody Fifth." On September 2, 1862, the Texas Brigade numbered 2,177 men. It is estimated that 854 men were present for duty at Sharpsburg. Out of this number, 548 were casualties; the overall casualty rate for Hood's Texas Brigade was 64 percent, the third highest for a brigade in any single battle.

Hood's Texans had been marching and fighting since April. Like much of Lee's army, their uniforms were ragged and many were without shoes. However, morale was high and combat efficiency had been finely honed fighting the many battles in Virginia. In an age where the average American traveled no farther than about 20 miles from their homes in a lifetime and with no television, cell phones, or computers, the Texans may as well been on the moon. These men were 1,500 miles from home in a strange land with barns described as bigger and better built than any of the buildings in Waco (a description written the following year on the way to Gettysburg), lush wheat and cornfields, and in many cases well-constructed macadam roads.

Although most of the men no doubt did not realize it at the time, from their positions in Western Maryland, the Shenandoah Valley of Virginia was less than a day's march away. There, not far from them across the Potomac River, was Martinsburg, Virginia (later West Virginia). Near here, Davy Crockett's grandfather settled in the mid-eighteenth century prior to moving to Tennessee. About 150 miles farther south, Sam Houston was born. So, in many ways, the roots of the Lone Star State were in the Shenandoah Valley with the Scots Irish settlers, many of whom would move farther south and westward to Texas.

For the Texans, Antietam (or, as the Confederates called the battle, Sharpsburg) was one of the bloodiest battles during their tenure with Lee's army. It was the bloodiest one-day battle of the War Between the States, as Lee's army suffered more than 10,300 casualties. Colonel Harold B. Simpson, in his seminal work *Hood's Texas Brigade: Lee's Grenadier Guard*, aptly points out that "the stellar performer at Antietam was the First Texas Infantry." Leading the advance of Hood's entire division, the First Texas took 226 men into the fight and came out of the fray with 186 killed, wounded, and missing. This staggering loss of 82.3 percent was the highest casualty rate in a single day's combat for either side during the war. The Texas Brigade lost sixteen color bearers during the bloody battle. Nine of them were from the First Texas. One soldier recalled that the Yankees were "cutting [them] down almost like grain before a cradle." Through all of this combat, the Texans made sites such as the Dunker Church and "The Cornfield" household names and among the greatest landmarks on any Civil War battlefields.

Hood's Brigade was one of the last Confederate units to cross the Potomac back to Virginia late on September 18. In three months of campaigning, the Brigade had marched approximately 500 miles, fought in seven engagements, and incurred 1,800 casualties. After Sharpsburg, the Brigade would never be the same numbers wise. However, it had two more years of hard campaigning and fighting at battles such as Gettysburg.

Joe Owen, Phil McBride, and Joe Allport have put together a masterpiece of combat history. With this book, *Texans at Antietam: A Terrible Clash of Arms, September 16–17, 1862*, the reader experiences the battle first hand with accounts by the men who were there. The editors are to be commended for their diligent research, which yielded rare accounts from letters, memoirs, and newspapers. This is a must read for anyone interested in the Texas Brigade and the Battle of Antietam.

Ted Alexander
Historian (retired)
Antietam National Battlefield

# Acknowledgements

Many people, organizations, and academic institutions were instrumental in the successful completion of *Texans at Antietam: A Terrible Clash of Arms, September, 16 17 1862*.

The authors would like to thank American Historical Artist Mark Maritato for providing the outstanding painting "Heart of Texas," which graces the front cover of the book. Artist Chris Collingwood for providing the outstanding painting "Bloody but Unbeaten, The Battle for Dunkard Church, Antietam, September 17, 1862," which graces the back cover of the book.

The authors would like to thank the outstanding publishing and editing team at Fonthill Media—Alan Sutton, Jay Slater, and Joshua Greenland. Alan, Jay, and Joshua's enthusiasm, profound patience, editing, and wise advice was greatly appreciated. Also, a special thank you to all the people at Casemate.

Antietam National Battlefield Historian (Retired) Ted Alexander, whose enthusiasm, support, and knowledge was crucial in the completion of *Texans at Antietam: A Terrible Clash of Arms, September 16-17, 1862*; author and historian John Schmutz, who graciously provided much of the information on the 5th Texas Infantry at the Battle of Antietam; noted Civil War author and historian John M. Priest, who allowed us to use the letters written by Stephen Elliot Welch in *Stephen Elliot Welch of the Hampton Legion*, as well as his great editorial advice was extremely helpful and appreciated; and John Wiley, one of the leading historians of author Margaret Mitchell and her famous book and movie, *Gone With the Wind*— John provided great information and history of Margaret Mitchell's grandfather, 1st Sergeant Russell Crawford Mitchell of the 1st Texas Infantry Regiment. Our thanks also go to Mark Lemon, great-great-grandson of Captain James Lile Lemon of the 18th Georgia Infantry Regiment. Mark graciously allowed us to publish Captain Lemon's letter about the Battle of Antietam.

Much admiration and appreciation to Civil War historians Scott Mingus Sr., Chris Mackowski, Randy Drais, and Jim Schmick, who is the owner of the outstanding bookstore "Civil War and More" in Mechanicsburg, PA. Jim's great knowledge of

Hood's Texas Brigade in the Antietam and Gettysburg Campaigns was very useful and appreciated in the research of the campaigns. Thanks to Zack Waters and Cooper Wingert—their knowledge, professionalism, and support is valued and appreciated; cartographer Natalie Wolchover, who designed and drew the outstanding map of Hood's Texas Brigade at the Battle of Antietam; a special thank you to Leah Krause of Brunk Auctions; a heartfelt thank you to Patty Branard Gambino, the great-granddaughter of the 1st Texas Infantry's Color Sergeant George A. Branard— Patty and her husband, Sal, provided the photograph and biography of Sergeant Branard; Cindy Harriman and Glenda Mounger of the Texas Division of the United Daughters of the Confederacy; Amy Bowman and Aryn Glazier of the Dolph Briscoe Center for American History; and Anne Peterson of DeGolyer Library at SMU. Appreciation to photographers Diane Kirkendall and Brian Duckworth; and to the Texas Heritage Museum–Historical Research Center Director and Curator John Versluis and his outstanding staff, Rica Acevedo and Mary Ann Schneider—their knowledge, kindness, and professionalism is unsurpassed. Thanks also to author Robert Reichardt for his advice and editing skills; Elsa Vorwerk, who graciously provided the letters and history of Adjutant Campbell Wood and 2nd Sergeant William L. (Bose) Campbell of the 5th Texas Infantry; John Hoopes, who allowed us to use the memoirs of his great-great-grandfather Private William Abernathy of the 17th Mississippi Infantry; Michele Lambing of the Texas State Preservation Board, Texas Historical Baptist Museum; Jerry Nelson, who provided much of the fascinating history of the 5th Texas Infantry at Sharpsburg; author and historian Steve Chicoine; Cynthia Dorminey for creating the image of the Hampton's Legion flag flown at Sharpsburg; Nancy Tilden and Stuart Smith; Keith Snyder of Antietam National Battlefield; Kenny Dee, who graciously provided the image of Sergeant D. H. Hamilton; Finney Clay; and Tom Stevens. Thanks to the State of Texas Archives; Library of Congress; Larry Terlecki; Alexander Shane; Patrick Pelarski; Brian Perry; and Brian Vickers.

Many thanks to Commander Bill Smith, 1st Lt. Commander Sanford Reed, and the rest of the men of Hood's Texas Brigade-Sons of Confederate Veterans Camp #153 of San Antonio, Texas, whose support, enthusiasm, and generosity is unsurpassed. Thanks also to Sam Hanks, a descendent of Amos Hanks of the 1st Texas Infantry, who generously provided much background material about Lieutenant Colonel Philip A. Work, commanding officer of the 1st Texas Infantry at the Battle of Antietam. We would also like to thank Bernadette Loeffel-Atkins and Kevin Drake, owners of "Battlefields and Beyond" bookstore in Gettysburg, PA; their welcomed advice about editing and publishing was valued and deeply appreciated. Thanks to the members and leaders of the great organization "Gettysburg Past and Present," an outstanding group of dedicated Civil War and battle of Gettysburg enthusiasts, their love and appreciation of the war and the battle of Gettysburg is outstanding, and their civic service to the town and battlefield at Gettysburg is unsurpassed. We would also like to thank author and great friend Lee Lawrence, whose support and advice was greatly appreciated. Much appreciation to Laura Munson Cooper, who graciously gave information about John W. Hanks of the 3rd North Carolina Infantry, and Dr. Shirley Beck of Blanco, Texas, whose knowledge of the men and women of Civil War Texas and their daily lives gave an invaluable insight to the mindset of the soldiers that fought in the Civil War and their families left behind in Texas. A special thank also goes to Wil and Debra Williams for their great support and enthusiasm.

Outstanding author, historian, and friend Stephen (Sam) M. Hood, a descendent of General John Bell Hood, provided great information and fact checking about General Hood and his Texas Brigade regiments. Miss Dollye Jeffus, the great-granddaughter of Colonel A. T. Rainey, who was the original commanding officer of the 1st Texas Infantry Regiment; Miss Dollye's support and knowledge of the soldiers of Hood's Texas Brigade, is an inspiration, and her approval and enthusiasm of *Texans at Antietam: A Terrible Clash of Arms, September 16-17, 1862* is valued and appreciated.

The authors also thank their wives, Cathy Owen, Debbie Morphew Allport, and Nita McBride for their love, support, and extreme patience in our endeavors of researching and writing *Texans at Antietam: A Terrible Clash of Arms, September 16-17, 1862.*

Joe Owen, Philip McBride, and Joe Allport
December 20, 2016

# Contents

# Introduction

Shortly after the first shots of the Civil War were fired at Fort Sumter, South Carolina, cadet Campbell Wood, a student at the Texas Military Institute in Fayette County, Texas, received a letter from his father. It read:

My Dear Son:

I hand you herewith a check on W. M. Rice of Houston. Pay your bills, come home and join the army.

Affectionately,
[signed] Green Wood.[1]

This brief letter by Texas plantation owner Green Wood to his son, Campbell, succinctly reflects the war fever that struck Texas in 1861. Thousands of young men, including nineteen-year-old Campbell Wood, flocked to county seats all over east Texas to do just as Wood's father directed: "join the army." A surge of volunteers across east Texas travelled to their county seats to enlist in newly formed independent companies, which elected their own captains and lieutenants. In the fall and winter of 1861, and in early 1862, thirty-two of these companies made their way to Virginia. They were designated the 1st, 4th, and 5th Texas Infantry Regiments, the core of Hood's Texas Brigade.

There were never enough Texas infantry in General Robert E. Lee's army for them to compromise a wholly Texan Brigade of four or five regiments. Therefore, during the first half of the war, including the three great battles at Gaines' Mill, Second Bull Run (Second Manassas), and Antietam (Sharpsburg), the 18th Georgia Infantry Regiment and Hampton's South Carolina Legion were brigaded with the Texans.

## Eltham's Landing to Second Manassas

On May 7, 1862, the Texas Brigade fought its first engagement at Eltham's Landing on the Pamunkey River, north of Richmond, Virginia. With orders to "gently feel" the enemy, the Texans pushed the Union forces over a mile, all the way back to the banks of the Pamunkey. The Brigade's first battle casualties were incurred at Eltham's Landing, Virginia. Eleven enlisted men and four officers died in the relatively small battle, and another twenty-five were wounded. Most of the casualties were taken by the 1st Texas Regiment, which led the brigade formation.[2]

The following month, the Seven Days Battles around Richmond provided the Texas Brigade another chance to cover itself in bloody glory and begin to win its nickname, "Lee's Grenadier Guard." At Gaines' Mill, on June 27, 1862, the Texans made an improbably successful attack through Boatswain's Swamp up Turkey Hill to break the strong Federal position on the slopes and hillcrest. The 4th Texas Regiment and the 18th Georgia Regiment incurred the most casualties. In the 4th Texas, half the riflemen and all the field grade officers were killed or wounded. In all, the five regiments in the Texas Brigade suffered 152 killed and 456 wounded at Gaines' Mill.[3] The building of the Texan's reputation as aggressive fighters had begun.

In late August, on the second day of the Battle of Second Manassas (August 30, 1862), the Texas Brigade was part of the attack of Longstreet's Corps. The 5th Texas Infantry went into its day of reckoning with over 400 men. Unrestrained, the 5th Texas, along with the 18th Georgia and Hampton's Legion, smashed into the 5th New York and 10th New York Infantry regiments, giving and receiving casualties at an appalling pace.

By dark on August 30, the 5th Texas had outdistanced their Georgia and South Carolina support and driven 2 miles into the flank of the Union Army, demolishing two Union infantry regiments and overrunning two enemy battery positions. The cost to the 5th Texas was high: fifty-four dead, 143 wounded, and seventeen missing—214 casualties, over 50 percent. As had happened to the 4th Texas at Gaines' Mill, all three of the 5th Texas regimental command officers were killed or wounded.

## A Perspective in Deaths

Two great American armies clashed on September 16 and 17, 1862, at Antietam, Maryland. Known as the Battle of Antietam by the Union and the Battle of Sharpsburg by the Confederates, the day-long battle near Antietam Creek on September 17 is widely recognized as the single bloodiest day in American history.

On that one day, 3,911 American soldiers died in battle, far more than during either day at Shiloh, Tennessee, four months earlier, or during the one-day bloodbath at Perryville, Kentucky, three weeks after Antietam. More soldiers died at Antietam than during any single day at Gettysburg, Pennsylvania, the following summer.[5]

More American soldiers died at Antietam, where muzzle-loading muskets and smooth-bore cannons dominated the field, than during any one day during the Battle of Argonne Forest in 1918, during World War I, where machine guns and artillery chewed men to pieces.

Twice as many Americans died at Antietam than the 2,499 American servicemen killed on D-Day, June 6, 1944, during World War II.[6]

Finally, the number of soldiers killed at Antietam surpasses the 2,996 deaths suffered during the terrorist attacks on September 11, 2001.[7]

As horrific as all those death numbers are, this author is compelled to note that Civil War deaths were caused by Americans engaged in war with other Americans. In 1862, we did not need a European army opposing us, a suicidal terrorist enemy, or modern weaponry to inflict the single most horrendous death toll in our nation's history. We did it to ourselves.

## The Brigade at Antietam

With virtually no time for new recruits to reach the Texas Brigade during the campaign, and having sustained significant casualties in three battles, the three Texas infantry regiments marching into Maryland in September, 1862, were small. The 1st Texas was comprised of 226 soldiers and the 4th Texas was even smaller, with 200 men in the ranks after their losses at Gaines' Mill. The 5th Texas, fresh from its bloody day at Second Manassas, could field only 175 riflemen.[8] On the eve of the Battle of Antietam, the combined strength of the only three Texas Infantry regiments in the Army of Northern Virginia was just 600 men, the whole brigade under 900 men.

Hood's Texas Brigade played its part early in the battle. During the late afternoon and early evening of September 16, the entire brigade deployed as skirmishers and engaged in hot firefight in Miller's cornfield and in the East Woods with the Union General Seymour's brigade of Pennsylvanians. With darkness, both sides withdrew for the night.[9]

The battle began in earnest the next morning, September 17, even before the men in the Texas Brigade could cook and eat a dawn breakfast—their first issued rations in three days. Leaving their half-cooked meals behind, the five regiments deployed in battle lines over the same terrain where they had skirmished barely twelve hours before. Their deployment from the left to right was 18th Georgia, Hampton's Legion, 1st Texas, 4th Texas, and the 5th Texas.[10]

By mid-morning, through notable sacrifice and bravery, Hood's Brigade lost over 60 percent of the roughly 900 riflemen and officers. During the intense fighting for Miller's cornfield, the 1st Texas suffered 182 casualties—82 per cent, the most of any Confederate regiment in one battle during the entire war. The 4th Texas, fighting along Hagerstown Pike to the left of the 1st Texas, lost 107 riflemen. Also on the Hagerstown Pike, the 18th Georgia took eighty-five casualties, and Hampton's Legion fifty-three casualties. Meanwhile, the 5th Texas regiment, engaged in the East Woods to the right of Miller's Cornfield, suffered eighty-two casualties—50 percent.[11]

The human cost was again horrifically high, but the Texas Brigade was instrumental at Antietam in stymieing the attack of the Federal right-most divisions.

This book is about those few early morning hours on September 17. However, the authors' intent is not to describe the actions of Hood's Brigade at Antietam in our words—many diligent historians and gifted writers have already done that. Rather, this book presents the reflections of the soldiers of Hood's Brigade through letters and official reports they wrote, newspaper articles, interviews, and speeches they gave after the war.

As the veterans aged, their interests in sharing their war experiences grew. In the early 1900s, city newspapers across Texas published a surge of memoirs written by the old Confederates. For over a century, many of these accounts lay ignored in dusty newspaper archives or on microfiche film in university libraries. Whichever the format, the newspaper articles have been generally overlooked by historians and uncatalogued for researchers.

The internet has finally brought many forgotten treasures back into the light. Diligent researchers can now do online word searches of electronically scanned newspapers to find veterans' letters, recollections, or speeches, bringing those languishing memoirs to the surface. The primary author of this volume, Joe Owen, has done just that. With relentless devotion, Mr. Owen has mined the archives of newspapers and other publications as no other has done. He has rediscovered the words set down by the Texas soldiers who were there, the first-hand accounts written by men for whom the carnage and chaos of Antietam left undeletable memories.

To appreciate a man's words, it is helpful to know something of the man. Therefore, we have included biographical information about most of the soldiers whose comments and reports are included in this volume so the reader might better connect with them.

Finally, we ask the reader to consider the time and place of the Battle of Antietam. Even though the three Texas regiments left the field at Antietam with cumulatively less than 300 riflemen still able to march and bear arms, their war was far from over.

## After Antietam

Impressively, Antietam was the third massive battle in a period of just four months in which one or more of the regiments in the Texas Brigade suffered a 50 percent casualty rate—Lee's Grenadier Guards indeed. Yet, Antietam was not even the halfway point in the Texas Brigade's four-year journey through the Valley of Death. The cycle of attrition from disease, battle transfers, and desertions was to continue for two more years.

Fortuitously, the Brigade was not engaged during the Confederate victories at Fredericksburg or Chancellorsville. A nearly year-long respite from battle allowed time to refill the extremely diminished ranks of the Brigade. The months from October, 1862, to June, 1863, allowed desperately needed weeks for wounded soldiers to heal, as well as time for new recruits to travel from Texas to Virginia. By the time Lee's army began its Pennsylvania campaign in June, 1863, the three Texas infantry regiments could again field over 400 riflemen each.

Even if nearly half the privates in each regiment were fresh replacements, green to the rigors of campaign and the horrors of combat, they were led by veteran officers and non-commissioned officers who had survived one maelstrom after another. The fighting spirit of the Texas Brigade was intact.

When Antietam ended, Gettysburg, in July, 1863, was just nine months away, and Chickamauga was just a few months after Gettysburg. The Texas Brigade was to play a key role in both of those great battles, and it again suffered casualties approaching 50 percent. At Gettysburg, the Brigade suffered 597 casualties, including Texas Brigade's Generals John Bell Hood and Jerome B. Robertson, the colonels of four regiments, and two lieutenant colonels.[12] At Chickamauga in September, the Brigade casualties were 570 men of the 1,300 who travelled from Virginia to Georgia.[13]

With the flow of replacements from Texas dried up, the 1st, 4th, and 5th Texas regiments began the year 1864 with about 200 riflemen in each regiment. In May, 1864, the Texans would again lose half their effectives at the Battle of the Wilderness. In September and October, Lee's stubborn defense of Richmond would cast the Texans into two more devastating battles at New Market Heights, Virginia, and Darbytown Road, Virginia.

When the war finally wound its way to Appomattox in April, 1865, a total of 467 enlisted men and officers in the three Texas infantry regiments of the Texas Brigade received paroles—about 155 men in each of the three regiments. In three and a half years of campaigning, the 1st, 4th, and 5th Texas infantry regiments had each lost over 300 men killed in combat, and over 600 men in each Texas regiment had been wounded once or more. Another 140-plus had died of disease in each regiment. The total attrition rate for the Texas regiments was over 80 percent for the course of the war.

Yes, the men of the 1st, 4th, and 5th Texas Infantry were Lee's Grenadier Guards.

# Uneasiness in Texas

Information about the Battle of Antietam (Sharpsburg) was reaching the Lone Star State at a very slow rate. There were incomplete casualty reports, different rumors of who won the battle, and what the fate of loved ones was. All of these together left many cities and towns in Texas on edge.

*Tri-Weekly Telegraph*
October 3, 1862
The Situation

The indefinite and meagre intelligence from the seat of war renders it exceedingly difficult to form anything like an accurate idea of the position of affairs. We have reliable intelligence of the crossing of the Potomac by Gen. Lee, after the battle at Manassas. From that time up to the date of the latest advices, all is uncertainty, save only that Jackson captured Harper's Ferry and a large number of prisoners; that another severely contested battle has been fought at Sharpsburg; and at Shepardstown. In the fight at Sharpsburg both sides claim a victory. McClellan is reported to have fallen back, and Lee is said to have recrossed the Potomac.

In another dispatch, we have it that only a portion of our army has crossed, while Lee is pressing McClellan with the bulk of his forces. Again, it is said that Lee only went into Maryland to meet and repel a flank movement by way of Harper's Ferry. This he is said to have done at Sharpsburg, and accomplished, he attains his object and recovered the river. But, then, what becomes of his promises to the people of Maryland in his address to them, issued at Fredericksburg?

We deem it a waste of time to endeavor to sift this mass of contradictions and upon the foundation of the most probable events form the most plausible conjecture. As it is impossible to penetrate the plans of our commanders, even when we have reliable advices of the movements in pursuance of those plans, and as we shall soon have intelligence of the development of those plans, we shall content ourselves with summing up the assumed results, and wait with patience further reliable intelligence.

1st. we gave the Yankees a terrible drubbing on the 30th ult., at Manassas; 2nd. on the 5th inst., our army crossed over into Maryland, and occupied the third city of the State; 3rd. on the 15th we captured Harper's Ferry, taking some 12,000 prisoners, large quantities of arms, ammunition, and stores, all of which we secured; 4th. on the 16th we encountered the enemy again at Sharpsburg, and if we didn't whip him, we gave him at least as good as he sent, and made him glad to get off, which was equivalent to a victory four us; 5th. on the 20th, it appears we met and almost annihilated Burnside's division at Shepardstown, taking a large number of prisoners and utterly routing the opposing force, after which Jackson re-crossed into Maryland.

These are results of importance enough to make us satisfied to wait to learn more before we embark upon the uncertain and profitless sea of speculation. Whether Lee has recrossed the Potomac or not does not affect these results; and if he has, we may rest assured it is to accomplish some important purpose, and not because he was driven back.

*Tri-Weekly Telegraph*
October 8, 1862
By The Central Train
The Glorious Victory at Harper's Ferry
The Battle of Sharpsburg

By the Central Train we have the Alexandria (Virginia) *Democrat* extra of the 25th, with the following important intelligences:

Richmond, Sept. 19.—Gov. Leicher has received letters today from Winchester of the 16th, confirming the report of the unconditional surrender of 11,000 Yankees at Harper's Ferry on Monday, without the loss of a man on our side.

General Jackson captured fifty pieces of artillery, ammunitions, stores, &c.

Letters also mention an engagement in Maryland, between Boonesboro and Middleton, in which the enemy were repulsed, with a reported loss of 2,000 in killed and wounded. The Confederate loss is heavy. No further particulars received.

Richmond, Sept. 20.—Col. Lindsay Walker arrived here yesterday from Harper's Ferry, which place he left on Wednesday last.

The cannon and stores captured by the Confederates have been removed.

There had been fighting since the recapture of Harper's Ferry on Monday.

Our army is in fine spirits.

Gen. McClellan, with his army, was in our front near Sharpsburg, and a general engagement was expected.

Gen. Reno (Yankee,) was killed in the fight near Boonesboro', Md.

Gen. Jackson's official report of the capture of Harper's Ferry says:

"Yesterday, God crowned our arms with another brilliant success in the surrender of Harper's Ferry, of Brig. General White and eleven thousand troops, an equal number of small arms, seventy-three pieces of artillery, and about two hundred wagons. In addition to other stores, there is a large amount of camp and garrison equipage. Our losses are very small."

From the *Louisiana Democrat*:

Richmond, Sept. 21.—The Enquirer has a dispatch, dated Warren, 20th, announcing a terrible fight at Sharpsburg on Wednesday. The advantage was on our side—great loss on both sides. Generals Stark, Manning and Branch were killed, and General D. R. Jones, R. R. Jones, Ripley and Lawton wounded.

The whole strength of both armies was engaged in the fight.

The report says the fight was renewed on Thursday, and the enemy routed and driven nine miles.

Richmond, Sept 21.—*The New York Herald* of the 18th claims a victory at Sharpsburg. Its dispatches are contradictory, but concur in stating that the Confederates were defeated.


*Tri-Weekly Telegraph*
October 8, 1862
(Second Column)
By The Central Train
More Heavy Fighting
Houston, Oct. 2d.


Augusta, Sept. 24.—Richmond papers of the 22d report that only a portion of our army crossed the Potomac, but letters from Winchester to the Dispatch say our army crossed without losing a man, or any commissary stores. Gen. Sumner and another Yankee General sent a flag of truce after the battle asking permission to bury their dead. Mr. Boteler says that the evacuation of Maryland is only temporary and that she must and will be redeemed.

Our loss is 5,000, that of the enemy about 20,000. The Enquirer says Major Gen. Anderson was severely wounded. Generals Wright, Lawton, Ripley, Armistead, Ransom, and Col. Cunnings slightly wounded. Gen. Starke and Branch killed. Gen. Toombs slightly wounded.

Mobile, Sept. 25.—A special dispatch to the *Advertiser and Register*, dated Charleston, Sept. 22d, says that the whole of our army has not recrossed into Virginia, but Lee, with the bulk of his army, is in hot pursuit of McClellan.

He came up with him and defeated him on Friday, and continued pursuing him towards Frederick.

Richmond, Sept. 24.—Lynchburg dates of today say that the Yankee column recently routed by Jackson near Sheppard's town was commanded by Burnsides.

Four brigades of the enemy, rushed across the river, when Jackson precipitated his whole force upon them.

They were literally mowed down; so many were killed that the stream was almost jammed up with their bodies.

About 15,000 prisoners were taken, and of the whole force estimated at 20,000, it is thought not more than 2,000 escaped. The casualties on our side are 250 killed, wounded and missing.

*Bellville Countryman*
October 11, 1862
The News

Either from the crookedness of the Potomac river, or the agility of our commanders and their armies, we are unable to tell from the dispatches on which side of the river our armies are at present. It seems certain however that there has been some heavy fighting in Maryland, there being two or three battles immediately succeeding that at Harper's Ferry. There was a heavy battle at Sharpsburg in which Gen. Lee claims a signal victory, altho' the Federals, as usual claim a victory also. Then followed a fight at Shepardstown in which Jackson met a force of 20,000 under Burnside, and *burnt* his *sides* a little more than was his custom. Of the whole force of the enemy but 2,000 escaped. The balance were killed, wounded, driven into the river or captured. There were 15,000 prisoners taken. So many were killed that the stream was almost jammed up with their bodies. Our side lost 250 in killed, wounded and missing.

The reason given for our army's recrossing into Virginia, is to procure supplies.

# 1st Texas Infantry Regiment

List of Companies and First Company Officers of the 1st Texas Infantry:

Company A: (Marion Rifles) Marion County—H. H. Black
Company B: (Livingston Guards) Livingston County—D. D. Moore
Company C: (Palmer Guards) Harris County—A. G. Dickinson
Company D: (Star Rifles) Marion County—A. G. Clopton
Company E: (Marshall Guards) Harrison County—F. S. Bass
Company F: (Woodville Rifles) Tyler County—P. A. Work
Company G: (Reagan Guards) Anderson County—J. R. Woodward
Company H: (Texas Guards) Anderson County—A. T. Rainey
Company I: (Crockett Southrons) Houston County—E. Currie
Company K: (Texas Invincible) San Augustine County—B. F. Benton
Company L: (Lone Star Rifles) Galveston County—A. C. McKeen
Company M: (Sumter Light Infantry)—Trinity County—H. Ballenger

The 1st Texas Infantry Regiment consisted of men mostly from East Texas counties, and was the first regiment from Texas to arrive in the Confederate capital of Richmond, Virginia, in August, 1861, where the Lone Star flag of Texas was presented to the 1st Texas by Lula Wigfall, daughter of the regiment's first colonel, Louis T. Wigfall.[1, 2] By the time of the Battle of Antietam, the regiment and the rest of Hood's Texas Brigade fought, as the battle honors show on the 1st Texas's Lone Star flag, at Eltham's Landing (May 7, 1862), Seven Pines (May 31–June 1, 1862), Gaines' Mill (June 27, 1862), and Malvern Hill (July 1, 1862). The Brigade also fought in the battles of Freeman's Ford (August 22, 1862) and Second Bull Run (Manassas) (August 29–30, 1862), where, on August 29, the 1st Texas lost the greatest number of men—four killed and sixteen wounded and South Mountain (September 14, 1862).[3]

The Battle of Antietam (Sharpsburg) commenced for the Brigade during the evening of September 16, 1862, when artillery action between two batteries

1st Texas Infantry Lone Star flag of Texas flown at Antietam. (*State of Texas Archives*)

1st Texas Infantry Army of Northern Virginia battle flag flown at Antietam. (*State of Texas Archives*)

supporting Hood and two Federal batteries commenced firing on each other.[4] The 1st Texas was the center of the advancing line of regiments led by the Brigade's commander Colonel William Wofford. About an hour before sunset, the Brigade drove part of the 1st Pennsylvania Rifles (Bucktails) and the 3rd Pennsylvania Reserves into the east woods.[5] The Brigade would then spend the rest of the night in the West Woods near the Dunker Church.

During the morning hours of September 17, the men of the Texas Brigade were held in reserve and attempted to cook breakfast as the fighting opened.[6] The Federal Army launched an assault on the Confederate left flank, interrupting the Texans' breakfast preparations. The 1st Texas passed to the rear of Law's Alabama Brigade and came up on its right near the East Woods. The other four regiments were able to maintain their original alignment for only a short time during the advance. Increasing Federal pressure on the Brigade's left flank forced Colonel Wofford and General Hood to shift the 1st and 4th Texas in that direction to Miller's Cornfield, a 40-acre plot that became the focal point of battle on the Confederate left.[7] This placed the 1st Texas in the center of the Brigade, while the 18th Georgia and Hampton's Legion were occupied holding off Doubleday's Division moving down the west side of the Hagerstown Pike and firing into the left flank of Hood's Brigade; Law's Brigade, supported by the 5th Texas, was engaged with the Union XII Corps elements in the East Woods. The 1st Texas then advanced far ahead of the other regiments in the Brigade. For two hours from 7–9 a.m., the 1st Texas barely held on to Miller's Cornfield and the section of the pike that ran along its west side but eventually retreated.[8] General Hood described the two hours of fighting as "the most terrible clash of arms by far that has occurred during the war."[9] As the 1st Texas withdrew from Miller's Cornfield, the ninth color bearer of the day was shot down and the colors lost.[10] Lt. Col. Philip A. Work, commanding the 1st Texas— who saw both the Lone Star flag and the Army of Northern Virginia battlefield flag fall in the cornfield—wrote in his official report of the battle that the 1st Texas could not retrieve them due to the intensity of the action in the cornfield.[11] Nine dead Texans surrounded the Lone Star flag when a Union soldier found it. Flags captured on the battlefield were highly valued prizes and they paraded it around the Federal campfires after the battle.[12] The 1st Texas advanced the farthest of the Brigade in the fight against the Army of the Potomac, but at a horrendous cost. Of the 226 soldiers in the 1st Texas, 186 were either killed or wounded. The 82.3 percent casualty rate of the 1st Texas dead and wounded made it the highest casualty rate of a regiment on either side during the war. In the days, months, and years after the battle, soldiers of the 1st Texas would write about the heroic and tragic action of the officers and enlisted men in the 1st Texas in official reports, speeches, letters to their families, newspapers, and diaries describing the battle and the heroic 1st Texas Infantry.

*Tri-Weekly Telegraph*
October 15, 1862

Our accounts from the terrible battle of Sharpsburg are still meager. We know it was a most desperate battle. We have heard that our own 1st Regiment was cut to pieces, and that not a full company is left of it. Such havoc is awful.

The bravery that encountered it was sublime. Thermopylae witnessed no greater heroism. We dread, but are yet anxious again, to get at the list of the killed and wounded. It must be here soon. The partial list in today's paper is not satisfactory because it is so incomplete.

*The Texas Almanac—"Extra"*
October 16, 1862

We find the following additional in the "News" of yesterday, communicated by Mr. F. L. Thompson direct from Richmond:

He states that the First Texas suffered awfully in the Sharpsburg Battle, in fact was nearly annihilated, only 24 out of the whole regiment escaping. He says, the regiment was ordered to occupy a certain position and hold it, and the position was taken, and for two hours struggled with a whole brigade of the enemy, unsupported as support could not be sent to them in time to save the heroes from the slaughter.

Mr. Thompson says that the only commissioned officer in the whole regiment to escape uninjured were Lieut. Col. Work and Captain Woodward. Capt. Bedell of the Lone Star Rifles was reported too severely injured to be removed from the field, and it is feared that his wounds will prove mortal. A private letter has been received here, stating that the number who escaped in the 1st Texas was 43, and we hope that this is below the real number.

Lieutenant Colonel Phillip A. Work
February 17, 1832–March 17, 1911

Phillip A. Work was born in Cloverport, Kentucky, on February 17, 1832. His family moved to Velasco, Texas, when he was eight years old. His father, John Work, established a plantation near the town of Pine Bluff.[13] He was admitted to the Texas bar in 1853 and began practicing law in Woodville, Texas. In 1853, he enlisted as a sergeant in Captain John G. Walker's Volunteers, fighting the Kiowas and the Comanches on the Texas frontier.[14]

Work represented Hardin and Tyler Counties during the Texas Secession Convention, and when Texas seceded in February, 1861, he returned to Tyler County and recruited men into the "Woodville Rifles," which later became

Lieutenant Colonel Philip A. Work, 1st Texas Infantry. (*Texas Heritage Museum–Historical Research Center*)

Company "F" of the 1st Texas Infantry Regiment.[15] He was elected captain by the company, and when Col. Alexis T. Rainey was wounded during the Battle of Gaines' Mill on June 27, 1862, he became the commanding officer of the 1st Texas. He commanded the regiment in the battles of Malvern Hill, Freeman's Ford, Second Bull Run (Manassas), Antietam (Sharpsburg), Fredericksburg, and Gettysburg. After Gettysburg, Work became seriously ill and was transferred back to Texas. After recovery, he raised and commanded a company in Col. David Smith Terry's Texas Cavalry until the end of the war. After the war, he moved to New Orleans, Louisiana, and in 1874, he moved to Hardin County, Texas, where he returned to his law practice and owned the steamboat, *Tom Parker*. Lt. Colonel Phillip A. Work died on March 17, 1911 and is buried near Kountze, Texas.[16]

Lieutenant Colonel Philip A. Work
1st Texas Infantry

Near Martinsburg, West Va.
September 23, 1862
Colonel W. T. Wofford
Commanding Texas Brigade

Sir: The following is submitted as a report of the part taken by the First Texas Regiment in the engagement of Wednesday, September 17, near Sharpsburg, Md.:

The brigade, having been formed in order of battle upon the ground occupied by it on the night of the 16th, in the following order, to wit, First Texas in the center, Eighteenth Georgia left center, Fourth Texas right center, Fifth Texas on the right flank, and Hampton's Legion on the left flank, was moved forward to engage the enemy about 7 o'clock, the latter having made an attack upon our forces occupying a position in front of this brigade. Advancing through the woods some 200 yards, under a heavy fire of grape, canister, and shell from the enemy's artillery, the brigade emerged into an open clover field some 200 or 250 yards in width, across which the forward movement was continued for some 150 to 200 yards, when it being discovered that the left flank of the brigade was exposed to attack, I was ordered to move by the left flank, following a corresponding move of the Eighteenth Georgia and Hampton's Legion upon my left, which I did until ordered to move by the right flank, which was also done. Advancing now by the right flank (my original front), I entered a corn-field and soon became engaged with a force of the enemy, driving them before me to the farther side of the corn-field. As soon as the regiment became engaged with the enemy in the corn-field, it became impossible to restrain the men, and they rushed forward, pressing the enemy close until we had advanced a considerable distance ahead of both the right and left wings of the brigade. Discovering that this would probably be the case when my men first dashed forward, I dispatched you two different messengers, to wit, Captain John R. Woodward, Company G, and Private A. G. Hanks, Company F, stating that I was driving the enemy, and requesting you to hurry up the regiments on my right and left to my support. It was not until we reached the farther side of the corn-field that I could check the regiment. By this time we had broken the first line of battle of the enemy and had advanced to within some 30 steps of his second line, secreted behind a breastwork of fence rails thrown in heaps upon the ground, when a battery of artillery some 150 or 200 yards in our front was opened upon us. My men continued firing, a portion of them at the enemy's men and others at the artillerists, the result of which was that the enemy's men and others at the artillerists, of the second line broke and fled on the artillery was limbered up and started to the rear, when the whole fire of my regiment was concentrated upon the artillerists and horses, knocking over men and horses with such effect that the artillery was abandoned. Very soon, however, a force of the enemy was moved up to the support of this artillery, when it again opened fire upon us.

Just at the farther side of the corn-field was the point where I was in great doubt as to the proper move to be made by me. I was aware that my regiment had advanced 150 or 200 yards farther than the regiment upon my left, so diverging as to leave a wide interval between the right flank of the Eighteenth Georgia and my left, thus exposing both regiments to attack-the Eighteenth upon the right and the First Texas upon the left flank. I was aware at the same time that a heavy force of the enemy was massed upon my left, and felt confident that in case I moved farther to the front I would be attacked upon my left and rear and annihilated. Had I moved forward to carry the enemy's battery I would have exposed the regiment to attack from three different directions, to wit from the front from infantry and artillery and upon the left and rear from infantry. I am told, also, by some of the men that had I advanced a little farther to the front my right would have become exposed to attack, and am assured that some distance to my front and obliquely to my right was a large force of the enemy. This I did not discover, myself. At this juncture I dispatched Actg. Adjt. W. Shropshire to say to you that, unless the regiments upon my left were moved up quickly to my relief and support upon the left, I would be forced to abandon my position and withdraw. Before the return of Shropshire, a fire of musketry was opened upon me from my left and rear, which determined me at once to withdraw, as I had but a handful of men left, all of whom must have been slain or captured had I remained longer. I at once gave the order to fall back, and the few men remaining to me retired, turning to fire upon the enemy as rapidly as their pieces could be loaded and fired.

I entered the engagement with 226 men, officers-field and staff-included, of which number 170 are known to have been killed and wounded, besides 12 others who are missing, and, doubtless, also killed or wounded.

During the engagement I saw four bearers of our State colors shot down, to wit: First, John Hanson, Company L, second, James Day, Company M; third, Charles H. Kingsley, Company L, and, fourth, James K. Malone, Company A. After the fall of these, still others raised the colors until four more bearers were shot down. Not having seen plainly who these others were, I am unable to give their names in this report, but will do so soon as, upon inquiry, I can ascertain.

It is a source of mortification to state that, upon retiring from the engagement, our colors were not brought off. I can but feel that some degree of odium must attach under the most favorable circumstances, and although such are the circumstances surrounding the conduct of this regiment, the loss of our flag will always remain a matter of sore and deep regret. In this connection it is but proper to state, in addition to that detailed in the above and foregoing report, the additional circumstances and causes which led to its loss. When the order to retire was given, the colors began the movement to the rear, when the color bearer, after moving but a few paces, was shot down. Upon their fall, some half dozen hastened to raise them, one of whom did raise them and move off, when he was shot down, which was not discovered by those serving. While falling back, and when we had nearly reached the clover field hereinbefore alluded to (being still in the corn-field), I gave the order to halt, and inquired for the colors, intending to dress upon them, when I was told that the colors had gone out of the corn-field. Then I gave the order to move on out of the corn and form behind the crest of a small ridge just outside of the corn and in the clover field. It was when I reached this point that I became satisfied our colors were lost, for I looked in every direction and they were nowhere to be seen. It was then too late to recover them.

There was no one who knew the spot where they had last fallen, and, owing to the density of the corn, a view of no object could be had but for a few feet. By this time, also, the enemy had moved up and was within some 35 or 40 yards of my left (proper) and rear, and another force was following us. No blame, I feel, would attach to the men or officers, all of whom fought heroically and well. There was no such conduct upon their part as abandoning or deserting their colors. They fought bravely, and unflinchingly faced a terrible hail of bullets and artillery until ordered by me to retire. The colors started back with them, and when they were lost no man knew save him who had fallen with them. It is, perhaps, due to myself to state that, when I determined to retire, I requested Captain [U.S.] Connally to give the order upon the right, and stepped to the left to direct Captain Woodward to give the order upon the left, from which point I moved on to the extreme left, to discover, if possible, the locality of the enemy attacking from that quarter, in order to be prepared to govern the movements of my regiment, so as to protect it as far as possible from danger and damage. While I was at the left thus engaged, the regiment commenced the movement to the rear, and not being near the center I was unable, owing to the density of the corn, to see where the colors were and when they fell.

Captain John R. Woodward, of Company G, acted in the capacity of major during the engagement, and aided me greatly in directing the movements of the regiment. Major [Matt] Dale, acting as lieutenant-colonel, had moved from the right, and was conferring with me as to the propriety of advancing or at once withdrawing, when he was killed. Feeling that it was madness to advance with the few men left me, I remained for several minutes after the fall of Major Dale, awaiting orders and information as to what my movements should be, being unwilling to withdraw as long as I had the ability to hold my then position without [orders] to do so.

Submitted herewith and as a part hereof is a list giving the names of killed, wounded, and missing, together with the character of wound of those wounded.

I am well convinced that had the Eighteenth Georgia and Hampton's Legion not met with the most obstinate and stubborn resistance from a superior force to their left, they would have supported me promptly and effectively upon my left, and that portion of the enemy's force in our front would have been routed, the tide of battle there turned, and the day been ours. The conduct of this regiment in the engagements of the 17th, and of the night of August 29 and 30, and that of the other regiments of the brigade in these engagements, demonstrates fully the necessity of having supports promptly and quickly upon the field. If required to carry strong positions in a few more engagements, and, after carrying them, hold them unaided and alone, this regiment must soon become annihilated and extinct without having accomplished any material or permanent good. I will also state that where I last halted, and where my dead and wounded fell, I halted in consequence of an order or direction to that effect from someone in the rear, said by Captain Woodward to have been Captain W. H. Sellers.

Respectfully submitted.

P. A. Work,

Lieutenant-Colonel, Commanding First Texas Regiment.[17]

## Lieutenant Colonel Philip A. Work
## 1st Texas Infantry
## The 1st Texas Regiment of the Texas Brigade
## Of the Army of Northern Virginia at the
## Battles of Boonsboro Pass or Gap and
## Sharpsburg or Antietam, MD, in September, 1862

By P. A. Work, Lt. Col. Commanding the 1st.

The part taken by the 1st Texas in the engagement at Boonsboro Pass during the late evening and early night of September 14th was so uneventful as scarcely to merit mention the Brigade late in the evening ascended from the North side to the crest of the ridge of South Mountain, westward from the Boonsboro Pass, through it, but in time to repel and drive back a force of the enemy found ascending from the South side. We continued to occupy this position until a late hour of the night, when we were withdrawn to the valley below and to the turnpike road, lending westerly from the town of Boonsboro to the town of Sharpsburg. By this road we began retreating to Sharpsburg—and so continued through the night—but occasionally halting and resting. During the 15th the rear of the army was protected by the Confederate cavalry against the pursuing enemy, the infantry being deployed from time to time in order of battle in support of the cavalry when too hard pressed, this Texas brigade taking its turn amongst other troops.

If the 1st Texas sustained any casualties on South Mountain or during the retreat to Sharpsburg, they are not now remembered.

Although our army had marched to near Sharpsburg, crossing Antietam creek on a bridge a short distance before halting and taking position, the enemy did not appear in front until during the evening of the 15th. No engagement other than some artillery firing occurred on that day. The morning of the 16th found General Longstreet's corps in position and battle array on a ridge between Sharpsburg on the West and Antietam creek on the East. The position of the Texas Brigade was almost immediately between Sharpsburg and the only bridge across the Antietam. Distributed along this ridge was artillery as well as infantry. This position was maintained through the night of the 15th and on the 16th until during the evening of this day.

During the 16th this artillery engaged in firing at the enemy's lines some miles from to our front and East of the creek. Whilst it was thus engaged General

Longstreet appeared, rode up to a gun quite near to and in plain view of the 1st Texas, dismounted and himself taking charge of it, lengthened fuses, elevated, aimed and fired it several times in an effort to reach the Federals, precious shots having fallen short, and only desisted upon the urgent insistence of his staff and the artillerists that such exposure of himself to danger and death was needless, the enemy's shells exploding continually all about him, in front and rear and overhead.

During the evening the division was moved by the left flank Northward from Sharpsburg along the Hagerstown turnpike road, passing *en route* and to its left Dunker's Chapel or Church, and placed in position on and constituting the extreme left of Longstreet's corps, the only portion of the army then on the field. Soon after passing this church the division was deployed and placed in order of battle with its left resting on or near the turnpike, waiting and in readiness to receive an attack from the enemy.

Soon the enemy's artillery opened fire in an effort to locate us and fix our range, but with very slightly damaging effect. Next, Federal infantry was advanced but was easily and quickly repulsed, and, again, with but slight damage to ourselves. This attack seemed more of a faint, or reconnaissance in force, for the purpose of feeding of us and ascertaining our position, than intended as an attack in force and a battle. After the repulse of the enemy we were again subjected to artillery fire until after dark but without serious results. As we rested in line of battle after dark but without serious results. As we rested in line of battle upon the grass in a field, the enemy's shells passed over and above us from twenty feet to fifty, the lighted fuses as plainly visible as the glowworm's light.

At about ten o'clock at night we were relieved by Lawton's Brigade (Georgians, is my recollection) and marched Southward to woods in the rear and halted for the night, with orders from General Hood to send to the rear a detail of two men from each company to gather and roast roasting ears; the 1st Texas (and presumably the remainder of the command) having been without food other than an occasional roasting ear snatched from the stalk as opportunity offered and eaten raw.

At the dawn of day the following morning (17th) the Federals began a heavy artillery fire upon our troops, and upon its cessation their infantry advanced and, attacking Lawton's force in our (1st Texas) front, soon drove it pell mell back upon the Texas Brigade, when the later moved and met and drove back the enemy. In following them up the 1st Texas encountered and entered a patch of green corn in an old clover field. Pursuing the Federals through it to near the farther (North) side a Federal battery came in view on a slight eminence at the distance of from seventy-five to one hundred yards beyond it and it being evident that it was limbering up and in front of the clover field, and in the act of withdrawing the regiment, of its own notion and of one accord, unheeding the reiterated the command to Forward, Load and fire at will, came to a halt and began shooting down horses and artillerists with the hope and expectation of capturing it, unmindful of the fleeing Federal infantry in our front who had taken refuge behind a tumbled-down rock fence just at the outer (Northern) edge of the corn patch and was pouring a galling and deadly fire into its ranks.

At this juncture, it becoming manifest that the left wing of the regiment was being fired upon from the left and rear. I sent Adjt. Shropshire to Col. Wofford, commanding the 18th Georgia regiment on my left, requesting him to move up his regiment if possible to an alignment of the left of the 1st Texas. Very soon afterwards I sent Amos G. Hanks, a private of Co. "F", upon the same errand, and following him sent Private Hicks. None of these returned. Nor, as I afterwards learned, did either reach Col. Wofford. Shropshire and Hicks were killed and Hanks lost a leg.

Just as messenger Hicks had left me on his mission, Major Matt Dale, commanding the right wing, came to me at my station at the center and reported that nearly every man of the right wing had been shot down, killed or wounded, and not a man would be left alive unless we withdrew at once. The roar all about us of nearby small arms and of artillery more distant was so deafening that the Major, in making his report, had to place his mouth over my ear. Just as he concluded and whilst we still were standing breast to breast, he with his right side and I with my left towards the front, he was stricken by a bullet, straightened, stiffened and fell backwards prone upon the ground, dead.

Immediately thereafter—scarcely a minute—Capt. John R. Woodward, acting Major, in command of the left wing, came to me with a like report as to that wing. As the regiment no longer had the ability either to advance or resist attack effectively, and in addition, as its line of retreat was in momentary danger of being cut off by the Federals who were firing into our left from the rear, I directed Capt. Woodward to retire the left and myself proceeded to with draw the right wing.

Falling back to the Southward limit of the corn patch, I directed the few who had emerged from the corn to rally upon a squad of perhaps thirty men who were gathered about a Confederate battle flag some thirty to forty yards to the Northwest of us and resisting the advance of a Federal infantry, whilst I remained to forward on others as they might appear from without the corn. Just as the few had started for the battleflag mentioned, Captain Woodward cried out substantially, "The flags, the flags. Where are the flags? The bearers are shot down and I'll get them." And suiting the action to the word, rushed back to the corn to recover them. He had proceeded but a short distance when he came face to face with the advancing enemy, and returned without them.

Simultaneously with Woodward's dash into the corn patch, the squad of men rallied about the battleflag mentioned gave way before the advancing Federals (who were moving from the Northwest to the Southeast) and fled South towards nearby woods. It was this woods in which the 1st Texas had rested during the previous night and to which it was intended to retreat when falling back through the corn. As this line of retreat was cut off by the advancing Federals and as to the Eastward there was an open but uphill route to the fence, running approximately North and South, which fence was constructed of split slabs from six to eight inches in width and some two inches thick morticed with posts. I directed the few (only some seventeen is my recollection) with me to flee to that fence. As the attention of the Federals was diverted to the battleflag squad fleeing toward the woods, we seemed to escape their notice until we had accomplished about half of the distance to the fence. Then they began firing upon us. Their bullets when striking the hillside ground raised puffs of dust, just as in the beginning of a shower do large drops of rain on a dusty road. Capt. Woodward's canteen, swinging against his left side and hop, was shot through from back to front. The scabbard of my light dress sword was stricken in such a way as it threw the lower end between my legs from in front and gave me a fall. Before arising I removed it in my hand the balance of the way. Upon reaching the fence some crawled through slabs and others climbed and bounded over. To our relief and great joy we found that this fence stood two to three feet West of the West side of an old road which from long usage and rain washing had been worn and been cut down for a depth of from three to four feet leaving precipitous sides. To us this was a "casemate." To the right and left of where we reached it we found men of various commands to the number of probably sixty who, also, had taken refuge there. Many of these still had their rifles and cartridge boxes. In addition the base of the road was littered over with castaway rifles and cartridge boxes, cast away by other fugitives who had continued on in quest of greater safety. Thus, there was the greatest plenty both of arms and ammunition. Whilst Capt. Woodward and myself became actively and sternly busy in requiring all of these other fugitives to take rifles and ammunition, "fall in" and open fire upon the advancing enemy, the numbers of the 1st Texas were pouring into them a deadly and telling fire, every shot counting. All told, about seventy-five rifles were brought to bear and soon the Federals were not only repulsed but routed.

The enemy having disappeared from view, the old road was abandoned and our retreat continued Eastward for a hundred yards or so and next Southward. Whilst thus retreating Southward we were discovered by General Hood, who conducted the squad (including the refugees found in the old road) to the woods to the Southwestward, where were already assembled perhaps six hundred men, the remnants of Hood's division of two brigades. All were placed in line of battle— officers, as well as men—with rifles in their hands. This weak force presented and covered a wide extended front, as it was in single file and each man separated several feet from every other. Indeed, it was but little more than a strong skirmish line. Up to this time the enemy had been repulsed and, at many points, driven back in their advance and assaults upon Hood's division and upon the corps of General Jackson adjoining it on the left. Quiet, except for artillery fire, continued for some hours before the Federals had advanced. Those attacking what I will term "Hood's Squad" were easily checked and turned back at each advance; deceived as to our own strength, no doubt, by the fire along our wide extended front sufficient for ten thousand troops. This position was maintained until reinforcements arrived and attacking drove the enemy back and regained and reestablished our original advanced lines on this part of the field.

During the night of the 17th the Confederate forces retired to and formed a new line of battle which, without molestation from the enemy, was occupied throughout the next day. During the night of the 18th the army crossed the Potomac River at Shepherdstown and entered Virginia. The loss of the 1st Texas in the corn patch fight on the 17th was fifty killed and one hundred and thirty six wounded of a total strength of only 226.

As all Muster Rolls, Battle and "Sick" reports, together with all military records, fell into the hands of the Federals at the capture of Richmond, Va., and as the Federal Government declines furnishing copies, it is impossible from the recollection of the now (1907), very few survivors of the 1st Texans to name more than a few only of those who were killed or wounded that day. As to name only the few who are remembered would seem invidious these are left unnamed here. Doubtless a few will survive who were members, respectively, of the twelve companies composing the regiment and it is probable that each of these companies composing the regiment and it is probable that each of these can named killed and wounded of the company of which he was a member. If these would communicate to the writer of this, such recollection as they may have in this particular, it would be a labor of love with him to complete a list of all killed or wounded as a supplement to this recital of the part taken by the regiment in that battle, such recital being the sum of the recollection, unaided by memoranda or data, of an event which transpired some forty-five years ago.

It is proper and it is but the due of the survivors, descendants and relatives of those who were members of the 1st Texas Regiment of the Texas Brigade of the Army of Northern Virginia, C.S.A., and but due the Texas public, to state that in a letter addressed to the writer of this, on January 8th 1895 by General E. A. Carman, Historical Expert of the U. S. Antietam Battlefield Commission, occurs this passage, namely, "As one etc."

It is but meet also to mention that in 1902 Representative Warnock of Ohio, in discussing in Congress statistics as to Confederate and Federal losses during the Civil War, said: "The First Minnesota Regiment has a record of losses. During the second day's fight at Gettysburg, General Hancock ordered that regiment to attack Wilcox's brigade which was advancing to take the position which he regarded as the key to his lines, and in holding the Confederates in check the 262 men were reduced to 47, a loss of 82.3 percent. General Hancock pronounced this feat of the First Minnesota the most gallant deed recorded in history. It was equaled, however, by the First Texas at Antietam (Sharpsburg). The 226 men of the First Texas in that battle were reduced to 40, also a loss of 82.3 percent."

Representative Warnock might have said, and with support, that the feat of the 1st Texas regiment surpassed rather than "equaled" that of the First Minnesota, as the figures given by him show that the loss of the latter was but 82 percent and one sixteenth of one percent, whilst that of the First Texas was 82 percent and forty-eight sixteenths of one percent, rendering the loss of the First Texas greater by 47/16 or two tenths and fifteen sixteenth of one percent, and confirming General Carman's statement that the First Texas at Antietam or Sharpsburg "suffered more in one battle than any other in the entire war."

Until now the 1st Texas has remained silent, content with the consciousness of duty well and patriotically discharged. Now, however, that this attempt has been made openly and publicly in the halls of Congress of the U.S. to deprive it of the honor that is due and confer in unasked and unsought upon the 1st Minnesota, it finds itself impelled in self-defense to herald its valor upon the field of Sharpsburg to the reading public.[18]

## George T. Todd
## May 6, 1839–January 29, 1913

George T. Todd was born in Matthew's County, Virginia, on May 6, 1839. His family moved to Boston, Texas, in 1840 when he was less than a year old; later, the family moved to Jefferson, Texas. Captain Todd attended college in Virginia for three years at Hampton Academy and one year at the University of Virginia. After graduation, Todd moved back Jefferson, Texas, to study law and later was admitted to the bar. In May, 1861, he enlisted as a private in Company "A" of the 1st Texas Infantry Regiment and was made captain in 1862. He participated in several battles and was wounded at Antietam. Resigning as Captain of Company "A," Todd returned to Texas in October, 1863, and served as adjutant of the 3rd Texas Cavalry Regiment. After the war, Todd again returned to Jefferson to practice law where he was involved in several important cases including the infamous Rothschild Murder Trial. In 1909, he wrote of his wartime experience in the 1st Texas Infantry in *Sketch of History: The First Texas Regiment, Hood's Brigade*. He later became a state representative from the 11th District. He was active in the Texas Democratic Party and ran unsuccessfully for Texas Attorney General in 1904. He died on January 19, 1913, and is buried in Jefferson, Texas.[19]

## Captain George T. Todd
## 1st Texas Infantry Regiment

On the 5th day of September, 1862, we started at sunrise and waded the Potomac river, the bugles and bands playing, "Maryland, my Maryland," and during the day we marched on the soil of three states, Virginia, Maryland, and Pennsylvania—crossing entirely through Maryland and going into camp beyond Greencastle, Penn. This march through three states was only about 25 miles as Maryland is very narrow where we crossed the state. In passing through Greencastle late in the afternoon, hot, dusty and weary our regiment was greeted by bevies of neatly dressed women lining the sidewalks, and wearing small U.S. flags pinned on their bosoms. They made all manner of jeering and slighting remarks as we passed, calling us "dirty rebels" and other opprobrious epithets. Finally a tall Texan was asked what command it was, passing. He replied: "This is Hood's Texas Brigade, and they are noted, madam, for storming and taking all Breast Works that carry those colors." This statement the lady received amid a general titter.

We were surprised at the abundance and cheapness of the supplies and eatables all along our route. Pennsylvania and western Maryland Dutch generally owned the farms. Bread baked in Dutch ovens, apple butter, buttermilk, eggs, chickens, ducks, geese were given us, for the same prices in Confederate "old issue" that they charged in greenbacks. We preferred buying to stealing, especially under Gen. Lee's stern orders to refrain from depredation. But our camps at night were alive with squawking chickens and quacking ducks. We lived high for about a week.

On 10th Sept. we began our return march towards Boonsboro Gap in South Mountains and on the evening of the 14th we met the enemy on Boonsboro Mountain and repulsed him. Next day, however, we were moved to the western side of the mountains, and heard of the surrender of Harper's Ferry, and took up our march up the dusty turnpike towards Antietam and Sharpsburg. We were the rear guard of the army, and retired slowly. We were also nearly barefooted and worn out with marching and skirmishing when we went into camp the night of 16th Sept. on the pike north of Sharpsburg upon the very ground destined to mark the bloodiest and most obstinate struggle of the great battle of the 17th. We were near the Dunkard church and the enemy (Hooker) in our immediate front. We drew no rations that night, and when we got them the next morning and were cooking, and before eating, the enemies advanced, and were ordered forward on a charge through the corn field, under heavy fire. Before getting through the field this writer was placed "hors de combat," by a shell or shrapnel crushing his foot. The regiment went on, and drove them back, but lost 82 percent of its members killed and wounded, Maj. Matt Dale, and several hundred officers and men of the old 1st Texas shed their blood, but held the field, although by death of its holders, our regimental flag was lost. Gen. Hood says: "The First Texas Regiment lost, in the corn field, fully two thirds of its number." But we drove the enemy at the close and held the field. This scribe had limped back to the field hospital, and declining the offer of the surgeon, Dr. Ewing, to cut off his foot, got into an ambulance and crossed the Potomac at Sharpsburg. He went on to Richmond, and was not again with the command during its delightful camp life in the Shenandoah Valley that fall. I again joined the regiment at Culpeper Court House, Va., on its way to Fredericksburg, November, 1862.[20]

## William Henry Gaston
## October 25, 1840–January 24, 1927

William H. Gaston was born on October 25, 1840, near Prairie Bluff, Alabama; his family moved to Texas in 1849. His father farmed on extensive farmlands and served twice in the Texas State Legislature. Along with his brothers, Robert and George, William enlisted in the Confederate Army in 1861, and later joined a volunteer company that became Company "H" of the 1st Texas Infantry.[21] He later commanded his company with distinction.[22] After the Battle of Antietam, he contacted Typhoid fever and was transferred back to Texas where he recuperated and later became a purchasing agent in the Confederate Trans-Mississippi Department for the remainder of the war. After the war in 1865, he became a farmer, and after a successful cotton crop where he made $20,000, Gaston and his wife moved to Dallas, Texas. He became a successful banker and helped transform Dallas into a successful city. He died on January 24, 1927, and is buried at Greenwood Cemetery in Dallas, Texas.[23]

Captain William Gaston, 1st Texas Infantry. (*Texas Heritage Museum–Historical Research Center*)

Captain William Henry Gaston
1st Texas Infantry
Fredericksburg, Va.
November 28, 1862

Pa,

I received your letters of the 5th Nov, a few days ago but have not had the opportunity of writing until now. I am surprised at you not receiving my letters written after the Sharpsburg fight. I cannot see why my letters should not reach home as soon as others. I wrote you soon after the fight & gave you all the information I could about Robert. I have been inquiring and hunting for him ever since he was lost. I can hear nothing from him. I feel that he was slain although I cannot give him up yet. There is some chance for him to be alive yet. He may have been badly wounded and still left in the hands of the enemy. There have been some of my boys sent back from Maryland that I thought was killed. They saw nothing of Robert but say he may be there somewhere as our boys were scattered all over Md. I hope he may turn up someday. I have felt miserable since he has been gone and it is with deep regret that I have to communicate his loss to you. I hope you all will not think hard of me for not giving you all the particulars of his fate when it was out of my power and as my letters failed to reach you. We were overpowered by the Enemy and compelled to give up the battlefield leaving behind our killed and wounded with some prisoners & were not permitted to go on the field after the fight. Consequently I cannot tell the result of the missing. We are now lying in sight of the Yankee tents. Only the Rappahannock River between us. May expect a fight any day but I do not think they will attempt to cross this winter. The weather is very cold but we stand it very well. Have plenty of clothes. Some shoes wanting. Our boys are in fine health and our army is in good condition. We expect to go into winter quarters shortly. I intend to come home this winter if I can. I may have to resign to do so but I want to come. My health has not been good for some time & I think I would advise you not to come as you cannot accomplish anything by the trip. If Robert can be found I will find him before I come. If killed we will have to give him up for a time.[24] I'm glad you sold Jake as Negroes are cheap. I think it is my duty to come home awhile at least. Excuse my writing with pencil as ink is scarce in camp. Write to me often. I will do the same. I close,

This from your Son,

W. H. Gaston[25]

## Major John Woodward and Colonel Alexis T. Rainey

Major John Woodward was commanding officer of the Reagan Guards, later Company "G" of the 1st Texas Infantry. Major Woodward was wounded at the battle of Gettysburg on July 2, 1863. He was mortally wounded at Fort Royal, Virginia, on July 22, 1863. Colonel A. T. Rainey was commanding officer of the Anderson County Invincibles, later Company "H" of the 1st Texas, until he was seriously wounded at the battle of Gaines Mill on June 27, 1862.

At the Battle of Sharpsburg (Antietam), Hood's Brigade was almost completely destroyed on the battlefield. Ordered to hold a position with little ammunition against one entire wing of the Union Army, Hood's Texans did just that. Heavily outnumbered and battle weary, these men held their ground and repulsed attack after attack until the battle died down. When asked by General Lee on the condition of the Texas Brigade, Hood replied: "The Texas Brigade is dead on the field." When the casualty reports were compiled at the end of the war, it was discovered that, at Sharpsburg, Hood's Texas Brigade had lost 82 percent of its fighting force in the battle, and that the 1st Texas Regiment of which Rainey and Woodward's companies had been assigned had lost close to 85 percent—the highest casualty rate inflicted on any fighting outfit during the four years of war.[26]

### D. K. Rice
### 1st Texas Infantry

Enlisted as a private in the "Palmer Guards," which later became Company "C" of the 1st Texas Infantry. He rose rapidly in rank by elections from his company, and by November, 1863, he was acting Lieutenant Colonel of the 1st Texas Infantry.[27]

### Captain D. K. Rice
### 1st Texas Infantry
### *Tri-Weekly Telegraph*
### October 15, 1862
### The Sharpsburg Fight.

The following letter is from Capt. D. K. Rice, of this city, to his uncle, Wm. M. Rice.

Martinsburg, Sept. 21, 1862

Dear Uncle.—Here I am, for a wonder still alive. On the 15th we had a fight on the Alleghany Mountains, in which we had but a small force engaged, who acted very badly—they were from North Carolina and Virginia. Our division was ordered to their report, but we did not arrive until almost night, when we attacked the enemy driving him back and occupying our just position with a very small loss. I suppose we had no object in holding that position any longer, so during the night we left for Sharpsburg, where we took our position to meet the enemy and await for our reinforcements, which did not arrive until too late. The fight commenced on the evening of the 16th, by shelling and skirmishing, with considerable effect. At daylight, on the morning of the 17th, the battle opened in earnest, and I do not believe that troops ever fought against such odds. I went into the fight with 23 men, and only escaped with myself and Orderly Sergeant, all the rest being either killed or wounded.

Hoffman was among the killed beyond a doubt, he did nobly doing his duty. You may judge our fighting, when I tell you we took 296 men into the fight, and only brought out 46. Among the killed and wounded there was 21 officers, our Major being among the killed. Six officers was all that was left to the regiment at the time our regiment reformed with the rest of our brigade, and went forward again to battle for its country, and was under fire the rest of the day. I was third in command on the second formation, and acted as Major and have been up to the present time. Our regiment lost its flag, but it was not taken from us. There had been eight men shot down with it, when we entered a cornfield, following the retreating foe, and were ordered to halt. After fighting awhile, we were ordered out, and on hand, 46 men, and none of them knew the flag was left until too late, the corn being so dense that it could be seen but a short distance when flying. To the credit of our brave Texas troops, not one man left the field until he was ordered to do so. On the 18th, Gen. Lee offered battle again, but the Yanks did not accept, so the 18th passed with light skirmishing. On the night following, we retreated across the river, the enemy started to retreat, but found us doing so, and followed a body of them crossed after us, but were driven back with heavy loss in killed and wounded, and 600 prisoners. The battle of the 17th was about as follows: on our right the Yanks were run across the river; on our left, Jackson drove them back some three-quarters of a mile, and in the center, each had their own position; but in the retreat, we lost all the arms of our killed and wounded, amounting to several thousand, and a great many of our wounded. At Harper's Ferry we took 14,700 prisoners, among whom there were some 2,500 negroes, 80 fine cannon, 200 new wagons, 2,608 very fine horses and mules, and 15,000 stand of small arms.

We have destroyed several fine buildings for them, and taken a great many stores for our army. At Winchester, we took several fine siege pieces, with all their best works. At Harper's Ferry the Yanks had re-built the armory, and were almost ready to manufacture arms again; but all their buildings have been destroyed with the bridge. Now they are at liberty to commence again. It is believed that Stewart has destroyed several hundred of the Yankees wagons at Boonesboro; but of that I am not certain. I think the Yanks are at Shepherdstown. We are taking it easy here to-day; I suppose to get the Yanks to cross and in force and fight them. A man cannot say his life is his own, now, from one day's end to another. Everyone here believes we will be in Maryland again soon—very soon. The loss in rest of our brigade was slight in comparison to ours; the B. C. G.'s lost four or five men.

I think it must be my turn to catch it next, I have had so many narrow escapes. My blanket was completely riddled; four different balls struck it, and as it was folded, they made over 70 holes through it, making it worthless. I was also struck on the hip with a piece of shell, which also disabled me, but I am all right and hope to remain so. The enemy has lost something over 40,000 prisoners in thirty days. Is it not glorious?

I would like to write you about Maryland and the people there, but I have no time. I am a long way from Richmond, and will write every time I possibly can.

Your affectionate nephew, D. K. Rice, Capt. Comd'g Co. C., 1st Texas

## Samuel "Sam" Andrew Willson
## January 9, 1835–January 24, 1892

Sam A. Willson was born on January 9, 1835, in San Augustine, (Texas) Republic of Mexico. In the late 1840s, his family moved to Peachtree, Village, where his father practiced medicine. At the age of fifteen, he began studying law in Woodville, Texas, and was admitted to the Texas Bar at the age of seventeen. He married Susan Priest in 1853, and in 1856, he became the district attorney for the Fifteenth Judicial District.

On May 28, 1861, after serving in the Tyler County delegation at the Texas Secession Convention, Sam was enrolled as 1st Lieutenant in the "Woodville Rifles," which later became Company "F", 1st Texas Infantry. One year later, when P. A. Work was promoted to Lt. Col., Sam was elected captain. At the Battle of Antietam, he was severely wounded. At the Battle of Gettysburg on July 2, 1863, Captain Willson participated in the capture of Smith's New York Artillery Battery at the Devil's Den. The next day, on July 3, Captain Willson was captured when Union Cavalry charged into the lines of the 1st Texas. He was sent to Fort Delaware POW Camp, and sometime between early October and mid-December, 1863, he escaped and returned to Richmond, Virginia. It was at that time that he received his orders dated April 1, 1863, which transferred him to the Trans-Mississippi Department to serve as an adjutant to Col. Greer. Before being discharged, Captain Willson was promoted to major.[28] After the war, Willson returned to Woodville and was elected as District Judge in 1866. He helped organize the Hood's Texas Brigade Association and served on the original board of directors; he also served two terms as a justice on the Texas Court of Criminal Appeals. In early January, 1892, Judge Wilson developed pneumonia following a trip by horseback from the Cherokee County Courthouse and succumbed to the illness on January 24, 1892. He is buried at the Cedar Hill Cemetery in Rusk, Texas.[29]

## Captain Sam A. Willson
## 1st Texas Infantry

Sept 30, 1862

Mr. President,

I beg to recommend for a formal promotion with the rank of Major: Capt. Samuel A. Willson of the 1st Texas Regiment, and to ask that he may be assigned to duty in the Trans-Mississippi Department.

Capt. Willson entered the service as 1st Lieutenant among the first young men in Texas. He came to Virginia in July, 1861, and was a member of the Texas Battalion organized under Maj, (now Senator) Wigfall. Since that time he has been constantly in the service and has participated in every battle in which the regiment has been engaged. He distinguished himself for gallant conduct in the Battles around Richmond, and in the Second Battle of Manassas. In the Battle of Sharpsburg Capt. Willson took only seven men into action and the whole of his command, himself included was either killed or wounded. Capt. Willson is a gentleman of fine intelligence & good social position. At home he was a lawyer of intensive practices having twice served as District Attorney. The severe climate of Virginia and the hard service by Capt. Willson together with his severe wound have severely impaired his health & I seriously doubt if he would be able to undergo another campaign in infantry. Under the rule adopted by your Excellency I think Capt. Willson has fairly "won his spurs." I feel quite sure that he has abundant intelligence and qualifications to discharge the duties of a staff officer.—

With Much Respect, I am Your Excellency's Obt. Servt.

F. B. Sexton[30]


To The President—

I cheerfully concur in the recommendation of Capt. Willson. Having known him well for many years. I can safely say that his character is such as to afford acceptable guaranty that he will do faithful service in whatsoever service in whatever position may be assigned him.

P. W. Gray[31]


I endorse the statement of Judge Gray and concur in the accommodation of Capt. Willson.

M. D. Graham[32]


## Captain Sam A. Willson
## 1st Texas Infantry
### *The Jasper Weekly Newsboy*
### July 6, 1876
### The Coming Man

Honorable Sam A. Willson, the nomination of Judge Willson by the district convention would probably more in harmony with the wishes of the people than any selection it can make. Judge Willson is a native Texan—was born and raised in this district—and his interests are thoroughly identified with the interests of the people of the district.

He was elected district attorney before he was of age, but arrived at majority during the time in which he had to qualify.

At the expiration of his first term, he was almost unanimously re-elected, but the war coming on soon after, he volunteered, went to Virginia, in the 1st Texas, and served in "Hood's Texas Brigade" until after the great battle of Gettysburg, at which place he was captured on the evening of the last day's fight. He made his escape and was promoted for his gallantry, but owing to starvation and sickness he underwent during a long imprisonment, he was unable to again enter active service.

Judge Willson always displayed the greatest gallantry, particularly distinguishing himself at Gaines' Farm, Manassas, Gettysburg, and Sharpsburg. In the last named engagement, in which his regiment went in about a thousand strong and came out with only 46 unhurt, he was severely wounded. When the regiment (which had been decoyed off) was ordered to retreat and rose to their feet, the historical flag presented to the 1st Texas rose and fell many times. Many gallant fellows were successively killed in attempting to bear it away. It seemed instant death to touch it. Judge Willson took it and carried it beyond the enemy's fire, when he became so weak and sick from his wound that he could bear it no further. His escape seemed miraculous.

After the war he entered the practice, but was soon elected judge over one of the best and most prominent lawyers in the state. He was about 30 years old when elected judge, but fully sustained the reputation his profound legal attainments had won for him. Since his term of office expired, he has been engaged in the practice with every increasing reputation. Farmer.

## Lieutenant T. P. Sanford
## 1st Texas Infantry
### *Fort Worth Daily Gazette*
## December 4, 1887

Among the collection of war poems in my old scrap book are several signed "Maggie," and written "For the Texas Republican." From one, which was written "In Memory of Lieutenant T. P. Sanford, of the First Texas regiment, who fell at the battle of Sharpsburg, Va., September 17, 1862, and who was the youngest brother of his gifted sister, I make the following excerpts":

War Scrapbook,
By T. B. Baldwon.

> *My spirit wondered far away*
> *Where fair Potomac's water glide,*
> *And seeking out the place where they*
> *Have laid you by its chilling side,*
> *In fancy knelt beside the mound*

*My weeping eyes could not behold;*
*And on the consecrated ground*
*To thee its deepest sorrow told.*

*The deepest prayer my soul had breathed*
*Was twined around my brother's name;*
*The fondest hopes my heart had wreathed*
*Were for my soldier brother's fame.*

*Those hopes, alas! Are faded now,*
*And must be laid upon thy pall;*
*The crown that should have bound thy brow,*
*Will fade in Azrael's cheerless hall.*

The subject of this poem was a young lawyer of bright promise, and one of the first to enlist in his country's cause; and whose untimely death was mourned by a large circle of friends and relatives in several of the states of his beloved sunny south.

## Russell Crawford Mitchell
### February 27, 1837–January 20, 1905

1st Sergeant Russell C. Mitchell
1st Texas Infantry
*The Alto Herald*
February 25, 1937

Note: Written expressly for the *Alto Herald* by his granddaughter, Margaret Mitchell, Atlanta, Ga., author of *Gone With the Wind*.

My father Eugene Muse Mitchell gave me the following information which was imparted to him by my grandfather, Russell Crawford Mitchell, during his lifetime.

Russell Crawford Mitchell was born in Georgia, February 27, 1837. His father was Reverend Isaac G. Mitchell, one of the earliest Methodist ministers in Atlanta. After attending Bowden College in Georgia, he began the study of law and decided in 1859 to locate in Texas. He continued the study of law at Alto, Texas, in the office of Colonel Thomas J. Jennings, a former Attorney General of the State of Texas, which admitted to the bar and began practice at Alto. He was influenced to settle in Alto by Col. Robert Mitchell whom my grandfather met on the stage coach on his way to Texas. Col. Mitchell, noted pioneer citizen of Alto, was born in Virginia and settled in Texas about the time of the Mexican War. Col. Robert Mitchell's ancestors came from Scotland to Virginia before the Revolutionary War.

First Sergeant Russell Crawford Mitchell, 1st Texas Infantry. (*Brunk Auctions*)

My grandfather and Col. Robert Mitchell decided they were cousins by descent from the same ancestors in Virginia, but the exact degree of relationship they were never able to determine. Though they were not closely related they became intimate friends and were devotedly attached to one another. As an evidence of this esteem, my grandfather named my uncle Robert for Colonel Mitchell.

Among my grandfather's intimate friends was Col. Hyde Jennings for many years afterward a leading lawyer of Fort Worth. Another close friend was a young lawyer of Alto, Mr. Adolphus Muse, of a prominent Texas family and son of Senator Muse. They decided to form a partnership but the Civil War broke up this arrangement. They were such good friends that they pledged themselves that when each should marry, he would name his oldest son after the other. Adolphus Muse died early in the war, but my grandfather faithfully kept his promise and named his oldest son, my father, Eugene Muse Mitchell, after his departed friend.

When war approached, my grandfather, Russell Crawford Mitchell, "stumped" Eastern Texas for the cause of secession, helped raise a company and was elected captain. The company voted to go to Missouri and join Gen. Sterling Price, but grandfather wanted to go to Virginia where he believed the big fighting would be. So he resigned and joined another company which became Company "I" of the First Regiment of Texas Infantry. He afterwards became first sergeant and participated in the Battles of Seven Pines, Second Manassas, Sharpsburg and a number of other engagements. This regiment was part of Hood's Texas Brigade, one of the most famous organizations in the Confederate army. General Lee once said to my grandfather, "We cannot do without you Texans." At the great battle of Sharpsburg on September 17, 1862, eighty-two percent of the First Texas Regiment were killed or wounded in Hood's famous charge upon the batteries in front of the "East Wood." The regiment captured the guns but, was nearly exterminated. My grandfather was shot down in front of the captured guns and his skull broken in two by minie balls. His recovery was almost miraculous and ever afterwards his children and grandchildren loved to put their fingers in the depressions in his skull. After he was able to be moved he was brought home to Atlanta. When he had recovered sufficiently he was detailed for duty in the hospital department and became general ward-master of the Institute Military Hospital at Atlanta. At the end of the war he married and went into business at Atlanta. He wanted to go back to Texas but the state was under military government and the courts were closed. His business expanded, he became wealthy, accumulated a large estate, held high municipal offices and his children grew up in Atlanta, the home of their ancestors. So he finally gave up the idea of returning to Texas. He had loved the little town of Alto in Texas. In the 1870s he acquired a considerable body of timber land on the Southern Railway about 80 miles northeast of Atlanta and laid out a small town which he named Alto. The town thrived for a time, then ceased to grow and has become a mere village, but the Georgia State Tuberculosis Hospital has been located near it on lands Mr. Mitchell owned at the time of his death.

Margaret Mitchell, author of *Gone with the Wind.* (*Library of Congress*)

This great institution has given the name Alto great publicity. My grandfather died in Atlanta on January 20, 1905. Notwithstanding his extraordinary success in Atlanta, he always looked back with affection to the friends of his youth at Alto and his old companions in arms of the First Texas Brigade. Several years ago my father and my brother went to the Sharpsburg Battlefield and found the spot marked by a bronze table where my grandfather and his companions fell in the famous battle.

*Cherokeean Herald*
July 20, 2011
By Chris Davis

I promised you last week that I would continue the story of Russell Crawford Mitchell, the grandfather of Margaret Mitchell, author of *Gone with the Wind* after he left Alto. This is a portion of a letter Margaret Mitchell wrote to Colonel John William Thomason Jr. in Washington D.C.

My Mitchell grandfather, though Georgia born, was one of Hood's Texans, First Regiment of Infantry Volunteers, Company I; he enlisted in Alto, Texas, July 10, 1861, fought in eleven battles and was severely wounded at Sharpsburg (Antietam)—so severely wound that when the litter bearers dumped him behind the church with the other wounded, his cousin by marriage, Surgeon General Roach, declared there wasn't any use in wasting time on him when he would only live a few hours. This incensed by grandfather for he felt that this was a reflection on his stamina. To be sure a minnie ball had gone through the back of his head, fracturing his skull in two places and he had minor abrasions, here and there, but he felt that Dr. Roach was speaking through ignorance. He said as much, rose up, and picking up another cousin, who was shot through the lungs, set out for Richmond. He walked, hitch-hiked or was carried all the way, swimming a river or two on the road and arrived in Richmond eventually, still carrying his cousin who was somewhat the worse for wear by that time. The Richmond hospitals were full of erysipelas at that time and Grandpa thought they might be unhealthy for a man with a head wound, so he swung on a flat car and went south to Atlanta. And very hot weather too. He lived till 1905, acquired twelve children and a considerable amount of the world's goods. He devoted a great deal of his leisure time to telling Dr. Roach what a poor diagnostician he was. Till I'm tolerable certain, the doctor wished that he died at Sharpsburg."— Margaret Mitchell.

Russell Crawford Mitchell was known to have a very short temper after the minnie ball split his skull, but I figure he was just permanently disappointed over not being able to return to Alto after the war. He practiced in Florida for a while, but was disbarred for assaulting a state official and returned to Georgia. I'm sure that Florida state official didn't realize that Mr. Mitchell had lived in Alto or he wouldn't have antagonized him to the point of assault. Alto folks don't normally take to that sort of thing well.

## David Henry "D. H." Hamilton
## August 8, 1843–May 30, 1929

D. H. Hamilton was born in Oxford, Mississippi, on August 8, 1843, and was a young boy when his family moved to Texas around 1850. When Texas seceded from the Union, Hamilton enlisted in the Sumter Light Infantry of Trinity County, Texas, which later became Company "M" of the 1st Texas Infantry. After the war, Hamilton was elected as sheriff of Trinity County, Texas, 1865–1867, and served in the Texas Legislature, 1893–1895. In 1925, Hamilton wrote about his memories of being a soldier in Hood's Texas Brigade in a book he titled *History of Company M First Texas Volunteer Infantry Hood's Brigade* (Waco, TX: W. M. Morrison). His wartime experiences have been referred to in many books over the years about Hood's Texas Brigade.

D. H. Hamilton died on May 30, 1929, and is buried at Bennett Cemetery, Apple Springs, Texas. His great-great-grandson is former Texas Governor Rick Perry.[33]

Sergeant D. H. Hamilton, 1st Texas Infantry. (*Kenny Dee*)

## Sergeant D. H. Hamilton
## 1st Texas Infantry

After the second battle of Manassas we waded the Potomac River and started on the march to Sharpsburg and encountered the Yankees, first at Antietam Creek in a minor engagement, Sept. 17th. We then crossed the creek and formed a line in front of Sharpsburg where we remained the balance of that day. The Yanks crossed the creek that afternoon. Jeff Bowman stole away from the company and secreted himself in the upper story of a building where the Yanks were crossing the creek and about one hundred and fifty yards from them. From a window in the house he could see them distinctly and he could not resist the temptation to shoot. He fired about sixty shots at them before they located him and dislodged him. They trained a piece of artillery on the house and when the first shot passed through it Jeff "skedaddled" back to camp. It is highly probable that Jeff did effective work in that little battle staged all by himself. We laid in line of battle all that night and next morning moved forward into the battle of Sharpsburg. On the first charge we drove the Yanks about one half mile in our front when they brought up reinforcements and drove us back. A desperate battle waged back and forth over the field during that day and the next, and finally resulted in what seemed to be a draw, but we held the battle field.

On the third day at night we started to fall back in the direction of Sheppardstown near the Potomac River. The battle ground at Sharpsburg during the two days fighting was littered with dead and wounded. J. T. (Turner) Evans was shot down in this battle just as we started to fall back in one of the retreats of the first day; W. J. (Bill) Towns picked him up and got him on his back and ran with him about a half mile and prevented him from being captured. He was wounded in the hip from which he finally recovered but being unable to do Infantry service as was discharged and returned home. When he had sufficiently recovered he joined a company of Rangers stationed in North West Texas to protect that country from the Indians, at that time constantly depredating on the settlements.

In the battle of Sharpsburg we lost a number of men killed and wounded. Lieutenant Thomas Sanford, Josh Boon, James Story, Wade Turner, Shady Roach, Vondry Wizby and Jeff Bowman, the man who but two days before had fought the Yankee army by himself from the upper story of a house, were killed and fifteen or twenty were wounded. On the retreat towards Sheppardstown, before referred to, our Brigade held the difficult position of rear guard. The Yanks followed along unpleasantly close. Every time they got close we opened fire on them and drove them back.

On arriving at the Potomac River we found that all the army except our brigade had waded across. The river was about a mile wide at that place and about a waist deep. There was no way to cross except to wade. When we got out of the water on the opposite side we discovered A. P. Hill's division lying concealed on the second bank, in line of battle. As we walked out of the river we were ordered to strike a trot. This was done as we afterward found out to deceive the Yanks and induce them to continue the pursuit. They walked—or ran—unsuspectingly into the trap. As soon as they got to the river they all plunged in and started to wade across. When the front half had reached a point about one hundred Yards from General Hill's position, and while the river was full of men from there back to the other bank, Hill's men were ordered to fire. Volley after volley was fired into them. The slaughter was terrible. All the wounded who could not stand up were drowned and those who survived scrambled back to the other side. So many were killed and wounded that the water was bloody for a mile down the river. This wound up the fighting for the time and all went into camp and rested a short while.[34]

## Val C. Giles
## January 26, 1842–January 15, 1915

Val C. "Valerius Cincinattus" Giles was born in Shelby County, Tennessee, on January 26, 1842. He was nine when his family moved outside of Austin, Texas, to settle a farm.[35] In the spring of 1861, he enlisted in the "Tom Green Rifles," which later became Company "B" of the 4th Texas Infantry. During the war, Giles kept a journal where he would write his experiences of camp-life, battle, and observations of the men and officers he served with. He fought in the major battles involving Hood's Texas Brigade: Eltham's Landing, Gaines' Mill, Second Manassas (Bull Run), Gettysburg, and Chickamauga. Shortly after the Battle of Chickamauga, he was captured by Union troops during a skirmish in eastern Tennessee and was sent to POW Camp Morton in Indiana.[36] After a year of captivity, Giles escaped from the POW camp and travelled southward toward Texas by foot. While in Kentucky, he learned of the surrender of his regiment as a part of the Army of Northern Virginia at Appomattox Courthouse in April, 1865. He arrived back in Austin in September, 1865, where he became a clerk at the Texas Land Survey Office and later married his wife, Anne, who he met while in Kentucky. He fathered two children and was active in Hood's Texas Brigade Association and the United Confederate Veterans throughout the rest of his life. He died on January 15, 1915, and he is buried at Oakwood Cemetery in Austin. His lively prose about being in battle would make his journal one of the most popular journals of the Civil War; it was titled *Rambling Reminiscences of the Stormy Sixties*, which became a popular read after its publication.[37] In 1961, Mary Lasswell edited his journal, which she titled *Rags and Hope: The Recollections of Val C. Giles, Four Years with Hood's Brigade, Fourth Texas Infantry, 1861-1865.*

Sergeant Val C. Giles, 4th Texas Infantry. (*Dolph Briscoe Center for American History-University of Texas-Austin*)

Sergeant Val C. Giles
4th Texas Infantry
*Confederate Veteran*
September, 1907
The Flag of the First Texas, A. N. Va.
By Val C. Giles, 4th Texas, Austin, Texas.

Hanging on the wall in the Texas State Library is a worn-out faded silken relic of the eventful sixties—a lone star Texas flag, so tattered and torn by war and time that the casual observer will pass by it unobserved. It has a history, but is silent now, as silent as the gallant fellows who carried it, fought for it, and died under it in the old cornfield at Sharpsburg, Md., September 17, 1862. Triumphantly it had waved over the old 1st Texas Infantry on the banks of the Potomac, at Yorktown, at Eltham's Landing, at Seven Pines, at Gaines's Mill, at Freeman's Ford, at Thoroughfare Gap, at Boonsboro Gap, and went down in blood on the cornfield of Sharpsburg. The 1st Regiment was so proud of this flag that they carried it in a silk oilcloth case, and never unfurled it except on reviews, dress parades, or in battle. The entire brigade was proud of it; and when we saw it waving in the Virginia breeze, it was a sweet reminder of home, a thousand miles away.

This prized flag was made and presented to the 1st Texas Infantry by Miss Lula Wigfall while her father, Louis T. Wigfall, was colonel of the regiment, early in 1861. Later on she made a beautiful flag out of her mother's wedding dress and gave it to the 4th Regiment while they were in their winter quarters on the Potomac, and it is now in the possession of the Daughters of the Confederacy in their room in the State Capital building in Austin.

When this old lone star flag, now in the Texas Library, was returned to the State some months ago by the Secretary of War, it was labeled: "Texas Brigade Flag, Captured at Antietam, Md."

Knowing that Hood's Texas Brigade, the only Texas troops that served in the Army of Northern Virginia, had no brigade flag, Gen. William R. Hamby and myself, members of the 4th Texas Regiment of that old brigade, visited the Capitol to see if we could discover wherein lay the mistake. General Hamby's recollections of Hood's Brigade and of their eventful campaign of 1862 is remarkably clear. Although, he had not recovered from a wound received at Second Manassas, he went into the battle of Sharpsburg barefooted, but came out unscathed and well shod. I know that our brigade quarter-master issued no shoes or clothing of any kind during Lee's first campaign into Maryland, but I never asked him where he got his shoes.

As soon as the librarian pointed out the flag we both recognized it, although it had been about forty-four years since last we saw it. It is the Texas flag lost by the 1st Regiment in the battle of Sharpsburg. Colonel Work, who commanded the regiment in the battle of Sharpsburg, in his official report in speaking of the lost flags: "During the engagement I saw four bearers of our State colors shot down, John Hanson, James Day, Charles Kingsberry, and James Malone; others raised the colors until four more were shot down. The colors started back with the regiment as it retired, but when lost no one knew save him who had fallen with it."

The 1st Texas went into the fight at Sharpsburg with two hundred and twenty-six, rank and file, and lost one hundred and eighty-three in killed and wounded, which is the heaviest loss of any regiment, either Union or Confederate, in any battle of the war. The loss of the entire brigade in that battle was unusually heavy. We went into the fight with eight hundred and fifty-four; came out with three hundred and nineteen, having lost on the field five hundred and thirty-five.

I have in my possession, a complete muster roll of the members of the 1st Texas Regiment who fell at Sharpsburg gallantly defending this lone star flag and their battle flag, also lost in the old cornfield. I believe a muster roll of these brave Texans should be inscribed in parchment and hung by the old flag in the State Library.

The two flags lost by the 1st Texas Regiment, now in the State Library, are the only flags lost, captured, or surrendered by the Texas soldiers in Lee's army. The three Texas regiments, the 1st, 4th, and 5th, stacked their guns at Appomattox on April 9, 1865, but they hung no flags on the muzzles of their faithful Enfield rifles. The truth is, the boys deliberately cut their old flags into little pieces and divided them among themselves, and those little fragments of faded silk were about all they got for four long years of devoted service.

The Lone Star Flag of the 1st Texas has had an eventful career. When presented to the regiment by a noble Texas girl on the banks of the Potomac, it was bright and glorious, and, like the character of the fair donor, was "pure as the beautiful snow." Twelve hundred Texans cheered it to the echo when it was kissed for the first time by the breeze of classic old Virginia. On the morning of September 18, 1862 only forty-three of its gallant defenders answered to roll call. One thousand and forty-seven were missing!

General Sherman was correct when he said "War is Hell."

> *This faded relic here today,*
> *So torn by shot and shell*
> *Waved proudly o'er Virginia's hills*
> *In the days when war was hell.*

> *No foeman's hand e'er touched the flag,*
> *And oft the rebel yell*
> *Has rung beneath these thirteen stars,*
> *In the days when war was hell.*

> *'Tis old and faded now by time,*
> *And torn by shot and shell;*

*'Twas never furled on any field,*
*In the days when war was hell.*

*This grand old flag so silent now,*
*A story sad can tell,*
*Of those who died beneath its folds*
*In the days when war was hell.*[38]

"The Days When War Was Hell"

## George A. Branard
## January 5, 1843–August 7, 1909

George A. Branard was born in Galveston, Texas, on January 5, 1843. On August 8, 1861, he enlisted as a private in the Lone Star Rifles, which became Company "L" of the 1st Texas Infantry, and was soon advanced to 4th Corporal. In the Battle of Eltham's Landing on May 7, 1862, Color Sergeant Thomas Nettles received a bullet in the shoulder and was unable to carry the Lone Star Flag of the 1st Texas Infantry. The flag was then transferred temporarily to Branard. In the engagement the following day, Branard got too far out in front of the regiment and someone called out to him to fall back. Although cut on the head by a passing bullet, Branard shouted that he would be "dammed if he'd fall back," and remained with the colors until the fight was over. Colonel A. T. Rainey, hearing the remark and admiring both his courage and spirit, ordered the regiment forward to form under the colors. Rainey then and there promoted Branard from corporal to color sergeant of the 1st Texas Infantry.[39] Due to many miles of marching with the Lone Star Flag, his feet became bloody and sore. Major Matt Dale who saw his bare feet ordered Branard to the hospital, thus he missed fighting at Antietam. At the Devil's Den, during the Battle of Gettysburg on July 2, 1863, Color Sergeant Branard led the charge of the 1st Texas Infantry, being so far ahead of his regiment that he won the admiration of the Union troops on Little Round Top. The rattle of muskets momentarily ceased, then a Union artillery battery fired a shell in his direction, which exploded at his feet. Fragments severed the flagstaff and struck him in the forehead, cutting a gash that marked him for life and destroyed the sight of his left eye.

Branard still clutched his flagstaff and attempted to go forward. The shattered remnant of his flagstaff was still clutched in his hand when, unconscious, his comrades, who thought he was dead, bore him from the field of battle.[41] During the Battle of Knoxville in November, 1863, he was seriously wounded, which caused him to lose the use of his left arm. After recovering, he was reassigned as sergeant in charge of Hood's Texas Brigade ambulance corps. After the war, Branard returned to Galveston, Texas, and was active in the United Confederate Veterans

Color Sergeant George A.
Branard, 1st Texas Infantry.
(*Patty Branard Gambino*)

(UCV) organization and Hood's Texas Brigade Association. He was greatly beloved, respected, and admired by his comrades of Hood's Texas Brigade and all who knew him. When Color Sergeant Branard died on August 7, 1909, his fellow comrades in Hood's Texas Brigade, as well as the entire state of Texas, grieved. He is buried at Washington Cemetery in Houston, Texas.

### Color Sergeant George A. Branard
### 1st Texas Infantry
*Houston Post*
November 7, 1902

George A. Branard, member of the Dick Dowling camp, received a request from the Antietam battle board, for information regarding the part played by the First Texas Regiment at that battle. The Texas regiment lost 82 percent of its men at the battle.

Color Sergeant George A. Branard
1st Texas Infantry
*Galveston Daily News*
That Little Gold Ring
Letter of Gratefulness to Branard for What It Told
September 25, 1904

Through the medium of a little gold ring that was taken from the finger-bones of a dead Confederate soldier at Sharpsburg, when the body was exhumed and reinterred, years after the Civil War, relatives in Texas learned where rested the bones of Lieut. C. M. Graham, their much beloved kinsman who on many fields proved himself a hero.

The information was obtained by them through the efforts of Mr. George A. Branard of this city, and secretary of Hood's Texas Brigade.

A letter of thanks to Mr. Branard was recently received, and it is as follows:

Temple, Tex., Sept. 20—Mr. George A. Branard, Houston, Tex.—My Dear Sir: It was a great pleasure for me to receive your letter as coming from one of the noblest band of men the world ever knew, and as coming from you as you have won a way into our hearts by your kindness to us in giving to us that which we had not hoped to have—a history of the long struggles of our brave kinsman.

And sincerely do we thank Dr. Campbell Wood for his kindly interest in telling us more of the noble man who gave his life on the battlefield.

There are not many of those grand men left, and it has been one of my greatest pleasures to contribute to the comfort of those men when it is in my power to do so. Noblemen by nature are those men who made the history of the South.

Father Ryan says: "A land without ruins is a land without memories; a land without memories is a land without history."

So, while we all acknowledge allegiance to our Government, we of the South will cling with a never-dying love to her history and the noble little band of men who made that history.

The Confederate army fought, bled and died for a principle, and just how well they fought was demonstrated by the results. Some time ago I was up North, and an old Union soldier, who, I think, was a Captain in the army, and he said at one time while we were discussing the war, "While Hood's Brigade sometimes retreated, they never were whipped." He said again, "Those Texans were the hardest fighters in the Confederate army, and that is saying a great deal." I told him that I expected that nearly all of the Union army found that out before the end of the war. He admitted that they did.

I want to thank you Mr. Branard, for the interest you have shown and assure you that you will always be a welcome visitor in our home.

Mother and sisters were very sorry, indeed, that they were not here to meet you, but hope that they will yet have the pleasure of thanking you in person.

I am writing to Dr. C. Wood today, Ever your friend,

J. M. McCuthchan.

Color Sergeant George A. Branard
1st Texas Infantry
*The Brownsville Daily Herald*
March 2, 1905
Not Exactly Captured
First Texas Flag Had Been Wrapped Around Dead Officer

In speaking of a letter from a staff correspondent in Washington City, printed a couple of days ago in a Texas daily, Mr. George A. Branard, a member of the First Texas Regiment of Hood's Texas Brigade, stated that the information concerning one of four Texas flags reported "to have been captured during the war was somewhat misleading in the use of the word "captured," as applied to the flag of his regiment. It was in the fierce fight at Antietam, that two or three men of the First Texas wrapped their flag, which had its staff shot away, around the body of an officer of one of the companies who had been killed in the fight. It was here that the flag was found later by an officer of a Pennsylvania regiment. Mr. Branard has it from Mr. W. E. Barry of Navasota, who was captured in the battle, that a private brought the flag to an officer of the Pennsylvania regiment after the fight. The latter asked him where he got it. He replied, telling him that the flag when found, was wrapped around the dead body of an officer and was take there from.

Mr. Barry, who heard the conversation, was asked by the officer if he knew the flag. He gave the information that it belonged to the First Texas Regiment. The officer then asked the private who had the flag if he could again find the body of the officer if possible to do so and bury the flag with it. The answer was that the officer had already been buried with many others and he could not identify the body. It seems that the regiment went into the battle with 289 men and came out with sixty.

The flag was easily identified because it had the names of several desperate battles the regiment had been in prior to that time. The flags are soon to be returned to the remnants of the regiments that they had belonged to. Mr. Branard himself was the flag bearer of the regiment, but was in the hospital at the time of the battle of Antietam on account of wounds previously received.

The Confederate officer, it seems, was killed while waving the flag.


Color Sergeant George A. Branard
1st Texas Infantry
*Dallas Morning News*
October 3, 1897
Battle Flags of Texas

During the journey to Sharpsburg, George Branard was bare-footed. His feet becoming sore, he was ordered to the hospital by Major Dale, when the lone star flag was committed to the care of another.

At Sharpsburg, much heroism was displayed by the Texan brigade, "whose achievements," says Hood, "have never been surpassed in the history of nations." Jackson complimented them "for their almost matchless display of daring and desperate valor." Lee has written that "the Texans fought grandly and bravely and the contest in the cornfield and lane was the hottest ever witnessed on any battlefield."

In that ever-to-be remembered cornfield, being overwhelmed by numbers, the first Texas to their great sorrow lost their flag. When the "fallen banner" was discovered by the enemy, eight dead and six wounded Texans were found around and over it. One of them was immortalized in death with—this beloved standard of the Texans wrapped around his lifeless body as his winding-sheet.

Someday the people of this grand Lone Star empire state in gratitude for their heroism will erect a monument to their memory. Let the granite from the laughing waters of the Llano be its pedestal and the marble glistening with the spray of the Colorado be its shaft. May dew-eyed pity engrave on the crowning stone, "Here lies embalmed in everlasting glory the bodies of eight Texans who met death with the lone star flag in their hands."

S. T. Blessing of Dallas was near, when the flag went down. As he fell he saw the foe rush to gather the sacred silk from the burial pile. W. D. Prichard, a color bearer with the battle flag of the first Texas in his hands, was shot down almost dead with painful wounds. As he lay prostrated at the feet of the foe, bleeding and suffering the agony of death, he wept bitter tears, not for his wounds, but because the "flag by angel hands to valor given," all stained with the blood of brave ones was trailing in the dust, a trophy to the foe.

With the reverence and holy love for the memory of the heroes, we commit to the youth of Texas the sacred names of those who fell with glory under the shadow of that lone star flag which is now in Washington City—Major Matt Dale, Lieut. James C. S. Thompson, Sergt. A. A. Congleton, Sergt. Stephen Carpenter, Sergt. J. C. Hollingsworth, Jacob Frank, William Zimmer, killed; John Hanson, William Leach, Peter Gillis, Chas. Kingsley, Joseph Ashbrook, Austin Jones, wounded.

On the tattered silk can yet be deciphered the words, Malvern Hill, Gaines Mill, Eltham's Landing. Blood stains are still visible. The bullet-holes and shell rents show that it went through the hurricane of battle "where thick and heavy was the work of death."

After the battle far in advance of anyone, the dead body of Lieut. R. H. Gaston was found by the foe. In acknowledgement of his heroism, he was accorded an honorable burial by them with a head mark over his grave extolling in conspicuous gallantry: "Tears and love for the gray."

In the cornfield lie the crumbling bones of Texas' beloved heroes, Capt. Cotton, Lieuts. Hoffman, Perry, Runnels, Waterhouse, Sandford, Drake, A. H. Baker, color bearer of the Fifth, and many others whose names, like shining stars on the milky baldric of the skies, glitter with perennial glory: whose heroic deeds the cherubim and the seraphim chant to rhythmic lays in angelic choirs: whose renowned exploits are carved on a monumental shaft made of the ruby, the emerald, and the sapphire.

After the battle of Sharpsburg, another silk flag was presented to the first Texas.

## Amos Hanks
## 1828–1870

Amos Hanks was born in San Augustine, Texas, in 1828, and was less than a year old when his family moved to Tyler County Texas.[42] He joined the Woodville Rifles, which became Company "F" of the 1st Texas Infantry. Hanks was severely wounded in the leg at the Battle of Antietam and had his leg amputated as a result. He was discharged for disability on January 28, 1863, and returned to Texas.[43] Amos Hanks died in 1870 and is buried in Jefferson, Texas.

Sergeant Amos Hanks
1st Texas Infantry
*Fort Worth Morning Register*
December 9, 1900
Amos Hanks and President Lincoln

Major C. C. Cummings: There was a Texas lawyer, Amos Hanks, who was first lieutenant in my regiment—First Texas, Hood's Brigade—and lost a leg in the cornfield on the fatal field at Sharpsburg (Antietam). It was there that occurred the heaviest loss of the civil war, as determined by the war department at Washington, and a monument is erected on the spot by this department, commemorating this fact, the loss being 82 and some odd percent. Hanks was taken prisoner and left in the hospital there on the battlefield. President Lincoln visited this hospital and passed Hanks in the rounds among the wounded. Hanks had been ordering the Federal Nurses around with a high hand, calling them his "niggers," and demanding extra attention, which they gave him—to humor the joke of this wild and wholly Texan. Hanks had all the earmarks of a typical Texan, away back from Bitter creek. Long hair and mustache so fierce that he kept it tied back of his neck for the queerness of the thing. As President Lincoln passed, Hanks hailed him in a shockingly familiar away, saying: "And this is old Abe? We're kin, Abe, shore's you're born. I'm a Hanks, and so was your ma. Mighty glad to see you, Abe, old boy: but would prefer that it would have been under circumstances more of an equality between us." Mr. Lincoln took his smiles as belonging to Texas style, and passed on with a good humored smile. I dare say Hanks was the only soldier of the war who ever became so familiar with the president on either side on so short an acquaintance.

## Malachiah Reeves
## September 26, 1843–December 4, 1929

Malachiah Reeves was born on September 26, 1843, in Bibb County, Alabama. As a boy, his family moved to Texas in late 1849 or early 1850. They first settled on a farm in Nacogdoches County, Texas. In 1856, he was chosen along with Elder R. R. Morrow to lead the new congregation forming a Baptist Church in Athens. In 1860, he was living in Houston County and attended his first school, a subscription school in the spring of 1861, and, in July of that year, enlisted in the Confederate States Army and served three years. He was a member of Company "I," First Texas Regiment of Hood's Texas Brigade, when he was taken prisoner at Mechanicsville, Virginia, in 1862. He was later exchanged and fought in the Battle of Gettysburg. He was promoted to 4th Sergeant on April 15, 1864, and was furloughed to Alabama in the early spring of 1865. He was paroled at Centerville, Alabama, in April, 1865. He married Jane Elizabeth Powers on September 23, 1875, and had a daughter named Leila. In August, 1876, Jane died. In January, 1877, he married Nancy Beall and they had eleven children. He was ordained a Baptist minister in 1888, and later was a postmaster for the town. Sergeant Reeves died on December 4, 1929, and is buried in Leaguesville, Texas.[44]

### Sergeant Malachiah Reeves
### 1st Texas Infantry

Boonsborough Gap was the first battle on this move. Lt. Col. P. A. Works had been the First Texas Regiment's commanding officer through several engagements, but our commander in the battle of Sharpsburg, Maryland was Capt. R. W. Cotton. Sharpsburg was on Antietam Creek. This was to prove one of our toughest fights.

Our regiment was led into Farmer Miller's tall cornfield. It was getting to be cold weather. It was in the fall; September 16 and this was harvest time. We did a right smart of harvesting for Farmer Miller! There was hand to hand fighting all along our lines as the Yankees attacked. Our Louisiana and Georgia comrades were bearing the brunt of the fire under the leadership of General Jackson. Our Brig. General John B. Hood led our forces into help and as First Texas Regiment opened fire, moving against fresh Union troops led by McClellan, believe me, child, this was a dreadful battle! By late afternoon the cornfield was full of my dead comrades, and the Yanks were sending in other fresh troops. By the time the sun went down, 50 had been killed and 132 were wounded. Only two officers and twenty two of our First Texas Regiment came out of that horrible fight. The report was 82.3% of our regiment came out of that field.

My company had only one officer, and Private Bill Berryman and I to survive this desperate conflict!

It was in this battle that I received my first and only wound. I couldn't recover, somehow, and they placed me on the register of the Medical Director's Office in Richmond, Virginia, Oct 18, 1862. I was not allowed to return to duty until Nov 25, but was just in time to get into the battle of Fredericksburg.

My comrades were under the leadership of my good friend, Lt. Col. P. A. Work. There was hardly 500 of us including the officers. Our Army of Northern Virginia, I was told, had been inactive since Antietam. The weather was beginning to get real sharp with cold, icy winds. It bit our bodies badly—you know our clothes were not heavy as they might have been. Our shoes were badly worn; we needed new issue, and were expecting to get some new ones real soon.[45]

## James M. Day
## 1833–1910

James M. Day, in early 1862, enlisted in Company "M," 1st Texas Infantry. He was promoted to corporal in July, 1862. According to Lt. Col. Phillip A. Work's official report on the Battle of Antietam, Corporal Day was the second out of four men to be shot by the enemy while carrying the 1st Texas Infantry's Lone Star flag. Although he was badly wounded at Antietam, he escaped from the hospital to rejoin his unit. He was paroled in 1865. After the war he became a farm laborer in Tyler, Texas, where he and his wife, Anne, raised six children.

## Corporal James M. Day
## 1st Texas Infantry
## Texas State Library Receives Historic Mementoes

A pen and a gun are amongst the possessions recently added to the Texas State Library. The pen is the one used by President Roosevelt on May 30, 1908, when signing the act of Congress granting pensions to the Texas Rangers for services before the war between 1855 and 1860, and the gun is the one with which Color Bearer James Day was armed when he was killed while carrying the colors of the First Texas Infantry in the Battle of Sharpsburg, on September 17, 1862.[46] The weapon was presented by James P. Wintermyre of Shepardstown, W. Va. What adds special interest to this memento of southern bravery is the fact that after Color Bearer Day was killed, the colors were raised by four other men until one after another they were also killed, the regiment losing 183 of the 216 men with which it went into the fight.[47]

Basil "Bass" Hallum
?–September 17, 1862
2nd Corporal Basil Hallum
1st Texas Infantry

Basil was shot in the Battle of Sharpsburg. He was in Captain Gaston's company and was serving as an officer in a most closely contested engagement. The color bearers were shot down one after another, and when others would not raise the colors, he carried them for a time; yet in the hot engagement, he, too, fell to rise no more. His two messmates, William and Clarence Wren, returned and told the sad news.[48]

Orlando Thacker "O.T." Hanks
January 17, 1844–April 24, 1926

O. T. Hanks was born in San Augustine County, Texas, on January 17, 1844. Near the outbreak of the Civil War, Hanks joined the "Texas Invincibles," which later became Captain Company "K" of the 1st Texas Infantry. After the war, he and wife, Susan, raised ten children. He died on April 24, 1926, and is buried in Dickerson Cemetery, San Augustine, Texas.

Hanks' recollections of the war have been published in *History of Captain B.F. Benton's Company, Hood's Texas Brigade* and *A Yellow Rose in Old Dominion*.[49]

4th Corporal O.T. Hanks
1st Texas Infantry
Fall 1862

The battle was over (Second Manassas). We took up line of march for Lee's invasion of Maryland. We frequently had nothing to eat only roasting ears. The cobs are strewn along the roadside. After having made their repast some fellow would boast that he had eaten a dozen ears. We were undergoing as hard or harder forced march as we ever accomplished. The men were taxed almost beyond human endurance; would think they could go no further, and then still go on.

Along the line of march, two spies were captured both of whom were executed. We pressed onward, past Leesburg, on to the bank of the Potomac. We were directed to take off our shoes, and wade across it, and to be careful not to get our ammunition wet. Into the river we went and were now on Maryland's soil. I am satisfied it was General Lee's object to get aid from Maryland, which he did not get, only a few sympathizers.

We took up our line of march and pressed forward, passing through Frederick, a beautiful southern city. The people appeared awe stricken. The women and children, of course, were gathered to the front to see the soldiers pass. One little fellow was perched on the fence and asked if these were Texicans. On being told, "Yes," he remarked "Oh, Mama, they look just like our folks." Another one was heard to say: "Here comes the Bonny Blue Flag now, come and see it." It was a large Lone Star flag carried by the first Texas Regiment. If I am not mistaken it was presented to the regiment by Mrs. Louis Wigfall.

On we went and finally struck camp, near Hagerstown. Here our boys took a general bath. To see hundreds of men bathing at once was a spectacle. The Baltimore and Ohio Railroad crossed the river at this point—I have forgotten the name. Our fellows blasted the R. R. bridge down over this river. It was a splendid structure. We could see them at work

We now set out on a line of march for South Mountain. We rambled about through it among the rocks and cliffs with orders not to make any noise, not even to let our cups and canteens rattle. Towards daylight we fell back across the Antietam River, and prepared for an attack from the enemy. In a few minutes we were advancing under heavy fire from the enemy. That night we had roasting ears and broiled beef for supper. They were gathered from the field which we fought in next day.

Next morning very early we were preparing hastily some rations we had received. We were in a skirt or mot of timber in rear of the old Dunker Church. Before we had finished our breakfast the bombshells commenced coming along us fast and furiously. We soon formed a line of battle [Antietam, September, 1862] and marched forward to meet the enemy.

In a few minutes we were advancing under heavy fire from the enemy. The field was open, they used their cannon freely and had some improvised breast works. We had nothing between us (and them) only the air. But onward we went until within thirty yards. The smoke at times was very heavy on the field. We could go no further. They were too strong for us, cutting us down almost like grain before a cradle.

While we were fighting I noticed a fellow on his knees peeping through an opening made by two rails placed on end forming a kind of triangle. He was about thirty yards distant and had on a double breasted shirt. I had a good gun and drew directly at his breast. I thought to myself, "If we whip I am going to see if I killed you." The boys had often said they did not get to investigate. Just at that time when I was raising my gun to my face to fire again, a bullet passed, struck me in the left side, close up under the arm, coming out under my should blade near my back bone.

The battle [Antietam] was over and fellows had all left the field in defeat. While I was moping along to the rear and being among the last, a bullet passed through my hat rim, just over my right ear. I made it back a short distance and was carried to the field hospital. Next day passed and neither of the opposing generals dared to renew battle.

Next day, General Lee recrossed the Potomac at Shepardstown, leaving his dead and such wounded as could not be moved. Lieutenant James Waterhouse, Lieutenant Sam Patton and Jesse Hale were killed, while William Gray, Ned Miller, and O. T. Hanks, as well as others of the company I do not remember, were wounded.

The Yankee army pursued, General Lee next crossed the Potomac at Shepardstown and went into an ambush laid by General Jackson, who placed a small detachment of troops at the crossing, and further in the rear placed a line of infantry with several pieces of cannon. The enemy came forward, attacked the advance line, which fought them furiously for a while then skedaddled, leaving one piece of cannon behind. The enemy pursued viciously and ran into the ambush which surprised them. They were literally torn to pieces and fled for their lives.

The citizens told us when we crossed the river at the crossing on parole that they actually jumped off the bluff at least ten feet high into the water. They sent the cannon back to their rear. It passed by where we were lying wounded. There never was such parading before over one little gun as they had. They seldom ever captured one from us.

The Maryland Campaign was now closed. I was now a prisoner of war, as well as scores of my comrades left on the battlefield at the field hospital.[50]

## H. Waters Berryman
## March 18, 1844–February 14, 1922

H. Waters Berryman was born on March 18, 1844, in Louisiana. He enlisted in the Confederate Army on March 22, 1862, as a soldier in the Crockett Southrons; later, it would become Company "I," 1st Texas Infantry. He was in all the battles that Hood's Texas Brigade engaged in. In 1864, he was wounded twice; the first was at the Battle of the Wilderness and later at Darby Town Road.

After the war, he settled in Cherokee County, Texas, and died on February 14, 1922. He is buried in the Cherokee County Cemetery.

### Private H. Waters Berryman
### 1st Texas Infantry

Camp near Martinsburg Va.
September 22nd 1862
My Own Dear Ma,

I received yours of August the 2nd the 17th of this month, also one from Georgia written the 20th of July the same day. We had another big fight, one of the hardest contested fights that has ever been fought in the East. This fight commenced on the 16th and ended the evening of September 17th. It was near a little town in Maryland called Sharpsburg, of course the Texas Brigade was in it and in the hottest part of the battlefield.

Poor Tom Cook was shot down and left on the field. It is not known whether he was killed or not, our Lt. saw him fall, but he says he did not think that he was killed. Newt was slightly wounded in the thigh, it did not break the skin. I think that it must have been done by a spent grape shot. It bruised his leg and it made him a little lame. Tom Boone was wounded slightly in the foot by a piece of shell. It don't impair his walking at all. Malachiah Reeves, Mr. Blakey's nephew was slightly wounded in the head. William Pritchard was wounded in the face with a buck shot, also in the breast. It struck him about the middle while stooping, ranged downwards and lodged in the skin of his belly. The ball has been taken out. His wound looks pretty bad, but he is able to walk about. He will get a furlough in a week or two and go home. Lawyer Mitchell was wounded on the head with a piece of shell, his skull is supposed to be fractured, the surgeons say it is not dangerous. Captain Cotton was shot in the head, he is still living, some hopes of his getting well. I was sent off the day before the fight commenced on skirmish and got cut off from the Brigade. I was not in the general engagement, it, was only in the skirmish. I was under the fire of the enemy's cannon where the grape and canisters fell as thick as hale. J. R. Jones, Mrs. West's nephew was shot through the thigh, he will get a furlough to go home.

We had to give up the battlefield to the enemy and all that were not able to walk off were taken by the Yankees. You have no idea how much I suffer on account of poor Tom, poor fellow, left in the hands of the Yankees and probably dead. Mort is at Winchester, he is Ward Master in a hospital there, he was not in the fight. Sam Stuart was wounded and left on the battlefield. Moore was not in the fight, he was sick when Company I came out to fight. There were only three men to come out unhurt. The Regiment only had three stacks of arms, our Major was killed and left in the hands of the Yankees and the flag that was presented to us by Mrs. Davis and Mrs. Wigfall was left on the field. Just as fast as one man would pick it up he would be shot down. Eight men were killed and wounded in trying to bring it off the field. I can't say that we were whipped, but we were overwhelmed. The Texas Brigade stood up and fought without any reinforcements three or four fresh Yankee Brigades until all of her men had fallen, or most of them. They always take the Texians to the hottest part of the field, but her best men have fallen now and they will be more particular now. I reckon where she is carried hereafter.

Mite Easter went through the fight safe, he is in good health now.

I hope Dishman will not have to go to war, for if he leaves, I don't know what you all will do if he leaves. If he must tell him to get a substitute, cost what it many, for there is no telling when this war will end, but I hope it will not be long, for if it lasts much longer we will be ruined forever.

Tell Georgia it is no use in her weaving me and Newt any clothes as she cannot send them here safely and it would be putting her to a great deal of trouble for nothing.

I was sorry to hear that Georgia was in bad health. I hope when this reaches home that she will be entirely well. Poor Julia, I reckon she had a time of it, her children being all sick and being alone. I would like to hear from Hous. It must be very sickly in our neighborhood, from the deaths that have occurred so recently in our country. I hope Ma, that you and Georgia and the balance of the family will be blessed with good health. I have not heard from Cousin Newt since the fight. I hope he is not hurt, when I next see him I will make him write.

There is some good news that I was about to forget to tell you. We took Harpers Ferry with fifteen thousand prisoners on the 15th of September with a great many cannons and commissary stores. The Yankees were fortified there and we stormed the place and they surrendered after two days resistance. I am glad to hear that Phil Wolfe arrived home safe. He can tell you what a soldier has to undergo. Give him my respects.

Newt and I have plenty of clothing and blankets so you need not get uneasy about our suffering from cold. We are camped here near Martinsburg, but I don't know when we will leave, but as we have been leading an active life, I guess we will leave pretty soon. I wish we could get stationed so that we could write to you often, but as it is we don't have an opportunity once a month. There was a letter came to Tom from Mr. Cook but the poor fellow ever had a chance to read it. One came for Tom Boone also.

You wanted to know how the sick were treated in the hospital, in the one that I was at in Lynchburg, they had Bakiso bread and coffee for breakfast, with meat added to it for dinner and bread and coffee for supper.

Hughes and Russell are still behind, they have not come up yet. I heard from Hughes the other day, he is at Winchester. I have not heard from Sam McBee in a long time, I reckon he is still in Richmond.

Give my respects to all the neighbors, to Parson Slover and Mr. Carter's family. Tell all the black folks howdy. Tell Dennis I would like to be home to coon hunt with him. Tell Aunt Sally she must not die until I get home for I want to eat more of her good cooking.

Kiss Georgia and the children for me. I will write to her as soon as possible. Love to Cousin Henry and Dishman and Julia's family. I must close.

Accept the love of your son

Waters Berryman

P.S. Tell Milly and Maria I can beat them at cooking all to pieces. When I come home I will show them how to make biscuits. I was sorry to hear of the death of Mr. Blanton. Gus Aldrich was wounded in the arm. Give my love to Cook and Martin families, Roark's too.

Cotton is dead.

H. W. B.[51]

## Solomon Thomas Blessing
## 1840–March 9, 1928

Solomon Blessing was born in Jefferson, Maryland in 1840. In 1860, shortly before the secession of Texas, Blessing set up a Daguerreotype photography school in Galveston, Texas. On August 1, 1861, he enlisted in the Lone Star Rifles, which later became Company "L" of the 1st Texas Infantry. He was wounded twice during the Battle of Antietam and spent nine months recuperating from his wounds. In June, 1863, he returned to active duty.[52] On October 7, 1864, he was captured at the Battle of Darbytown Road, Virginia, and spent the rest of the war at Point Lookout Prison, Maryland. He returned to Texas in 1865 and resumed his photography career in Houston, Texas. In 1866, he moved to Dallas, Texas, and opened another photographic studio and enjoyed a successful business for many years. He died on March 9, 1928, and is buried at Greenwood Cemetery in Dallas, Texas.[53]

### Private Solomon Thomas Blessing
### 1st Texas Infantry

On Sept. 17 we fought the battle of Sharpsburg, or as the Federals call it, Antietam. I was in the charge in the cornfield and was near our regimental flag when I saw the bearer fall. My first impulse was to pick it up, but then thought I could do more good shooting. This flag was made from the wedding dresses of Mrs. Jefferson Davis and Mrs. Louis T. Wigfall, and presented to the regiment at Camp Wigfall. Very shortly I fell, shot through the leg and a buckshot in the hand which I carry yet. I managed to hobble back to the woods and was carried back to the field hospital. When Lee crossed the Potomac at Shepherdstown he was unable to carry all his wounded and I was among those left. We were paroled only six miles from mother's home. My sister and her husband, Mr. A. C. Castle, came for me and as I had been paroled was allowed to be taken home, where I remained till the next June, when I went to Baltimore and gave myself up and was sent to Fort McHenry, shortly after was sent to James River and exchanged.[54]

## The Perry Brothers and the Battle of Antietam

All four Perry brothers of the "Marshall Guards," which later was renamed Company "E," of the 1st Texas Infantry—Second Lieutenant Clinton Perry, Corporal H. Earl Perry, and Privates E. O. and L. F. Perry—were casualties at Antietam. The lieutenant and corporal were both killed and the two privates wounded. Thus, the Perry's accounted for one-sixth of the company's total casualties at the Battle of Antietam.[55]

John P. "J. P." Cook

J. P. Hook enlisted in the "Star Rifles," which later became Company "D," 1st Texas Infantry. He was wounded at the Battle of Chickamauga on September 20, 1863.[56] After the war, he settled in Harper, Texas.

Private J. P. Cook
1st Texas Infantry
The *Daily Express*
March 29, 1908
Historical Reminiscences
A Review of Times that are Past but Live in History—Prepared by J. B. Polley, Floresville, Texas.

We had intended in publishing Col. P. A. Work's report of the part taken by the First Texas Regiment of Hood's Texas Brigade in the battle of Sharpsburg, in which he accounts for the loss of its flag, but have been anticipated by Colonel Phelps. It appeared in last Sunday's issue of the *Express*. Mr. J. P. Cook of Harper, Tex., writing of the same battle, but before seeing Colonel Work's report, has this to say:

I have been reading W. E. Barry's and General Hamby's reminiscences of the battle of Sharpsburg, and having been a member of Company D of the First Texas and taken part in that battle, I can vouch for the truth of all they say concerning it. We made the charge with the rest of the brigade and, having driven back the first line of the enemy, went on to their second line, charged it and did not stop as long as there was a Yankee in sight. They ran through the cornfield and we had nearly gone through it when Colonel Work called a halt to reform our line and await the arrival of the balance of the brigade. While thus halted a Federal battery some 250 yards distant from us gout our range and began making it hot for us. The boys wanted to charge and capture it, but Colonel Work objected.

We began firing at the men around the battery, and after we had given them a couple of rounds they abandoned their guns and took to flight. Just as they did so a body of Federals who lay behind a rock fence fifty yards away, and partly hidden from our view by the standing corn, poured a volley into us. Turning our eyes in this direction, we began firing at them, taking the precaution however, to lie down and do our shooting. You can imagine how brisk the firing was from both sides when I tell you that within five minutes not a stalk of corn was left standing between us and the rock fence. But we stayed there and continued the fight until most of our men were killed or wounded, and then, ordered to retire, fell back and got in touch with other regiments of the brigade. Of my company only Captain Connally and myself were left.

While ramming the thirty-fourth cartridge down my gun it stuck about half way. Just then the order to fall back came, and having no time to tinker with a choked gun I picked up that of one of my wounded comrades. Getting back to where we had routed the first line of the enemy. I found a comrade named Dixon—we called him Dixie—lying down and severely wounded. He asked me to help him off the field, and I did, and although for 150 yards the air was full of lead fired at us by the Yankees, neither of us got scratched. About this time other troops relieved our brigade and we went back to the camp we had occupied the night before. When Captain Connally learned that he and I were the sole representatives of Company D he said that as we did not need any officers for so small a squad he would get a gun and fall in with me, and that we two would do the fighting for Company D as long as we lived. Captain Connally was one of the bravest men in the army. He was in the last stage of consumption and had to be hauled to the battle field that morning. But the day overtaxed his strength. He was sent back to Richmond and thence went to Georgia, where he died a few months later.

The last I saw of our regimental flag that day was at the time we were ordered to retire. I saw the flag fall, its bearer being killed, then I saw it grasped and raised by another man, who started back with it, furling it around its staff as he walked, then I lost sight of it, and am sure that this last man I saw in possession of it must have been killed in the retreat. Anyhow, the flag was not captured and was not secured by the Federals in any way of which they had a right to be proud.

Not one of the regiments that composed Hood's Texas Brigade ever had its flag captured in battle. The man who got credit for capturing the First Texas flag picked it up as it lay beside its dead or mortally wounded bearer, after all the fighting of the day was over. No doubt, however, he told his superiors that he had wrested it from the hands of its bearer. It put a feather in the cap of a Federal soldier to be credited with the capture of a Confederate flag, for in most cases not only was his name mentioned in general orders, but he was likely, if at all qualified, to receive promotion. The Confederate soldier, though, was offered no incentive of that kind; his regiment got all the credit, no matter what the risk he took. The best that the Confederate authorities did to encourage gallantry was to offer gold medals to the bravest man of a regiment. But as these superlatively brave were usually selected by the vote of the regiment, personal popularity had much to do with the awards.


## James J. "J. J." Hale
## 1840–January 1, 1926


J. J. Hale was born in San Augustine, Texas, in 1840, and soon after Texas seceded, he enlisted as a private in the Texas Invincibles, which later became Company "K" of the 1st Texas Infantry. Private Hale fought in all the major battles that Hood's Brigade was involved. On April 10, 1865, the day after the surrender of General Lee at Appomattox Court House, Hale and seven other men from Texas, who had been keeping the Confederate generals informed as to the movement of the United

States forces, gave their report. They immediately started for home in Texas. On that day, they captured fourteen prisoners, thirteen whites, and one African-American. Among the prisoners were several lieutenants and one captain. They marched their prisoners 13 miles and then paroled them. Hale signed General Lee's name to the parole.

He was elected sheriff of Navarro County, Texas, in 1902, serving until 1904, and was elected for another term of office from 1906 to 1908. He raised a family of ten children. He was a member of the Cumberland Presbyterian Church and of the Masonic Lodge. Hale was universally respected as a good sheriff. J. J. Hale died January 1, 1926, and is buried in Birdston, Texas.[57]

Private J. J. Hale
1st Texas Infantry
*The Eagle*
June 27, 1924
In a Hundred Skirmishes

I enlisted in St. Augustine County, Texas, in 1861, volunteering for service in the Confederate army. My first captain was B. F. Benton, who was killed at the battle of Gaines Mill where we broke McClellan's right wind with our left. I was sent direct to Richmond and was a member of Hood's Texas Brigade. It was the early summer of '61 that we arrived in Richmond, just a little while after the first battle of Manassas.

I participated in the following battles: Yorktown, Eltham's Landing, Seven Pines, 7 Days' Battle, Second Manassas, two Fredericksburg, two at Cold Harbor, Chickamauga, and the battles of the Wilderness to Petersburgh, where it was constant fighting for 26 days. I expect I have been in a hundred skirmishes which are about the same as a battle. I was never wounded and never had a bullet through my clothes.

I missed the battle of Sharpsburg because I hurt my knee a few days before when I fell off a pole across the top of a dug-out. Two other brothers enlisted with me; one of them was killed at Sharpsburg and the other at Gettysburg.

John C. "J. C." Robinson
August 6, 1839–June 9, 1924

J. C. Robinson was born on August 6, 1839, in Demopolis, Alabama. As a young boy, his family moved to Douglassville, Texas. On May 27, 1861, he enlisted in the "Star Rifles," which later became Company "D" of the 1st Texas Infantry. He was wounded in the battles of Second Manassas, Antietam, and Chickamauga, where he was severely wounded and was discharged in October, 1864. After the war, he settled back in Douglassville, where he and his wife, Emily, raised six children. He died on June 9, 1924, and is buried at the Union Chapel Cemetery in Douglassville, Texas.[58]

## Private J. C. Robinson
## 1st Texas Infantry

I was in the battles of Eltham's Landing, Seven Pines, Fredericksburg, Gettysburg and Chickamauga. Had an attack of slow fever by which I missed the Seven Days Battle around Richmond. Was at the second battle of Manassas and Sharpsburg. Here I was wounded and taken to Augusta, Ga., where we received much kindness from the ladies. Was given a furlough from that place to some relatives in Butler County, Alabama, and remained with them eighteen months on furlough.[59]

## S. O. Young
## 1848–1926

S. O. Young was a lifelong resident of Houston, Texas. During the Civil War, Young served with the 5th Texas Infantry. After the war, he graduated from Washington and Lee and later received his medical degree from New Orleans Medical College. He practiced medicine in Houston until the death of his mother in 1882. He then helped found the *Houston Post*. Later, Young became managing editor of the *Galveston News* and secretary of the Galveston Cotton Exchange. After retirement, Dr. Young was active as a writer of Houston and Texas history and participated in the many reunion events of Hood's Texas Brigade.

## Private S. O. Young
## 5th Texas Infantry
## The First at Sharpsburg

It was reserved for the First to give to the world an exhibition of cool courage and to undergo the hardest of all tests—endurance. At Sharpsburg for hours the First Texas held a position that was of vital importance to General Lee. They knew that it must be held at all cost, even though every man should be slaughtered. The idea of their driving back an inch never entered their heads. They knew they were simply a human wedge placed there by General Lee to prevent the Federal advance. There was not faltering. They simply stayed there and did what lee had placed them there to do, though at such frightful loss that today the military records of all civilized nations on earth have recorded the fact that the First Texas Regiment lost over 82 percent of its numbers at Sharpsburg, the largest record for any regiment in any army.

When did the Japs ever show greater eagerness to die than the First Texas at Sharpsburg?

This it will be seen that each of the Texas regiments in Virginia had an opportunity of reflecting honor on the whole brigade, and that each seized the opportunity.

The First Texas at Sharpsburg

The Fourth Texas at Gaines' Mill

The Fifth Texas at Manassas[60]


*Tri-Weekly Telegraph*
October 31, 1862
Richmond, VA., Oct. 8, 1862
"God bless the ladies of Virginia"

Such will be the prayer of the mothers, wives, sisters and sweet-hearts of the Texas Brigade: for when the gallant wounded were retracing their weary steps from the bloody battle-field of Sharpsburg, Md., across the river to Shepherdstown, the ladies in the vicinity came out into the public streets with wash-bowl, soap and towel, and there, before high Heaven, exhibited that peerless nobility of washing and dressing the wounds of our soldiers. Again I say, God bless the ladies of Virginia!

A. H. E. (Arthur H. Edey)


*Tri-Weekly Telegraph*
November 19, 1862

There were several Confederate flags captured by the abolitionists in Maryland, and among them as our readers are aware, was that of the 1st Texas. The first Texas was resting in a cornfield, and somehow forgot their flag. It was of course captured. An abolition correspondent thus describes it.

A large and very splendid silk flag, with the staff shot in two in the middle. The flag is composed of silk of three colors, and when new must have been a very superb one. The field is of deep blue, with a single large straw-colored star in the center. The bars are of straw color and delicate purple. On the field the top is inscribed "Seven Pines;" on the yellow bar, "Gaines' Farm" and "Eltham's Landing, and "Malvern Hills," on the purple bar. It is much torn and stained, and is bordered with heavy, but tarnished, silver fringe. This is evidently a Texan standard. I regret that I could not learn its history.

We believe this flag was made by Mrs. Wigfall and Mrs. President Davis, and by them presented to the 1st Texas when Wigfall was Colonel of it. It is a sad thing to think of that it should now grace the trophies in the hands of the Abolitionists.

### Austin Weekly Statesman
### June 30, 1887

The *San Antonio Express* says: "As will be seen by the Washington letter published elsewhere, the battle flag of Hood's Texas brigade is among the captured Confederate banners now in the war department; also, the flag of the "First Texas," though whether of infantry or cavalry the correspondent does not state. The government is fully entitled to keep these Texas flags, as it had a devil of a time getting possession of them. And from the way the survivors of that famous Hood's brigade deported themselves yesterday, it looked as if they had not a single thought or regret for that lost flag. Its absence did not bring forth any expressions of regret, and not even a passing allusion. Yes! the government can have a fee simple interest in that bit of silk, if such can be, and the gallant remnant of Hood's brigade will never give voice to the contrary."

### Fort Worth Star-Telegram
### September 2, 1907
### Texas Flags Bring Tears
### Emblems at Bowie Reunion Hall Recall Stirring Events
### Carried By Hood
### State Colors Presented to Col. Wigfall's Regiment by his daughter

Special to the Telegram

Austin, Texas. Sept. 1—The governor has just received a letter from General K. M. Van Zandt of Fort Worth, division commander of the United Confederate Veterans, thank him and also the adjutant general for the use of the Texas flags which were sent to the state reunion of Confederate veterans recently held at Bowie. The writer states that the flags were greatly admired and brought tears to the eyes of many. The flags were presented at the reunion by Colonel McGaughey.

These flags are three in number, and all have historical value. One is a battle flag of the First Texas infantry, Hood's brigade, army of Virginia; one of the Third Texas cavalry and one of the Texas state colors of the First Texas regiment. The following is a description of the last named flag by General Wm. R. Hamby, Fourth Texas infantry, Hood's brigade, which is quite interesting.

## The Lone Star Flag

The Lone Star flag was presented to the First Texas infantry in the summer of 1861 by Miss Wigfall, her father being the colonel of the regiment, and afterward the commander of the brigade, composed of the First Texas, Fourth Texas, Fifth Texas, Eighteenth Georgia and Hampton's Legion, but when General Wigfall was elected to the Confederate senate, General Hood was placed in command of the brigade, and as the brigade had not seen any fighting previously, it was ever afterward known as Hood's Texas brigade.

This flag was one of the handsomest in the Virginia army and was carried by the First Texas infantry thru the battle of Eltham's Landing, Seven Pines, the seven days' battle around Richmond, Freeman's Ford, Thoroughfare Gap, Second Manassas, South Mountain and Sharpsburg.

## At the Battle of Sharpsburg

In the battle of Sharpsburg, fought Sept, 17, 1862, the regiment was commanded by Lieutenant Colonel Work, and went into battle with 226 men and lost 186 on the field, killed and wounded, including nine flag bearers. To keep from being annihilated, they finally retired and when the flag fell, no one knew it save him, who had fallen with it.

Official records show that the First Texas infantry lost nine men killed and wounded in the battle of Sharpsburg in proportion to number engaged than any other regiment either Union or Confederate in any battle of the war.

Hood's Texas brigade did not have any brigade flag all of the flags in the brigade belonging to the individual regiments."

**The *West Weekly News and Times***
**February 18, 1921**
**In the House**
**Austin, Texas**

The bullet riddled and blood stained flag of the First Texas Regiment of Hood's Brigade, that was almost annihilated in withstanding an attack of federal troops at Sharpsburg, Md., be placed on the walls of the house. The flag which has been resting in the state library was presented to the house Wednesday by J. O. Bradford of Austin, only survivor of this famous regiment.

*The Eagle*
March 5, 1921

Austin, Texas, March 6—In presenting the battle flag of Hood's Brigade of Texas duly framed with its history by the following resolution was adopted by the House: Austin, Texas, March 2, 1921. Hon. Charles G. Thomas, Speaker of the House of Representatives.

Dear Sir: We, your committee appointed to have framed the old Battle Flag of the First Texas Infantry of Hood's Brigade, have performed our duty.

The flag was framed by C. M. Miller of Austin, for which there was a charge of $46.80.

We suggest that the survivors of the battle of Sharpsburg, Maryland, where this flag was defended to-wit: J. O. Bradfield, N. Hollingsworth, A. D. Oliphant and Captain W. H. Gaston, present this flag personally to the House and that J. O. Bradfield be requested to address the House. Horton, Roundtree and Perry.

*El Paso Herald*
March 21, 1921
Tattered Flag of Battle is Given Honor

Austin, Tex., March 21.—Torn and tattered and besmeared with the blood of its brave defenders, the Texas flag carried by the First regiment of Hood's brigade of the army of the Confederacy will be placed in a glass case and hung in a conspicuous place in the hall of the House of Representatives.

A resolution to that effect was unanimously adopted by the house. The resolution was offered by representative Horton of Dallas, and the tattered flag was unfurled in the house by J. O. Bradfield of Austin, the only member of the First regiment now living. As the gray haired old man unfolded the remnant of the banner that was carried by the men of Hood's regiment until they were practically annihilated, the members of the house rose to their feet and cheered. The flag was made by Miss Lula Wigfall of Marshall, Tex., daughter of Louis T. Wigfall, the first colonel of the regiment. When the regiment was met by overwhelming union forces at Sharpsburg, Maryland, on September 17, 1862, the flag was about to be captured. The regiment was almost wiped out and the banner was later found beneath the bodies of 16 brave Texas soldiers, who died while defending the emblem.

*Bryan Weekly Eagle*
February 24, 1921
Hood's Brigade Battleflag to Belong to Texas

Austin, Texas, Feb. 18.—The committee, Representatives Horton of Dallas, Horton of Dallas, Roundtree of Brazos, and Perry of Erath presented the following report to the legislature:

"This flag was made and presented to the First Texas Infantry by Miss Lula Wigfall of Marshall, Texas, early in 1861, while her father, Louis T. Wigfall was colonel of the regiment. The stars on the flag were cut from the wedding dress of Miss Wigfall's mothers.

"This flag received its first baptism of fire under Stonewall Jackson, and was borne triumphantly by the old First Texas Infantry on the banks of the Potomac and through many battles, including Yorktown, Eltham's Landing, Seven Pines, Gaines' Mill, Malvern Hill, Freeman's Ford, Second Manassas, Boonsboro Gap and finally went down in blood on the battlefield at Sharpsburg, Maryland on September 17, 1862, where the regiment which bore this flag was engaged by twelve thousand Union troops and thirty-six pieces of field artillery.

"When the battle was concluded, the flag was recovered beneath the bodies of sixteen Texas soldiers who died in its defense. By order of Congress, this flag was returned to the State of Texas by the Secretary of War."

The resolution was adopted and with the flag will be made a permanent memorial of Texas.

*Morning Herald*
January 25, 1965
Texas Marker in Rose Hill Recalls Fury of 'Cornfield'
By E. Russell Hicks

On April 9, a dramatic epoch in our country's history will close and a new era will begin. On that date just a century ago, General Lee surrendered to General Grant at Appomattox, bringing an end the Civil War and an end to ante bellum America.

A new age burst on the country. The footsore Confederate soldier, ragged, half-starved, heavy-footed, enfeebled by want and wound, returned to his devastated South and began building an agricultural and industrial empire destined to be a marvel in the modern world. The Northern soldier went home to translate his tremendous energy of the battle line into the creation of a new North and West which excelled the wildest dreams of the sages of the ages. Who will vision for us what the next hundred years will bring?

One thing the past century did for Washington County (Maryland) that gives it great priority in time. It made it a land bridge that unites Dixieland with Yankeeland, geographically, historically, economically, culturally and socially. Hagerstown as a gateway makes North and South one and inseparable.

Tremendous Stakes

Both North and South have stakes in Washington County. Antietam Battlefield and the Confederate Cemetery prove this. It was made still more evident last Nov. 11

when Texas dedicated a stone marker in memory of her heroic dead who did such terrific fighting in the Cornfield at Antietam on Sept. 17, 1862. It shows what it cost Texas in blood, suffering and sacrifice to feel the unity of our land bridge.

Sept. 17, 1862, at Sharpsburg, the Confederate Army, compared with its adversary, was alarmingly weak. A strong united attack by the whole of McClellan's command would not have threatened defeat merely, but run Gen. Lee's 45,000 men compared to the Union forces of 87,000. He would have to surrender or perish in the Potomac.

When the red day dawned, the Federal artillery opened furiously. Hooker's First Corps began moving down the Sharpsburg Pike against Lee's left wing, commanded by Stonewall Jackson. Jackson realized the ground had to be held at any cost, but he had no reserves. He had relieved Hood, one of the bravest of the brave, and his gallant fighting Texas Brigade so it might cook its rations. Hood and his men received some very rough treatment from Yankees in Turner's Gap above Boonsboro. They had gone hours without food; they were hungry and weak; some fainted.

## Furious Attack

Jackson placed his fighters in a fine field of corn about 500 yards north of the little white-washed Dunker Church that overlooked the ground of the Federal advance. Hooker's sunrise attack was furious and overwhelming. Its fire mowed down Jackson's depleted divisions; they suffered a frightful loss. Jackson had to order Hood to come at once to his support.

The hungry privates had not finished their cooking. They had to throw away their uncooked food and fall in for what they knew was going to be a desperate, death struggle. As they pushed into the cornfield, they saw that over half the Confederate force had been slaughtered. Never in all the army's battles had so many high officers been put out of action so quickly.

Hood's men had but one choice, hold on or perish. The enemy had cut a terrible gap on both sides of the Hagerstown road. Hood's hungry, mad Texans could muster about 2,000 muskets. They formed a death pocket into which the Union forces advanced. "Never," said an officer, "had I seen such a storm of balls—shot and shell, shrieking and crushing canister and bullets, whistling and hissing most fiendlike through the air."

Hood held his ground. Dead men lay in rows and rows; his men had to pass over them. The Federal fire grew fiercer, fresher and faster. Jackson had not a soldier to send to Hood. But just then, Gen. Lee withdrew Walker's Division and McLaw from his right, and sent them to Hood's aid. The Federal attack was repulsed. Hood's Division slowly drew back to the Dunker Church. It had used up its last cartridge. When Hood was asked, "Where is your division?" he pointed to the Cornfield and said: "Dead on that field!"

Miller's Cornfield. (*Brian Duckworth*)

# 4th Texas Infantry Regiment

Below is the first of two battle flags carried by the 4th Texas Infantry during the war until October 7, 1862. The flag was made by Lula Wigfall, daughter of Brigadier General Louis T. Wigfall, and was retired after the Battle of Antietam (Sharpsburg) due to the fact that it was riddled with so many bullet holes. On the top of the flagstaff was a spearhead with the engraving: "Fear not, for I am with thee. Say to the north, give up, and to the south, keep not back."[1]

List of Companies and First Company Officers of the 4th Texas Infantry:

Company A:    (Hardeman Rifles) Goliad County—J. C. G. Key
Company B:    (Tom Green Rifles) Travis County—B. F. Carter
Company C:    (Robertson Five Shooters) Robertson County—W. P. Townsend
Company D:    (Guadalupe Rangers) Guadalupe County—J. P. Bane
Company E:    (Lone Star Guards) McLennan County—E. D. Ryan
Company F:    (Mustang Greys) Bexar County—E. H. Cunningham
Company G:    (Grimes County Greys)—J. W. Hutcheson
Company H:    (Porter Guards, Walker County—P. P. Porter
Company I:    (Navarro Rifles) Navarro County)—C. M. Winkler
Company K:    (Sandy Point Mounted Rifles) Henderson County—W. M. Martin

The citizen soldiers of the 4th and 5th Texas Volunteer Infantry Regiments were primarily recruited in Central Texas under a levy imposed on the state by President Jefferson Davis on June 30, 1861 that called for 2,000 troops. An Austin newspaper editor, John Marshall, was convinced that most of the fighting would take place in the East and he made his plea with Davis so that Texas would have a sizable representation.[2] Colonel John Bell Hood was appointed as the regimental commander for the 4th Texas until his promotion to brigadier general on March 3, 1862.[3]

Of the aforementioned battles of Hood's Texas Brigade, the 4th Texas fought with distinctive valor at the Battle of Gaines Mill on June 27, 1862, when General

4th Texas Infantry flag
flown at Antietam. (*Texas
Division-Daughters of the
Confederacy*)

Lee ordered General Hood to break the Federal line of battle. General Hood led the regiment that indeed did break the enemy's formation as they were marching through heavy artillery fire and then charging with fixed bayonets into a searing barrage of bullets. Immediately afterwards, they fought alongside the 18th Georgia and captured fourteen cannons. At the conclusion of this bloodbath, Union General Phillip St. George's cavalry reserve came charging upon the brigade's left flank in an attempt to recapture these guns. Several companies in the 4th Texas wheeled around and decimated these horse soldiers with just one volley. Of the 506 enlisted men of the 4th Texas Regiment engaged at Gaines Mill, seventy-five were killed and 180 were wounded—a casualty rate of 50 percent. Here they earned the name "Hell Roaring Fourth" because Hood had proclaimed that when he was leading them, he "could double-quick the 4th of Texas to the gates of Hell and never break their line."[4] All of Hood's Texas Brigade had become famous for their awe-inspiring bravery, refusal to lay down or run, and stunning ability to turn the course of battle in the summer months leading up to the Maryland Campaign.

## Antietam (Sharpsburg)

Never before was I so continuously troubled with fear that my horse would further injure some wounded soldier lying helpless on the ground.

General John Bell Hood.[5]

At Sharpsburg, the 4th Texas Infantry was positioned to the right of the 1st Texas, who advanced ahead of the rest of the Brigade into Miller's Cornfield. The soldiers of the 4th were marching across the Hagerstown Pike towards the Cornfield, but just as they crossed it, they found Union troops approaching from both sides of the Pike. Hood ordered his men to the left oblique at the double-quick in order to take a small hill that overlooked this area of battle. Though the 4th managed to reach the top with bloody hand-to-hand fighting, they were raked with a fearsome deadly crossfire of bullets from the Pike and the Cornfield. At the same time, Confederate units to their right were retreating, so Lt. Col. B. F. Carter instructed his men to retreat to the other side of the Hagerstown Pike and take a defensive position. After several more minutes of fierce combat, the 4th Texas was low on ammunition and they found still more Rebel troops were retreating, so Carter led his men from the field of battle as General Hood withdrew the remnants of his division.[6] Lt. Col. Carter later wrote that his regiment was fighting admirably even while assaulted by "a tremendous fire from superior numbers.... The courage, consistency, and patience of our men is beyond all praise."[7]

## Lt. Colonel Benjamin F. Carter
### 1831–July 21, 1863

Benjamin F. Carter moved from Maury County, Tennessee, to Austin, Texas, in 1852 and began practicing law. He married Miss Louisa Oakley Rust in 1856 and they had a son and two daughters. Tragically, Mrs. Carter and two of their children died early in the war.[8]

Carter was the mayor of Austin, Texas, prior to being elected captain of the Tom Green Rifles, later Company "B", 4th Texas Infantry. Upon receiving the Stars and Bars flag made for the Rifles, he proclaimed: "Should it be our fortune to meet the enemies of our country on the field of battle, with that flag floating over us, who would not nobly dare to die beneath its folds."

Captain Carter was promoted to major on June 27, 1862, following the Battle of Gaines Mill and sometime prior to the battle of Second Manassas on August 30, 1862. Major Carter was promoted to lieutenant colonel and leader of the regiment. His account of the Battle of Sharpsburg (Antietam) is below. He led 200 men into battle that day and 107 of them were killed or wounded.[9] Lieutenant Colonel Carter was mortally wounded at the Battle of Gettysburg on July 2, 1863, and captured by Union troops. He died on July 21, 1863, and was buried in the Methodist Cemetery in Chambersburg, Pennsylvania.[10]

This letter composed by Lt. Col. Carter five days after the Battle of Antietam along with the subsequent accounts attest to the supreme importance of the regimental flag—symbolic and intrinsic. Many men died on the battlefield to "save the colors," and at times the mere sight of the flag brought brave men to tears.

Lieutenant A. H. Patton,
Acting Assistant Adjutant-General
September 22, 1862

Lieutenant: I have the honor to report the part taken by my regiment in the battle of the 17th instant near Sharpsburg, Md. Owing to the severe illness of Colonel Key, I was in command of the regiment during the day and succeeding night.

Soon after day light the brigade formed a line of battle in regular order, the Fifth Texas being on my right and First Texas on my left, and, about 7. a.m., were ordered to advance. I received no order as to which was the directing battalion, but, advancing diagonally to the right through the woods, we entered the open field on the right of the turnpike road. Here the fire upon us became sever, and, owing to our troops being in front of us and the dense smoke pervading, we were unable to return the fire or see the enemy clearly. Still advancing, I came directly behind the Eleventh Mississippi, when I received the order from Captain Sellers for the Texas Brigade to halt. Halting, I ordered the men to lie down. At the same moment the Eleventh Mississippi was ordered to advance, and a portion of two companies on my right, mistaking the order, advanced with them. After a moment I received an order from General Hood to move to the left until the left of my regiment rested on the crest, in advance, next to the turnpike road. Moving left-oblique in double-quick, I occupied the position indicated, and was then ordered by General Hood to move directly up the hill on the left of the troops then advancing. The enemy then occupied the hill in strong force, which receded before our steady advance. Arriving on the top of the hill, at the intersection of the corn-field with the turnpike, I found the enemy not only in heavy force in the corn-field in front, but occupying a ravine in the field on the left of the turnpike, from which my position they poured a destructive fire upon us. I discovered at once that the position was untenable, but if I fell back the troops on my right who had entered the corn-field would be surrounded; so, wheeling my regiment to the left, I posted the men along the fence on either side of the turnpike, and replied as best as we could to the tremendous fire of the enemy. We held this position for some time, until the troops in the corn-field on my right were falling back, when I ordered the regiment to move along the line of fence by the left flank. This movement, however, exposed us so much that we fell back directly under the hill. Here I ordered the regiment to halt and form but at the same moment received an order from General Hood to move by the left flank into the woods. Forming here I advanced on the left of the turnpike up to the fence at the edge of the field, and rested in this position until I was ordered by Colonel Wofford to fall back to the point we started from in the morning, where the remnant of the brigade was formed. We moved about to various points during the day and succeeding night, but nothing worth reporting noted.

Enclosed I forward you a list of the casualties in this regiment. I carried into action about 200 men, and you will see how heavy our loss was. In our loss we embraced many valuable officers. Lieutenant [N. J.] Mills, of Company I, was severely wounded on the 15th instant. On the 17th, Lieutenants [L. P.] Hughes, commanding Company F; [A. J.] McKean and [H. M.] Marchant, of Company A; [J. T.] McLaurin, commanding Company B; [J. C.] Billingsley, commanding Company E; and [John] Roach (of Company G,) commanding Company H, were all wounded. Lieutenant Roach was left on the field, and I fear was mortally wounded. Color-bearer Parker, of Company H, was severely wounded and left on the field. At his fall Captain Darden, of Company A, seized and carried the colors until we fell back to the woods. Many who are reported missing I fear were killed, or so severely wounded as to unable to leave the field.

To Captain E. H. Cunningham, acting field officer, and Adjut. F. L. Price I am indebted for the great assistance rendered me on the field. I cannot speak in too high terms of the conduct of both officers and men of my command. Exposed to a tremendous fire from superior numbers, in a position which it was apparent to all we could not hold, they fought on without flinching until the order to fall back was given. These men, too, were half clad, many of them barefooted, and had been only half fed for days before. The courage, constancy, and patience of our men is beyond all praise.

Very respectfully,

B. F. Carter,

Lieutenant-Colonel, Commanding.[11]


## Lt. Colonel Benjamin F. Carter
## 4th Texas Infantry
*Fairmont News*
## November 15, 1900

An unidentified soldier said to Colonel James Birch of Plattsburg, Missouri, that there was a Col. Carter of the 4th Texas who sat overseer fashion upon the top of a post and rail fence on the west side of the Hagerstown road at Sharpsburg when hundreds of men in the Federal army within 150 yards in front were blazing away at him, and a howitzer was enfilading the line from the left. Scores of men were killed within a few yards of Carter, and he didn't receive a scratch.

Gen. Hood a few minutes later, when we had driven across the Hagerstown road and were holding the line of fence on the east side, rode quietly the length of his brigade, and spoke to many of his men by name. All this time, remember, shot and shell from the Federal batteries and bullets from the rifles of the Federals just across the road were making the regimental line almost like a slaughter pen. My own idea is that General Hood and Colonel Carter were truly daring.

## Clinton McKamy "C. M." Winkler
## October 19, 1821–May 13, 1882

C. M. Winkler was born in Burke County, N.C., on October 19, 1821, and his family moved to Indiana in 1835. In July, 1840, eighteen-year-old Winkler struck out to live in Franklin (Robertson County), Republic of Texas, and lived with his uncle, Harrison Owen. This was frontier country and he served with "minutemen" on several occasions to fight marauding hostile Indians. Between 1843 and April 27, 1844, Winkler became district clerk *pro tem*, and was admitted to the bar as an attorney. Within two years, Robertson County was split for the creation of Navarro County.[12] In the spring of 1861, C. M. Winkler was elected as captain of the Navarro Rifles, who were mustered into service as Company "I," 4th Regiment Texas Infantry. After the Battle of Gettysburg, he was promoted to major and then lieutenant colonel. Lt. Col. Winkler was in command of the 4th Texas at the time of General Lee's surrender at Appomattox.

C. M. Winkler was married twice and raised nine children. After the war, he helped to organize the volunteer fire department in Corsicana. In 1870, he was chosen as Grand Master of the Texas Masonic Lodge, and in 1872, Winkler was elected to the state legislature for the second time (first time was prior to the war). In 1876, Winkler was elected as a judge to the Texas Court of Criminal Appeals, where he served alongside his former comrade-in-arms, Captain Sam A. Willson (1st Texas Infantry) of Rusk, Texas. Judge Winkler, a co-founder of Hood's Texas Brigade Association, passed away on May 13, 1882, in Austin, Texas.[13]

## Lt. Col. C. M. Winkler
## 4th Texas Infantry
## Near Culpeper C.H. VA Nov. 18, 1862

Lt J. R. Loughridge
Dear Friend

I have received two letters from you recently and have also shown one to Genl. Hood. I have also received the Dr.'s certificate as to your physical condition. I need not say that you have my sympathies in your affliction I know full well the great anxiety you feel to be with your comrades in arms but an overruling Providence shapes our course such it is our duty humbly to submit. No one here doubts your patriotism or your courage, and a will shout with delight when you return we miss you very much and I hope the day is not far distant when the smile of the great [?] shall thaw out your [?] and allow you to take again your place in the gallant 4th. This campaign this army has made since leaving Richmond in August last is one that has rarely been equaled and surpassed in ancient or modern times, no army ever made harder forced marches or fought more bloody battles in the short span of two months, in fact within less than that time [?]'s larger force organized and sent forward with the avowed purpose of overpowering the Confederate forces in Virginia and taking the Southron's capital has shelter beneath the guns and fortifications of Washington, Maryland invaded, the federal capital seriously threatened and the whole north thrown into a fun excitement from fear for their own houses and firesides. The battles of Cedar Mountain, Freeman's Ford, the second Manassas, Fairfax, Boonsborough Gap and Sharpsburg have been fought and still are in good condition and ready for anything that may time up. History shows nothing to surpass is and will do [?] Our company carried the battle flag at Freeman's Ford, at Manassas, Boonsborough Gap and Sharpsburg in the latter engagement it was fearfully riddled with bullets and nearly torn from the staff by a shell it had been so badly used up in the recent battles as to be unfit for use and has been sent to Austin to be laid away among the archives of the State, its place being supplied with a new one, many and peculiar are the recollections that cluster around that gallant old flag, now laid aside to be reproduced when the God of battles shall [?] [?] final and complete success to our armis and our deeds are being celebrated in peaceful groves & arbors, none daring to molest or make afraid.

The cost at Manassas, Morris, M. Morris, Beasley, Spruce & R. N. Rice, at Sharpsburg E. M. Garnir, besides many wounded at Mills was wounded in the leg at Sharpsburg on the 1st day of the fight (we were under fire four days) which left me without any officers Dr. Beasly joined me the day before the army left Md. [?] and has had command of the company, most of the time since, I have been playing Major for a while in the absence of Maj Townsend [?] who lost his leg at Manassas. This is only temporary, if Maj Townsend resigns as they [?] say he will, Capt [?] will take his place, by the way Capt [?] is likely to lose the use of his arm from the wound he received at Gaines' Mills, he is with us now but not on duty, Gen' Hood has been promoted Major Genl, and commands the Division formerly more Gnl Whitney, Capt Cunningham has gone to Texas for men to fill up the Texas Regs in VA he tales a place in the Staff of Maj Gen'l Hood with the rank of colonel, which makes ours the second company, position on the left Col J. B. Robertson of the 5th Texas has been promoted to Brigadier and commands the Texas Brigade. Col Key now commands the 4th. Lt Col Carter commanded at the battles of Manassas & Sharpsburg. Hampton's Legion has been transferred to Walker's division, our Regiment is in good health and will [?] in here [?] received a [?] uniform suit is gray [?] and light blue pants which looks [?] grate a change from this ragged dirty, lousy, bare footed condition which we returned from Maryland. A [?] [?] at Sharpsburg. Plate has procured his transfer to La, and old man Smith has been discharged. I commanded the company in all the recent battles in which we have been engaged and am thankful to be able to say I have escaped without a [?] Both at Manassas and at Sharpsburg the Regiment lost more than half the members engaged [?] killed or wounded. The properties [?] as Sharpsburg than any other.

I will keep you all night as to your absence. McClellan has been removed and Burnside takes his place, the principal cause assigned for McClellan's removal is that he failed to advance though ordered by the Federal Secretary of War so to do, and it is therefore expected that Burnside will endeavor to subdue the army under Gnl Lee before winter sits in and everything is held in [?] accordingly, so we may have another general engagement soon in [?] [?] sure to expect it, my own opinion however is that our company is about over. My regards to Mrs. L, and the children. God bless the war and [?]

Yours Truly C. M. Winkler[14]


Sergeant Val C. Giles
4th Texas Infantry
*Galveston Daily News*
December 14, 1896
Battle Flag of the Fourth Texas


Austin, Tex., Dec. 13.—To The News: The old battle flag of the Fourth Texas regiment was never surrendered and is now in the possession of one of the old command residing in this city. I have in my possession a little faded volume printed on paper manufactured in Richmond in 1862. It was presented to me by the late General W. H. Hammon during one of his visits to Austin, when a candidate for governor of this state on the greenback ticket. He was a member of my old regiment, and although I never voted for him we were always warm personal friends. He did me a favor on the battle field on Gaines' Mill while he was quartermaster sergeant of the regiment, which I have never forgotten. Peace to his memory.

The title of this little book is *Campaign From Texas to Maryland*, by N. A. Davis, chaplain of the Fourth Texas regiment. It is a history of the Texas brigade from the time it left Texas up and including the battle of Sharpsburg. The battle flag of the Fourth and the lone star flag of the Fifth Texas is referred to below by Chaplain Davis, were both brought back to Texas by Captain Stephen H. Darden and deposited with the archives of the state just before the federal soldiers reached Austin in 1865. Captain W. C. Walsh and Randolph R. Robertson, members of company B, Fourth Texas regiment, who was at home at that time, secured both flags from the old capitol and hid them away to prevent them from falling into the hands of the enemy. If my memory serves me correctly at the request of Bolling Eldridge and other members of the Fifth Texas residing at Brenham, the flag of the Fifth was shipped to them and lost or destroyed by fire in transit.

The next annual reunion of Hood's Texas brigade association meets at Floresville June 27, 1897, and I would suggest to the members of the Fourth regiment who may be present that a resolution be adopted requesting that the flag be returned to the care of the state.

I here give an extract from Mr. Davis' book, also Colonel Carter's letter to Governor Lubbock, which will explain why the old flag was sent home:

October 7 and 8 I was again in the camp, and Generals Longstreet and Hood were reviewing the troops. On the 8th, as I sat looking on while one regiment after another passed in review (eighteen in all). I saw one flag in which were many holes made by bullets of the enemy.

I watched it until it had gone some distance past. It was a matter of great interest to me to see an object upon which the history of the recent battle was so plainly and truthfully written.

From the manly steep of the ensign one could easily see that he was proud of his colors. It was a 'Lone Star' flag and belonged to the Fifth Texas regiment, and after the parade I learned that it had been pierced forty-seven times and seven ensigns had fallen under it.

By the time I turned from looking after it another was passing me. I knew it. It was an old acquaintance.

Many times had I seen it on dress parade, but never with such mingled feelings of pride and sorrow.

It called to mind all the hardships and suffering, fire and blood, through which we had passed. It was made and presented by Miss Lula Wigfall to Colonel Hood for the Fourth Texas regiment with the motto: "Fear not, for I am with thee. Say to the north, give up, and to the south, keep not back," which was graven on the spear head.

Nine ensigns had fallen under it on the field, and it had brought off the battle scars of sixty-five balls and shot, besides the marks of three shells.

It was the only flag to be seen that had gone through so many battles and had so many marks of honor.

It was understood that this was the last time it would appear upon parade. For it is an object of too much pride to the regiment and honor to the state of Texas to be kept in the camp. On tomorrow it is to be committed to the care of Captain Darden, to be sent home to report our conduct in the hour of our country's struggles, and to be deposited among the archives of the state. And knowing that hundreds would desire to see it I had a drawing made, and here present it to our friends and relatives at home that they may see the battle flag around which the old Fourth rallied in so many struggles for our country's liberty and beneath which so many of our brave men have fallen.

It is with great pride that we can send it home without a single stain, and to it the men of the Fourth can point for the record of their deeds as long as Texas exists as an independent and sovereign state.

Headquarters Fourth Texas Regiment, Near Winchester, Va., Oct 7, 1862—To His Excellency F. R. Lubbock, Governor of Texas—Sir: I have the honor to present to you, by the hand of Captain S. H. Darden, the battle flag of the Fourth Texas regiment, borne by them in the battles of Eltham's Landing, Seven Pines, Gaines' Farm, Malvern Hill, Freeman's Ford, Manassas Plains, Boonsboro Gap and Sharpsburg. From its torn and tattered condition it can no longer be used, and it is returned to you that it may be preserved among the archives of the state as a testimonial of the gallantry of her sons who have fought beneath its folds.

I need not dwell upon the services of my regiment. Its deeds in battle will go into the history of our country and speak for themselves, and this silent witness bears eloquent evidence that the men who followed it in action were where shot fell thick and death was in the air.

More than 500 of our comrades in arms have fallen beneath its folds. And it is to us an emblem of constancy under multiplied hardships, gallant and dauntless courage in the storm of battle and devotion unto death to our cause.

Let it be preserved sacredly that the remnant of our little band may, in the future days, gaze upon its battle stained colors, recall to mind the suffering they have endured in their country's cause and their children incited to renewed vigilance in the preservation of those liberties for which we are contending.

Our general has presented us with another "battle flag" and we hope to be able to acquit ourselves as well with that as we have done with the old one.

Respectfully, your servant,

B. F. Carter

Lieutenant Colonel Commanding.

## Stephen Heard Darden
### 1816–May 16, 1902

Prior to leading his company of volunteers from home, Captain Darden was offered a position as major from the Secretary of War. He declined the offer so he could remain close to his friends and neighbors.[15]

Darden resigned his commission after the Battle of Antietam due to poor health, and he later accepted an appointment as colonel of the 5th Regiment, Texas State Troops, to guard the Gulf Coast in 1863. On November 21, 1864, he replaced a vacant seat in the Second Confederate Congress until the end of the war.

After the war, Colonel Darden returned home to his farm in Gonzalez County, Texas. At the end of Reconstruction, he was appointed comptroller of public accounts and served from 1873–1879. Afterwards, Darden continued to work in public service up until his death on May 16, 1902. He is buried at the Texas State Cemetery in Austin, Texas.

### Captain Stephen H. Darden
### 4th Texas Infantry
### *Tri-Weekly Telegraph*
### July 22, 1863

Editor *Telegraph*—The Texans have always distinguished themselves by their valor on every battlefield where they have met the enemy, and their gallant conduct justly render the participants in our many sanguinary conflicts, worthy of the thanks and admiration of every patriot in our land. We were glad to observe in your paper that the name of one of our gallant officers is announced as a candidate for Lieut. Governor. We refer to the name of Capt. S. H. Darden, of the county of Gonzales. Under the very first call the President made of this state for volunteers, Capt. Darden enlisted, and gallantly led his company in those memorable battles in Virginia, under Gen. Hood, in which Texas Brigade in the Army of Northern Virginia, has not only sustained the character of Texans for bravery, but even added some additional luster to her fame. Capt. Darden gallantly, led his company in the battles of Eltham's Landing, the Seven Pines, Gaines' Mill, and the seven days battles around Richmond, the second Manassas and Sharpsburg. He was wounded in the shoulder in the memorable charge of the Fourth Texas Regiment on the fortifications of the enemy at Gaines' Mill, and at the sanguinary battle of Sharpsburg, after several of the flag bearers of the Fourth Texas had been shot down, he seized our battle flag, and bore it proudly amidst a heavy hail of minnie balls and exploding shells.

During the hard campaign of last summer, his health and strength failed so completely as to compel his resignation; but now he stands ready as a volunteer under the order of Governor Lubbock, to serve his country again in the field the moment it becomes necessary.

Capt. Darden was also a soldier in the Texas revolution of 1836, and emigrated from his native state, Mississippi, to the Republic of Texas in an early day, and settled in Gonzales county with his family, where he has ever since continued to reside. He has several times represented Gonzales County in the House of Representatives, and was State Senator from his District, and made an efficient and able legislator.

We feel proud of him as one of the brave sons of Texas. His intelligence and high moral character, his devoted patriotism and experienced statesmanship, will qualify him for the high position of Lieutenant Governor. Should he be elected, he will ever be found a true friend to Texas and a firm and judicious supporter of our Confederate authorities.

F. Chenault.                            C. C. Dewitt.
WM. Thomas.                       R. N. C. Tate.

## Private John J. Stacy
## Fourth Texas Regiment
*Galveston Daily News*
June 4, 1894
## What Became of the Colors at Sharpsburg?—The Color Bearer

Alvin, Tex., June 2.—As there has been some controversy concerning the flag of the Fourth Texas at the battle of Sharpsburg. The News correspondent interviewed Mr.

J. J. Stacey, who was with that regiment through all of its campaigns in Virginia, and the following version of the affairs is related by him:

At one period of the battle, by some error, we were placed in position that a battery on our right mowed us down with an enfilading fire, while in front we confronted vastly superior numbers of infantry. At this juncture the color bearer was shot down and the regiment fell back under the hill and reformed. Captain S. H. Darden rescued the colors and brought them behind the hill, where he delivered them to me, and I bore the colors until Captain Darden came to Texas and brought the flag with him, and the flag is now in Austin.

Major Pinkney, now district attorney, was present when Captain Darden gave me the colors. The color bearer was named Walker, from company H, and we never heard from him again.

Mr. J. J. Stacey is now a citizen from Alvin and can relate many thrilling incidents connected with his regiment during the Virginia campaigns.

This correspondent was one of Stonewall's foot cavalry from North Carolina, and well remembers the reputation the Texas troops had. They were looked upon as something wonderful as the reputation of Texas was then noted for her desperate characters, and the few men she sent to the army of Northern Virginia felt that they had to sustain this reputation, and nobly did they do it.

**Captain Stephen H. Darden**
**4th Texas Infantry**
*Galveston Daily News*
**June 5, 1894**
**The Battle Flag.**

Captain Stephen H. Darden was the last man who bore the flag of the Fourth Texas Regiment alluded to in yesterday's *Daily News*. This was after four others had fallen as the standard-bearers of the regiment. Col. Carter, of Austin, who was commander of the regiment, died of wounds in the service.

The Flag of our Regiment
Sergeant Val C. Giles
Company B, Fourth Texas Regiment.

> *The old battle flag of our regiment,*
> *How oft with wear feet*
> *Have we followed its fold to victory,*
> *And guarded it in retreat,*
> *In the red hot glare of battle*
> *Where carnage and death were supreme,*

*We have seen the flag of our regiment*
*Like a star on the horizon gleam.*

*The flag of the old Fourth Texas*
*Through many a conflict shown*
*O'er the red clay hills of Virginia,*
*As she swept through tempest and storm,*
*And when the battle was over*
*There was many a saddened brow,*
*When the boys would gather around it—*
*In memory I see them now*

*But we'll gather no more around it,*
*The star of her glory has set,*
*Gone down in a cloud of oppression,*
*But we cherish the old flag yet,*
*We have seen the flag of our regiment*
*On many a gory plain*
*An emblem of victory, and pity*
*A half-mast o'er her stain.*

*Though the old flag's furled forever,*
*'Tis free from dishonor's stain,*
*That noble old regiment's disbanded—*
*Their hears, thank God, are the same,*
*We love that dear old banner,*
*We love the cause we lost,*
*And though some see it treason,*
*God bless St. Andrew's cross.*

## Nicholas A. Davis
## August 24, 1824–November 19, 1894

Nicholas A. Davis was born on August 24, 1824, in Limestone County, Alabama. His father, Nathaniel, served eleven years in the Alabama legislature. Young Nicholas studied theology under the guidance of a Presbyterian minister and eventually became ordained in that church.

By November, 1857, Chaplain Davis was married and had two daughters. That is when he moved to Bastrop, Texas. A son was born in 1858, but both the boy and his mother died prior to Davis's journey on August 16, 1861, to report for duty as a chaplain in the 4th Texas Infantry, Confederate States Army.[16]

In February, 1865, after his discharge from the army, Davis married a widow and had four more children. Through this marriage, he also acquired 2,000 acres of land in Sabine County. He continued to preach while he also tended to various business ventures. His children said they were not allowed to ask questions or discuss the War in his presence. He died on November 19, 1894.[17]

## Chaplain Nicholas A. Davis
## 4th Texas Infantry
## Sharpsburg

Soon after night, orders were received to withdraw from this position. All our forces were to fall back in the direction of Sharpsburg, or Antietam River; and we were again to act as the rear guard of the army. But there was little or no annoyance on the march. Arriving on the heights beyond the Antietam river, near the Town of Sharpsburg, about noon on the 15th, we took position on the right of the road leading to Boonsboro. But, as it was found that the enemy was threatening an immediate attack on the other flank, we were ordered to the extreme left, and take position on the Hagerstown road, near St. Mumma Church. Here we remained, under the shot and shell of the enemy, until near sunset, on the evening of the 16th, at which time the enemy made a vigorous attack upon our left. They had crossed in great force higher up the Antietam, at Smoketown. Hood's Division, of two small Brigades, were all the troops in this portion of the field; Yet he succeeded in checking, and then in driving them back for some distance, when night put an end to the contest. During the night, General Jackson's troops having arrived, they were thrown to our left, and at almost a right angle with our line, and with a space of some little distance between our left, and his right; his line facing west, and ours north.

The officers and men of this Division, having been without food for three days, except half rations of beef and green corn, General Lawton, with two Brigades, was ordered to relieve us, that we might have a chance to cook. On the morning of the 17th, the firing commenced at 3 o'clock, along the line of General Lawton. At 6 a.m., General Hood received notice from him, that he would need all the aid he could render, in order to hold the position. In a few minutes, another courier arrived, and informed him that General Lawton was wounded, and he must come forward immediately and take the command. His men were ready for the word, and were instantly moved out upon the field, where they met the advancing lines of an immense force, consisting of not less than two entire Corps of their army; and according to their own statements, were soon reinforced by several Brigades.

"Here," says General Hood, "I witnessed the most terrible clash of arms, by far, that has occurred during the war." A little world of artillery was turned loose up on—and the line of their shot and shell screaming, blazing and bursting as they flew, made a perfect network in their passage through the air. "And here," says he, "the two little giant Brigades of my command, wrestled with a mighty force, and although they lost hundreds of their officers and men, they drove them from their position, and forced them to abandon their guns on our left."

Thus the battle raged furiously until 9 o'clock. The enemy had been driven some four or five hundred yards by this little band of gallant men. But, fighting at right angles, with our general line of battle, it afforded the enemy an opportunity to pour a heavy fire into the right and rear of Colonel Law's Brigade, which made it necessary for the Division to move to the left and rear, into the woods, to close up the unoccupied space, between our left and Jackson's right, at the angle of the two lines, near the St. Mumma Church. And especially was this move necessary, as Jackson had moved the troops from his right flank, without our knowledge, thereby leaving our left entirely exposed. Moving back near the Church, they formed and held their position bravely until 10.30 a.m., when General McLaws arrived with his command, which, being formed, was immediately thrown forward upon the field, and becoming engaged, Hood's Division was withdrawn to the rear, to replenish their cartridge boxes. At noon they returned, and were ordered to form in rear of the Church, and hold their ground, which they did until about 4 p.m., when the Division moved to the right, near the center, and there remained until the night of the 18th. During the day, we waited their advance, but they did not move. Two or three guns were fired, as a challenge to the contest, but still they did not come. They had received a shock, so severe, and lost so many officers and men, that they were not willing to hazard another attempt. And they felt so proud that they had not been run entirely off the field as usual, they were perfectly willing to make the child's bargain with us. "I'll let you alone, but if you'll leave me alone." They knew from their facility at lying, that they could manufacture a splendid victory out of the fight, and not fire another gun, notwithstanding we had waited all day, and challenged them to renew the fight. And, sure enough, they have so published it to the world. But it is like those splendid victories won by McClellan, around Richmond—and by Pope at Manassas.

## Hood Sends for Aid

On the morning of the 17th, Major Blanton was dispatched to General D. H. Hill, to ask for troops to assist in holding the left of our position, but he returned with a negative reply—"He had no troops to spare." Again and again, General Hood sent for aid, which his little devoted band of heroes were struggling with the many thousands of the enemy, who were pouring in, in a constant flood. In the hopes of aid, they held their ground, and even drove them back over the field, long after every prospect to the eye of the observer of their final success had fled. They were frequently cheered with the indefinite promise, "You will be reinforced soon, hold on a little longer." They had never been beaten upon the field, and knew not how to give up the ground. They were out-numbered, twenty to one. But there they stood, amid the storm of death, until they became the astonishment and admiration of their enemies. And in their report of the fight, they pay this Division, the following well-earned tribute of praise.

## The New York Herald, Sept. 20

General Ricketts at once assumed command. But our victorious movement has lost its impulse. Our right had advanced and swept across the field so far, that its front, originally, almost in a line with the front of the center and left, formed almost a right angle with them. While our lines rather faltered, the rebels made a sudden and impulsive onset, and drove our gallant fellows back over a part of the hard won field. What we had won, however, was not to be relinquished without a desperate struggle. And here, up the hills and down through woods and standing corn, over the plowed land and the clover, the line of fire swept to and fro, as one side or the other gained a temporary advantage. It is beyond all wonder, how such men such as these rebel troops are—can fight as they do. That those ragged and filthy wretches, sick, hungry, and, in all ways miserable, should prove such heroes in the fight, is past explanation. Men never fought better. There was one regiment that stood up before the fire of two or three of our long range batteries, and two regiments of infantry. And though the air was vocal with the whistle of bullets and the scream of shells, there they stood, and delivered their fire in perfect order.

As to the regiments here referred to, it will distract nothing from the honor of our troops, to tell the reader that this was our whole Brigade. Numbering in all, when this fight begun, only eight hundred and fifty-four men. Not the number of one full regiment. They had passed through so many battles, that regiments looked like companies, and brigades looked like regiments. Yet, small as they were, they did the work of strong, full commands.

The great misfortune on that day was, that our higher officers did not discover in time, that it was on this part of the field, that the enemy had stacked the fortunes of the day. Of this, they could not be convinced, though frequently advised by General Hood and Staff, that they were moving in sight, and in tremendous force. And in connection with this matter, General Hood remarked, that he was "thoroughly of the opinion, that the victory of that day, would have been as thorough, quick and complete, as on the Plains of Manassas, on the 30th of August, if General McLaws had reached the field with his men, even as late as 9 o'clock." The reasons for his tardiness, we hope, will be satisfactory, when he renders his report. But, if he moved carelessly up, stopping at the river and losing two hours, as we are told he did, waiting for his men to strip and roll up their clothes, to prevent getting wet, and then halting for some time, to make their *toilette* on the other side, not only the loud condemnation of a country, which had, in part, entrusted him with its destiny, should fall upon him, but the strong arm of the law should he take hold, and by one way or another, remove him from a position, in which he is able to jeopardize her future weal. This is not the first time that a single man has thwarted the plans of a great army, and made its victory only half complete.

## Evacuation of Maryland

On the evening of the 18th, we received orders to recross the Potomac. Our march to and across the river was undisturbed. This, of itself, will show the world the nature of McClellan's victory. And if he had beaten and driven us, as he publishes, why did he allow us to pass quietly away, after holding the field a whole day and night? Why did he not follow our army as we did his, near Richmond, forcing him to turn and fight, to save his routed men?

We had accomplished our object, as far as we were able, and, of course, were ready to return. Harper's Ferry had fallen, and it rich prizes were ours. They, it is true expected us to move against Washington, Philadelphia, and Baltimore; and whether we would capture one or all of them, they could not tell. But we had started out for Harper's Ferry, and as much else as circumstances would allow us to accomplish. And having won it, we saw that the magnitude of further invasion was greater than our preparations, and we returned to await another "on to Richmond." Our loss will not exceed seven thousand men, in killed, wounded and missing, while McClellan's friends set down his killed and wounded at fourteen thousand seven hundred and ninety-six, up to the 18th. And, by adding about two thousand for the number that were slaughtered and drowned, in attempting to follow us across the river, and thirteen thousand killed and captured by Jackson on the 14th and 15th instants, you can see whether our Maryland campaign was a failure or not. The sum total of their loss in men, is twenty-nine thousand seven hundred and ninety-six; and in property we captured seventy-three pieces of artillery, fourteen thousand muskets, great quantities of ammunition of every kind, and finest quality, with quartermaster's and medicine stores to the amount of thousands of dollars, and two hundred wagons, with fine teams, all in harness made by Yankee labor, with which to haul the other property away. And so ends the brilliant campaign of twelve days across the Potomac.

It is due to the memory of those who fell, either killed or wounded, that their names be written and preserved for the pen of the historian, who will write them with other fallen sons of the South, and that Texas may see that her brave men were at their post when her honor and her liberty called for a sacrifice of blood. We have given them a place.[18]

## Joseph Benjamin "J. B." Polley
## October 27, 1840–February 2, 1918

J. B. Polley, born on October 27, 1840, was the son of pioneers who came to Texas and married in 1826 when it was part of the new Republic of Mexico. At the age of twenty-one, he enlisted in the Mustang Greys, which became Company "F," 4th Texas Infantry at the time of its first muster in 1861. He was 5 feet, 11 inches tall with blue eyes and "light" hair.

Polley survived the war, though he lost his right foot due to a wound sustained in combat on October 7, 1864, at the Battle of Darbytown Road near Richmond Virginia. He returned to his home in Wilson County, Texas. After the war, he married and practiced law. He was selected by his fellow soldiers to become the official historian of Hood's Texas Brigade. Later, he served in the Texas legislature. Polley fell upon hard times late in life and died poor on February 2, 1918, and is buried at the Floresville City Cemetery in Floresville, Texas.[19] Quartermaster Sergeant Polley is the author of the article about Wintul E. Berry.

Quartermaster Sergeant Joseph B. "J. B." Polley, 4th Texas Infantry. (*Texas Heritage Museum–Historical Research Center*)

## William E. Barry a.k.a. Wintul E. Berry?

There is no record of a Wintul Berry in this regiment, but it could be a *nom de plume* for William E. Barry who enlisted in the unit later named Company "G" on July 19, 1861, in Harrisburg, Texas, at the age of twenty-two. He was wounded in one arm at the Battle of Gaines Mill and captured at the Battle of Antietam. After being exchanged from the POW camp, Fort Delaware, Barry was elected third lieutenant in March, 1864. He was wounded in the arm at the Battle of the Wilderness on May 6, 1864, and resigned his commission and retired due to disability on November 28, 1864.[20]

Wintul E. Berry
4th Texas Infantry
The *Daily Express*
October 20, 1907

Wintul E. Berry, of Navasota, who in the sixties followed the Stars and bars into many great battles, writes as follows of the Battle of Sharpsburg, or as named by Federals, Antietam.

On the 4th of September, 1862, Hood's Texas Brigade crossed the Potomac River into Maryland, and after a few days of much-needed rest at Frederick City, marched on to Hagerstown via Boonesboro Gap. September 14th it made a forced return march to Boonesboro Gap, and assisted in the hold of that position long enough for General Lee to make sure that a point near Sharpsburg he would be rejoined by Stonewall Jackson, previously sent to capture Harper's Ferry and the troops there. Then, acting as rear guard of the Confederate Army, it proceeded toward Sharpsburg, and on the night of September 16th took position in an open field between the Old Dunkard Church and the large force of the Union Army which had crossed the Antietam River. Jackson's troops, as they came up, coming into position confronting the enemy on its left.

Later in the night, the little brigade was withdrawn from the front and marched into the grove surrounding the Dunkard Church where rations of beef and flour were issued to it. These were most acceptable, for since leaving Hagerstown we had been compelled to subsist on green corn and coffee alone. While engaging in cooking, day began to dawn, and with it came the sound of musketry and artillery drawing rapidly nearer and nearer. When shells began sweeping through the tree-tops, breaking limbs and hurling them at us, we formed in line of battle in rear of the brigades of Lawton, Hays and Tremble, parts of Jackson's command, which immediately moved forward to meet the Federals. In a little while, though, these gallant brigades were overpowered, Generals Walton and Lawton severely wounded and most of their regimental officers and hundreds of the men in the ranks wounded or killed. The Texas brigade and Law's Alabama brigade moved forward, at once, to the relief of the three brigades, and found themselves confronted by two corps of the Federal army. The situation was one of extreme peril both to the Confederate army as a whole and to the Texans and Alabamans on whose pluck and endurance depended the holding of the Confederate line unbroken. Realizing the danger that threatened, General Hood asked for reinforcements, but none could be spared without endangering other parts of the Confederate line, and so, all unaided, we stood our ground and charged and countercharged until the dead and wounded almost literally covered the ground where we fought. Like heroes, the ragged, starving men of the two brigades loaded and fired, and like heroes, they fell, wounded or dead.

In his official report of the battle, General Hood said: "Here I witnessed the most terrible clash of arms by far that has occurred during the war. The two little giant brigades of my command wrestled with the might force, and although they lost hundreds of their officers and men, they drove them from their position, and forced them to abandon their guns on our left."

In front of the line occupied by the Texas brigade at the commencement of the fight lay a cornfield. Into this the First Texas charged, holding it against ten times their number, until more than two-thirds of its men were killed or wounded: until, in fact, its loss was eighty-three and one-third percent of the number engaged— the greatest loss suffered by any command on either side during the war. Mowed down, like the corn surrounding them, they held their ground unflinchingly until their ammunition was exhausted—then falling back with stubborn slowness, they still bade defiance to the enemy, meeting his loud, triumphant huzzas with the blood-curdling Confederate yell. It was then about 10 o'clock a.m., and McLaws' division having reached the battlefield and pressing forward to take the places of the two brigades they retired to the rear, renewed their supply of ammunition and again took position in the wood near the church. When the close of that bloody day ceased the hardest fought battle of the war.

In front of the cornfield where the First Texas played so gallant a part ran a line parallel with our front. Into this about fifty Texans rushed, myself among the number, thus securing a position in front and to the left of the First Texas. Here we knelt, and resting our guns on the planks of the fence, loaded and fired at the enemy until our guns grew almost too hot to handle. The pall of smoke that hung over the cornfield was too dense for me to see what individuals were doing there, but once I glanced in that direction, I distinctly saw the fragments of one poor Texan's leg fly up in the air above the smoke—his body having, evidently, been dismembered by a bursting shell.

So intent was our squad of fifty in dealing death and destruction to the enemy in our immediate front, that before any of us realized the possibility of it, the First Texas, their ammunition exhausted, and but fifteen or twenty of them left, fell back from the cornfield, and the enemy pushed forward and got in to our rear. It was a nasty predicament to be in, and to escape it, three of us made a break down the lane, leaving, as we thought, the most of our comrades in the lane, wounded or dead. But we had gone but a hundred yards when we ran into a New York regiment—the Thirty-Third, I think. They were lying down as we came up, but no sooner saw us close to them, than they rose and poured a volley into us, killing two of my comrades, but, wonderful to relate, never touching me. Of course, I surrendered: what else could I do? For a while though, after I did, I wished I had not, for when it was discovered that I was a Texan, the New Yorkers got in a terrible rage. They had belonged, they said, to Franklin's division which we had encountered and repulsed at Eltham's Landing, near West Point, Va., on the 7th of May preceding, and they insisted that on this occasion we had not only fought them with negroes, but had also cut the throats of wounded Federals who had fallen into our hands.

Indignant and truthful as I was my denial of both charges, it was of no avail, and to punish me they forced me, over my solemn and energetic protest, to take a place in the front rank of their line and join in the attack they immediately made. With nothing in front of them to impede the advance, they moved rapidly forward several hundred yards when reaching a fence, and discovering a hundred yards beyond it a skirt of dense timber, they came to a sudden halt, in evident dismay. But their halt did not relieve my apprehensions, for many of them appeared to be under the influence of liquor and to be seeking a pretext to kill me. In the timber, perfect quiet prevailed. But feeling sure we had troops there, and not wishing to be killed by my friends, I asked permission of the Yankee who had me especially in charge to lie down. He consenting, I dropped at full length on the ground, my head toward the timber, and drew a flat rock up against my head. The Yankee inquiring why I did that. I told him, loud enough to be heard by half the regiment that I know the men who were in that timber, and that in a few minutes there would be the awfullest wool-tearing right there where we were that the world ever witnessed.

Nor was I a false prophet. Five minutes had not elapsed when there was a flash, and a roar and rattle of artillery and musketry, and out of the timber came a sheet of fire, gleaming bayonets and a rebel yell so terrifying as to make my blood run cold and my hair stand on end. Instantly, my escort gave me a punch with the barrel of his gun, and as I sprang to my feet, ordered me to hike to the rear at the best gait that was in me. And were not alone in the race—the whole regiment got up and got with clarity of movement that beat anything in the way of running it had ever seen done. Such speed soon brought us to another fence. Just as we mounted that and began to throw our legs over it, we heard an extra loud roar from the Confederate artillery, and a storm of shot and shell coming pouring in on us, many of the New Yorkers fell down dead or wounded, backward or forward off it. Thinking it a good time to escape, I made an attempt to do so, and failed.

The gallant New Yorkers having, at last, got pretty well out of range of the Confederates my special escort proudly marched me back, about two miles—on the way pass Gen. Joe Hooker, who, wounded in the leg, was having the leg of a boot cut off—and delivered me to a major commanding two or three companies of cavalry. We were on the main road from the battlefield.

A seemingly endless procession of ambulances, loaded with Federal wounded, was passing on their way to the field hospitals further in the rear, and blood sprinkled the roadway until it look as if a street-sprinkler had been at work. Up the road from the firing line, came about this time a squad of men escorting a Confederate flag. As they came opposite us, the Major inquired where they got the flag and when they answered, "Down in the cornfield," he turned to me and asked if I knew the colors. "Yes," said I, "I do know them. It is the flag of the First Texas, and there was many a dead Texan around it before you captured it." "Indeed there were," said one of the escort: "there were thirteen men lying dead or wounded on it and around it." Then I asked him to let me have it a moment, and when he handed it to me, I kissed it reverently, with tears in my eyes.

A few minutes later, noticing that the main signal station of the Federal army was but a short distance from us, I asked permission of the major to climb a fence near it and observe the battle, adding that it was a privilege I had never enjoyed. "All right," he kindly said: "I'll put you under parole to that extent, but do not get near enough to the signal men to hear anything they say."

From the position thus secured on a high fence I saw Burnside's corps cross the Antietam and form in line of battle on our side of the stream, the sun flashing from their muskets and the shining musical instruments of their regimental bands, and their flags waving in the breeze. Off in the distance was the thin line of the Confederates. Standing on a hill appeared a man, looking intently over at the serried ranks of the Federals, though, I thought, field glasses. My heart sank low, and I thought the battle lost to the Confederates. Then I saw a cloud of dust rising above the tops of the trees near the old Dunkard Church, and a man dashed forward on horseback, and in a swift gallop approached the lone man. A second or two later, a long line of Confederates, double-quicking came out of the timber and quickly formed in line of battle: Officers and couriers galloped back and forth in their rear and along their front, and when at last, the alignment was accomplished, the artillery on both sides let loose its thunders, and for a minute or two the space between the lines soon to meet in the shock of battle, was clouded by shot and shell and puffs of white smoke. Then, while cannon roared, shells bursting their fragments in every direction, and solid shot dug long furrows in the ground, the Confederates moved forward—at first, slowly and steadily, and then with a rush they hurled themselves against the outnumbering Federal force, the wild, reckless Confederate yell and a quick, sharp rattle of musketry that in a moment deepened into a roar, drowning the noise of artillery and bursting shells. For probably two minutes, the smoke from the musketry firing hid the combatants from my view, but when it lifted, Burnside's corps was making tracks toward the safe side of the Antietam.

The lone man I first saw observing the movements of the enemy, was, I believe, General Lee—the man who approached him on horseback was, I have no doubt, Gen. A. P. Hill, who, with his corps, reached the field of battle just in time to save the day to the Confederates. Four days later, General Lee wrote the following letter:

Headquarters Army of Northern Virginia, Sept. 21, 1862—Gen. L. T. Wigfall—

General: I have not heard from you with regard to the new Texas regiments which you promised to raise for the army. I need them very much. I rely upon those we have in all the tight places and fear I have to call upon them too often. They have fought grandly and nobly, and we must have more of them. Please make every possible exertion to get them on for me. You must help us in this matter. With a few more regiments such as Hood now has, as an example of daring and bravery, I could feel more confident of the campaign. Very respectfully yours, R. E. Lee, General.

Mr. Barry, the writer of the foregoing, in mentioning Law's Alabama brigade unintentionally does an injustice. Up to and during the battle of Sharpsburg, General Law commanded the Fourth Alabama, the Second and Eleventh Mississippi and the Sixth North Carolina regiments. After that battle the Mississippians and North Carolinians were transferred to other brigades—Law getting in their places Alabama regiments exclusively. In the Texas brigade at the time of battle were the Eighteenth Georgia and Hampton's South Carolina Legion. In the reorganization that followed the battle these regiments were transferred, and the Third Arkansas became a part of the Texas Brigade.

In another respect, also is Mr. Barry mistaken. But few of the Texans whom he and his two unfortunate companions left in the lane when they sought to escape capture by flight, were wounded or dead—they were playing "possum," or at least, did play that game when they discovered the enemy both in front and rear of them. This we say on the authority of E. R. Crockett, now living in Temple, who was one of the squad, and inherits from his famous ancestor, Davy Crockett, an immense amount of coolness and tact. When the lines of the advancing Federals came within a hundred yards of the lane, and looking back, he discovered that the main line of the Texans had withdrawn, it at once occurred to him that "discretion was the better part of valor." Posted as the squad was, in a sunken road that would prevent the Federals from seeing them until right on them, if they were caught with arms in their hands, or even sitting erect the Federals would be sure to fire on them at first glimpse. To avoid this, Crockett suggested that each of them lie down and pretend to be dead or wounded, and thus, surely, escape a volley. After the Federals passed they could surrender at their leisure, and without danger.

The ruse was an unqualified success. Although at first sight of the Texans the Federals leveled their guns and were about to fire, they did not—a cool headed officer shouting, "Don't shoot, boys—don't shoot!! Those fellows are all dead." Telling us the story, Crockett said: "The only time in my life that I felt myself in mortal peril was when I heard the click of the gunlocks, and the second that intervened between that sound and the "don't" of the officer was one of intensely agonizing suspense. You may imagine the surprise of our enemies when, after they passed over our recumbent and presumably dead bodies, they heard one of us say, "We surrender gentlemen—we surrender." Luckily, though the joke was on them, they were not blood thirsty.

## Private William Barry
## 4th Texas Infantry
*Galveston Daily News*
June 23, 1896

President of Hood's Texas Brigade Association William Barry referred to the correspondence between General E. A. Carman of the United States war department and himself, the former asking him to locate the position of the brigade in the battle of Sharpsburg, and showed a map sent to him by the war department of the battlefield. A committee of participants in the battle was appointed to mark on the map the position of Hood's Texas brigade.

Captain Barry destroyed all the romance of the flag lately sent to Secretary Branard as the First Texas flag by stating the flag in the secretary's hands prior to the receipt of the last one was the true First Texas flag.

## Private J. M. Polk
## 4th Texas Infantry

The Federal army was close behind us, and I could see from the movements that we would soon have another bloody conflict. About that time the sergeant ordered me to go back to the banks of the Antietam on the picket line. I remained there all day and after dark returned to my command, which was located near the old Dunkard Church.

The next morning a small amount of bacon and flour was issued: I was trying to cook some bread; I took the ramrod out of my gun, wet up the flour without grease or salt, wrapped it around the ramrod, and was holding it over the fire when a shell from one of the Federal batteries fell, bursting near me, and breaking a man's leg. In less time than it takes to tell it we formed a line of battle, and the command was given to "forward." Our ranks were so reduced that regiments looked like companies and brigades like regiments; and this was about the condition of General Lee's army that day. I don't remember the date, but it was between the 12th and 20th of September, 1862. Some were in hospitals, sick or wounded; some discharged; some dead. The Federals must have had about three or four to our one, and it was as near a knock-down and drag-out as anything I have ever seen or heard of. The air was full of shot and shell and we were in an open field, with no protection, and it seemed almost impossible for a rat to live in such a place. The dead and dying were in every direction. I heard that the First Texas regiment lost nineteen color-bearers and finally lost their colors. I didn't take time to load my gun, for there were plenty of loaded guns lying on the ground by the side of the dead and wounded men, and they were not all Confederates; the Blue and the Gray were all mixed up. The New Jersey men were in front of us; this I found out the next day, after Generals Lee and McClellan had agreed upon a cessation of hostilities in order to take care of the dead and wounded. I saw a great many men go in that day who never came out, but it has been so long ago that I do not remember their names, not even the members of my own company. I saw Milt Garner go in, but never saw him again. He was an old friend and neighbor of mine, and his people now live in Navarro county, Texas. I can remember a little fellow by the name of Paul. I was on picket with him the day before. He was the only Jew I ever saw in the army, and belonged to Martin's company, from Henderson county, Texas but I never saw Paul any more. I can remember that all that was left of our company, out of over 100 after we came out of that fight, was Captain Winkler, Lieutenant Mills and eight men. We had hardly stacked our guns when a shell from one of the Federal batteries exploded near us, knocked the guns down and came very near killing the balance of us. I could not help but think how different this was from the way it was pictured out to us in war speeches at the commencement. It reminded me of what one of our men by the name of Brooks told me. He was on the picket line with an Irishman. The Federals outnumbered them and they knew it, and it began to be a serious matter. So Mike said to the captain: "We must be getting away from here. They will kill us all." "No; you must stand your ground Mike," said the Captain, "If you should happen to be killed here, there will be a great big monument erected to your memory, with great big letters on it, "Sacred to the memory of Mike Donohue who died in defense of his country." "Yes, and be Jesus and it might stand here one hundred years," said Mike, "and I would never read a word of it, sir."

The next day I went out with the litter bearers among the dead and wounded near the old stone church. The first man I noticed was a wounded Federal soldier. He made motions for me to come to him. He asked me if I would give him some water. He said he had been lying there twenty-four hours and was nearly dead from thirst. My canteen was full, as well as I can remember, and I handed it to him. I think he drank it all, or most of it. He then said he felt better, and that he could not have lived much longer without water. I think he said he belonged to the Thirteenth New Jersey, and had been in the army only about two weeks. He said he was a shoemaker by trade, and supported himself, mother and sister, but now he was crippled and did not know what would become of them, or whether he would ever see them again. About that time my attention was attracted to the litter bearers trying to move a man who had been killed the day before. There was a dog lying beside him, and every time they started toward the man the dog would jump at them and growl; he thought the man was only asleep. They were meditating about what to do—to move the man they would have to kill the dog. I started toward them, and in passing a tree I heard a minnie ball strike the tree, and one of the litter bearers cried, "Drop that gun. We are under a white flag here. You ought not to come out here with a gun." Well, it didn't take me long to drop that gun. The best friend to man is the dog; next is the horse, and many a poor horse loses its life trying to serve the man. That night between midnight and day, we crossed the Potomac.[21]

**Private James C. Murray**
**4th Texas Infantry**
**Camp Near Martinsburg**
**Sept. 22, 1862**

Dear Sister Mary:

It is once more my privilege to write you a line or two. Since I last wrote to you it has been a hard time on the Soldiers, we have been fighting every few days. I have been through 3 hard battles, have not received a scratch as yet, though it is my painful duty to inform you that John and Bob are both wounded in the last battle, the Battle of Sharpstown in Md. It was fought on Wednesday 17th. Bob was shot first in the charge, he is not dangerously wounded by any means, mere skipped in the jaw and neck. We were repulsed by the enemy and had to fall back under a deadly fire. John was shot in the retreat, he is skipped across the back, his is also a slight wound.

Mary do not be uneasy about these poor fellows, they fought bravely until wounded, though their wounds are painful they are not dangerous. Tell Mother not to be uneasy about them. The Battle raged from sunrise until dark and quit just about where it began, the loss was very heavy on both sides, the enemy say they lost 30,000 men and ours could not have been less than theirs. Both sides stood their ground, and both sides were badly whipped, we lay there all next day, neither side was willing to make another attack, so we waited until dark then fell back across the Potomac. Both sides now are reinforcing as fast as possible so we will probably march against them in a few days.

John and Bob are now at Winchester. Some of our wounded were left in the hands of the Yankees. Our company went into the fight with 33 men and came out with nine, lost 24, we now have about 18 men in the company, though only 9 of these that went in came out again. I will name some of the wounded. Sam Hughes lost left arm above the elbow, Wm Floyd in side and arm badly, Wm Hollander lost an arm, Peter Mans wounded badly and left on the field, supposed to be killed. Ben Henderson missing, supposed to be mortally wounded or killed, Eli Park and

J. O. M. was not in the fight, don't know where he is, haven't seen him for some time, suppose he is with the wagons. I will not name the rest of the wounded, time will not permit and then you do not know them, it looks like there will not be a Texan left if this little fuss is not settled soon. Charley Mc had the top of his hat shot off, the same ball just did miss the small of my back, we were laying down and shooting some and I was almost touching where he was shot, poor fellow he now has the fever and I fear will die. I will not attempt to give you a description of any of the other battles, though you may be sure they were hot enough.

I will send this by an old man who is on a visit he will start day after tomorrow, excuse me for not writing often as I cannot carry papers with me, we are never still long enough to write.

Mary, I spent about 2 hours with Cousin Obed Carr today, he is Captain of a company, he is a fine looking and intelligent man. I saw Cousin W. B. Player on the day of the battle, he told me our relatives had suffered very much. Dick Cowan lost a leg in the Battles around Richmond. Asa G. Murray was killed the other day near where our Regt. Fought. George Cowan was shot and left in the hands of the enemy. Captain A. J. Williams was killed in the last battle. Cousin Obed belonged to the 46 N. C. Regt. The others which I have mentioned belong to the 3rd N.C. Regt. I am very sorry to hear of the death of Asa G. William. Cousin player told me that he (A. G.) was almost crazy to see us, he was Color Bearer and will liked throughout the Regiment, and then I suppose there was a great deal depending upon him at home.

Our Color Bearer, E. M. Francis, was severely wounded at Manassas, he was doing well last heard from. Wesley Francis is well, but was not in the fight. Capt. Cunningham in now acting. Major H. Bradshaw is now (illegible).

Well Mary, I must say to you that I got the letters that you, Ma and Pa wrote, they did me more good than all the letters I ever got in my life, I have worn them out reading them. Tell Pa I will write to him soon as possible and give him a great big hug.

Goodbye,

J. C. Murray

I suppose John and Bob will write soon and often now. Where is Asa, what is Nancy doing, has she moved to our house or does she live at home?

Well Mary I saw Cousin Morris Bowden the other night, he is one of Aunt Alley's sons. I also saw Murdock Wood though you don't remember him. Morris told me all about the N.C. Boys, all that has not been killed in battle are well. Capt Obed W. Carr has gone home on sick furlough. John has not yet returned from N. C. We got a letter from him the other day. He said he would be here in a few days though he has not come yet. I am anxious to see him or hear from him. Wm. Morris is not very well, it is a cold that ails him. J. O. Wiseman and Charley McAllister are well, R. Houston is in very bad health. I wish he could get a discharge.

Oct. 11, 1862
Texas Brigade Hospital

Dear Father,

General Hood has been made a Major General, he now commands four brigades, I think he is one of the best generals we have in this army. If he could have had his was at the Battle of Sharpsburg, we would have routed the entire Yankee Army in 3 hours. He told them where the attack would be made, he first sent to D. H. Hill four men at three o'clock in the morning, he refused to send them. He then set to Longstreet, he also refused to send them, by this time the battle had opened and in a few minutes it was terrible. Hood seeing that it was impossible to hold his ground, sent a third message to Longstreet, and from Longstreet to Gen. Lee. In the meantime our brigade was formed and marched forward. Many of our own were already wounded by the grape from the Yankee batteries, we being in the direct range of their guns. Every discharge I could hear some poor fellow shriek out, it was a trying hour. We drove into it (Yankee lines) 20 times our number, (50 says General Hood), one thing I do know, we fought until we were completely flanked and nearly all killed and wounded. Our brigade went into the fight with 860 men and lost 554, killed, wounded and missing, the whole brigade was not as strong as one full regiment. At the time of the battle our army was nearly one third bare-footed, but now they all, or nearly all, have shoes. Our clothing is very bad now but we will get better in a few days.

I am very sorry you made such poor crops in Tex, this season though I hope you will not suffer for want of something to eat.

I must close for this time, I will write often as I can, for the present, fare you well.

Your unworthy son,

Jas C. Murray[22]

## Private Lawrence A. Daffan
## 4th Texas Infantry
## April 30, 1845–January 28, 1907

On the evening of the 16th we crossed the Antietam Creek, falling back from Boonsboro Gap. This occasioned some skirmishing and artillery duels across the creek, as we had taken a stand near Sharpsburg. We had orders the evening of the 16th to cook up three day's rations, and to be ready to move at a moment's warning. We were located nearly a half mile south of an old Dunkard church. There was heavy timber between us and the church; north and west of us there was a large stubble field where wheat was cut. North of this stubble was a large cornfield of considerable dimensions. Corn there in September is as high as it is here in July; fodder was about ready to be gathered. By daylight the pickets commenced firing.

By sunrise we were ordered forward in line of battle. We stopped near the church in the heavy timber, the branches were falling on us, and many spent balls played around us.

A short time after this we were ordered "forward." We emerged from the timber into the stubble field; some of it I think had recently been plowed.

As we emerged from the timber, a panorama, fearful and wonderful, broke upon us. It was a line of battle in front of us. Immediately in front of us was Lawton's Georgia Brigade. After we left the timber we were under fire, but not in a position to return the fire. As we neared Lawton's Brigade, the order came for the Texas Brigade to charge. Whenever a halt was made by a command under fire, every man lay flat on the ground, and this was done very quick. Lawton's Brigade had been on this line fighting some time before we reached them. Lawton's Brigade attempted to charge and did charge; their charge was a failure, because their numbers had been decimated; they had no strength.

Then the Texas Brigade was ordered to charge; the enemy was on the opposite side of this stubble field in the cornfield. As we passed where Lawton's Brigade had stood, there was a complete line of dead Georgians as far as I could see. Just before reaching the cornfield General Hood rode up to Colonel Carter, commanding the Fourth Texas Regiment (my regiment), and told him to front his regiment to the left and protect the flank. This he did and made a charge directly to the west. We were stopped by a pike fenced on both sides. It would have been certain death to have climbed the fence.

Hay's Louisiana Brigade had been on our left, and had been driven out. Some of their men were with us at this fence. One of them was a better soldier than I was. I was lying on the ground shooting through the fence about the second rail; he stood up and shot right over the fence. He was shot through his left hand, and through the heart as he fell on me, dead. I pushed him off and saw that "Seventh Louisiana" was on his cap.

The Fifth (Texas), First (Texas) and Eighteenth Georgia, which was the balance of my brigade, went straight down into the cornfield, and when they struck this cornfield, the corn blades rose like a whirlwind and the air was full.

The First Texas here lost her colors and eighty percent of her men. There was a Yankee battery playing down this pike at the fence where we were. As the rock and shell were flying in every direction, I can't understand why more men weren't killed, as were under fearful fire from the time we passed the Dunkard church until we reached the fence, in fact, all the time we were there.

But the climax was reached in front of the First Texas regiment, right in front of the cornfield.

Longstreet's Corps here were fighting all of McClellan's army. As Jackson had not reached us, we had orders to fall back and rally at the timber near the Dunkard Church.

I was there very thoroughly impressed with the power and effect of thorough organization. As we reached the timber, near the church, every man fell in right at his place, and in a few minutes we were as thoroughly organized as when we started in, except a very heavy loss, both killed and wounded.

We were under terrible fire from the time we emerged from the timber until the time we rallied in the timber near the church.

We then proceeded where we started from in the morning. Jackson came in to relieve us about 1.00 or 1.30 o'clock p.m.

He had been detained at Harper's Ferry, where he had captured General Miles with 10,000 prisoners, artillery, wagons, etc., as an army of this size would have. This was not the General Miles of the Jefferson Davis affair. Jackson's troops passed over us and took up the fight where we left off.

The most remarkable thing which happened to me that day was my reckoning of time. I thought we had been in action an hour, and asked, when we came out it was after one o'clock. I had a haversack full of fine rations, not altogether furnished by the Confederate Government, which was shot off and lost near the fence at the pike.

In all the battles in which I took part, General Lee brought on the attack, whether we were retreating or advancing, as the attacking party has the advantage.

We lay on the battlefield all day on the eighteenth. It rained. About seven or eight in the evening we filed off quietly and crossed the Potomac at Shepherdstown. As we were passing from the battle field to the river, I came in contact with a horrible sight. We passed an old school house, or an old church, where our wounded been carried that day and the day before to have their wounds dressed and their limbs amputated. There was a dim light burning in the church and the doctors were at work. At each window was a pile of legs and arms nearly as high as the sill. The men were being placed in ambulances and carried to Richmond.

There was no attempt to follow the enemy that night. But I understood that Jackson had allowed some of the Federals to cross the river, as many as he thought he could do without much trouble; this he did and got them all.[23]

## Sharpsburg—Navarro County Casualties

Casualties among the Navarro County men are high—37%. Wounded in the battle are Privates Frank Dillard, Robert Holloway, and J. B. Lanham; wounded and captured are Privates A. Barry and H. L. W. Killian. And one of the men wounded in the Gaines's Mill battle—Private E. M. Gardner—is killed in action. In all, seven Corsicanans felt the sting of Yankee bullets or the thud of grape or shrapnel that day near Antietam Creek.

The day before the battle, W. R. Jefferson and J. T. Green had fallen into enemy hands, and on September 15, Lieutenant Nat Mills had been wounded severely in the arm. This left only 12 men, including Captain Winkler, to answer roll call and build camp fire the night after the Sharpsburg battle. And these remaining men were almost killed by a Federal artillery shell that exploded near their camp, knocking over their stacked guns. James Polk said that he couldn't help but think how different this was from the way it was pictured to them in speeches at the beginning of the war.

The Corsicana Invincibles fought in the same battle, along with the rest of their regiment. Private J. R. Marshall, one of the few remaining members of the first men from Corsicana to answer the call for volunteers, was wounded in the engagement.

That night, sometime between midnight and dawn, the Corsicana men crossed the Potomac along with the other members of the Texas Brigade. Marching about two miles, they lie down beside the road to rest. About daylight artillery roars and musketry rattles behind them, and they know that the Federals are not far behind them. Stonewall Jackson's men held them off, however, and the Texans march on to another skirmish at Port Royal. While on the march they stop to rest along the road, and Bill Fuller of Corsicana comes in with some whiskey, James Polk said that Fuller is an old man, and that Captain Winkler never tries to control him, because although he didn't keep up with the company very well, he is always present to go into a fight.[24]

Anonymous
4th Texas Infantry
*Confederate Veteran*
December, 1914
The Texans at Sharpsburg
By a Member of the Fourth Texas.

On the morning of the 16th of September 1862, just after sunrise, the Texas brigade crossed the Antietam bridge, and as we climbed the hill on the other side I caught sight of Gen. R. E. Lee and a part of his staff. The head of our column filed to the right and formed line of battle facing the creek, with a cornfield between us and the bridge. Our picket line was in the cornfield and some of the boys had a hard time in getting their breakfast of corn without being shot, for wherever a stalk would shake a volley of bullets followed from the enemy's sharpshooters. But this was not the cornfield that the 1st Texas Regiment got into on September 17, 1862, and they stopped to rest and wait for the enemy and rations. The latter came about dark and consisted of scorched beef and corn. Our position faced the Antietam bridge, with a road running just in our rear nearly parallel with our line, and across this road was a mat of timber. Immediately after dark we moved some distance to the left and very close to a battery of the enemy.

Here we lay down on the ground and let the shells fly over us, looking like balls of fire in the heavens. I didn't know how long this lasted, for I went to sleep; but sometime around midnight we moved back into the timber and camped for the night. About four o'clock in the morning we were aroused and give some flour, and we had begun to cook our dough on sticks and ramrods when the enemy commenced to shell the woods and spoiled most of our hoecakes. At daylight we were in line of battle, and about sunrise we marched out into the open field across the road. Here I saw Whiting's old brigade in front of us. It moved on after a while, leaving a line of dead men where they had fallen.

We later changed front to the left, and the charge then commenced in earnest. The brigade was formed with the 18th Georgia in front or on the right, then the 5th Texas, then the 1st with the 4th on the left. The ground in front of the 1st rose gradually, but in front of the 4th it was more abrupt, forming some protection against the fire of the enemy: and right there, when we reached the top of the hill, was the hottest place I ever saw on this earth, or want to see hereafter. There were shot, shells, and Minie balls sweeping the face of the earth; legs, arms, and other parts of human bodies were flying in the air like straw in a whirlwind. The dogs of war were loose, and "havoc" was their cry.

Reaching the road again, with a fence on each side, we found Hooker's Corps, 18,000 strong, in front of us, and to our right was a batter of at least six guns, and the most effective I ever stood before. The only thing I saw during the entire engagement, that was all funny occurred right there. Captain Cunningham, a fine, large, two-hundred pounder was squatting behind a 2 × 6 fence post where Capt. R. H. Barrett compared him to "a big yaller dog basking on the sunny side of a house."

As our brigade did not number a thousand men, we could not stand this racket; so we fell back under the hill, moving to the left across the road, and formed a line of battle at right angles to the road, with the right of the brigade resting on the road. As we had no troops on our left, this was done to protect our flank. We had a rail-fence for breastworks, behind which we lay down under a heavy fire from sharpshooters, doing us little or no damage, however.

We waited until ten o'clock or after, when we heard something drop on our left, and what do you think it was? Why, it was that grand old war horse, Stonewall Jackson. And what the enemy caught when Stonewall struck him on the flank is too well known for me to attempt any description of it here. The Texas brigade then retired to the rear for a rest.

The 1st Texas lost eighty-three men, out of one hundred in this charge, which is the heaviest percentage of loss in our war or any other that history has any account of.

After our rest we formed into line at about three o'clock on the same ground where we camped at daylight, and then we stayed until about sunset, when we moved to the right and remained in line of battle all night. During this night I met an old friend who had lost his haversack and said he was hungry. I handed him my haversack, and he did not leave me a crumb.

By ten o'clock that night the fighting had entirely ceased, and we all had a much needed sleep. We held our position all day and sometime after dark we moved out, wading the Potomac River about ten o'clock to the tune of "Carry me back to old Virginia."[25]

## William Robert Hamby
## July 24, 1845–January 23, 1913

William R. Hamby was born on July 24, 1845, in Paris, Tennessee, as the only child of his family. His father died when he was eight years old and his mother moved with him to Austin, Texas, for the purpose of getting him an education. At the outbreak of the war, in April, 1861, William enlisted in the Travis Rifles (later the Tom Green Rifles; later Company "B") at the age of fifteen.[26]

He was the youngest soldier in the company: a boy in years, but a man in duty. He was sixteen years old at the beginning of the Peninsular Campaign and only seventeen at the Battle of Antietam. When the war was over, Hamby went to Nashville, Tennessee, and after trying a number of jobs, he was appointed Adjutant General by Governor James E. Porter. He returned to Texas and represented Travis County in the state legislature; became a cashier; and finally President of the American National Bank of Austin.[27]

Pvt. Hamby was wounded at the battle of Second Manassas (August 30, 1862); fought at the Battle of Antietam; detailed to nursing duty at Winchester, VA on September 30, 1862; and discharged for disability on November 4, 1862. After the war, William Hamby became President of the Hood's Texas Brigade Association and treasurer of the committee who raised the monument to the Brigade on the Capitol Grounds in Austin. He died on January 23, 1915, and is buried at Mount Calvary Cemetery in Austin, Texas.[28]

Private William R. Hamby
4th Texas Infantry
*Confederate Veteran Magazine*
January, 1908
Hood's Texas Brigade at Sharpsburg
Sketch of the Battle by W. R. Hamby, 4th Texas, Austin, Texas.

The Librarian of Congress in a recent letter to the Texas State Librarian, asking for information touching Hood's Texas Brigade, says: "The known statistics of these regiments are so remarkable that if missing figures can be obtained it will establish a record equaled by few, if any, organizations in the Civil War, or indeed in modern warfare."

Private William Hamby, 4th Texas Infantry. (*DeGolyer Library-Southern Methodist University*)

When a soldier has been wounded, he has the scar to show for his wound. When a regiment or brigade claims to have suffered heavily in battle, you ask for the list of killed and wounded. Judged by this standard, no brigade in the Confederate army has more bloody laurels or stands higher on the roll of honor than Hood's Texas Brigade. This article, however, will only attempt in an imperfect way to describe the action of the brigade in the battle fought near Sharpsburg, Md., September 17, 1862.

On the first campaign in Maryland our brigade was commanded by Colonel Wofford, and was composed of the 1st Texas, Lieutenant Colonel Work commanding; 4th Texas, Lieutenant Colonel Carter; 5th Texas, Captain Turner; 18th Georgia, Lieutenant Colonel Ruff; and Hampton's South Carolina Legion, Lieutenant Colonel Gary. The three Texas regiments were the only Texas troops in the Virginia army, hence we were always known as the Texas Brigade. The 18th Georgia had been associated with us from the first organization of the brigade, and from a spirit of comradeship was called the "Third Texas."

After the battle of South Mountain. September 14, we were the rear guard of the army on the march to Sharpsburg. On the morning of September 15, with a detail of one hundred men under Major Sellers, I was with the rear guard of the rear guard;

and after the army crossed the Antietam, we were on the skirmish line along the west bank of that stream until the 16th. In the meantime the brigade had formed a line of battle along the Hagerstown and Sharpsburg Turnpike, near the Dunkard church. This modest and hitherto unknown church was destined soon to become historical, as it was the storm center of the great battle fought September 17, 1862, called Sharpsburg by the Confederates and Antietam by the Federals. The church was about a mile north of the town of Sharpsburg and about a mile west of the Antietam River.

From the church north, along the west side of the pike, the woods extended about a quarter of a mile to an open field, extending still farther north several hundred yards. Across the pike east of the church were open fields, somewhat rocky and hilly, extending about half a mile north and intersecting with a cornfield. East of the fields were woods extending toward the river.

About sunset the evening of the 16th the Federal skirmish line was seen advancing through the woods east of us, closely followed by lines of battle in echelon with banners waving, drums beating, and bugles blowing. It was a magnificent spectacle, and looked more like they were on a grand review than to battle. Our thin single line presented a striking contrast. Since leaving Richmond, about one month previous, we had marched over two hundred miles, and had participated in engagements at Freeman's Ford, Thoroughfare Gap, Second Manassas, and South Mountain, and had lost six hundred and thirty-eight nun, killed and wounded. For the past several days we had subsisted chiefly on apples and green corn. Many of us were barefooted and ragged, and all of us were footsore, weary, and hungry, but full of patriotic ardor and inspired faith in the justice of our cause. The fight was opened by the artillery on our right, between us and Law's Brigade, which was composed of the 4th Alabama, 6th North Carolina, 2d Mississippi, and 9th Mississippi. They were as gallant soldiers, collectively or individually, as ever fought a battle. Among the first to enter the field, they were on the firing line when the last shot was fired. Both brigades advanced across the field with our skirmish line in front, which fell in with the main line as we entered the woods. The action continued for some time after dark; and when firing teased, the two lines were so close together that they could hear each other speak. We knew this was only a preliminary skirmish, as we could tell from the sounds in front of us that the Federals were massing their troops for a desperate battle the following day. In this position we remained until far into the night, when we were relieved by General Lawton's Division and marched a short distance to the rear. After a long delay, some flour was issued to us, which was the first ration of any kind we had received since leaving Hagerstown; but before the flour could be cooked and eaten the battle of Sharpsburg had begun.

It was scarcely daylight Wednesday morning, September 17, when the Texas Brigade was ordered in line of battle, and by sunrise had crossed the pike in front of the Dunkard church and entered the meadow to take the place of the troops who had relieved us only a few hours before.

The 5th Texas was on the right of the brigade, and as it entered the field was ordered into the woods east of the cornfield, where the fighting had occurred the previous evening. The 4th Texas, 1st Texas, 18th Georgia, and Hampton's Legion entered the meadow in the order named, and at once encountered a heavy fire. The troops in front had lost half their numbers, had exhausted their ammunition, and were retiring, and the smoke was so dense that the enemy could scarcely be seen to return his fire. The 4th Texas was ordered by the left flank to the left of the brigade, up the side of a hill toward the pike. In this formation the 4th Texas, Hampton's Legion, 18th Georgia, and 1st Texas advanced and drove the Union lines out of the open fields back upon their reserves across the pike on the west and beyond the cornfield on the north.

The enemy's reinforcements appearing in strong numbers on the left, the 4th Texas changed from front to left flank and took position along the pike near the south edge of the cornfield. A short distance to the rear were some stone bowlders, behind which some of our wounded were placed to protect them as far as possible from further injury; but even then several were struck the second time and some the third time. Hampton's Legion and the 18th Georgia were farther into the cornfield, facing a galling fire from infantry and artillery with a steadiness unsurpassed. The 1st Texas had advanced some distance beyond the remainder of the brigade toward the north side of the cornfield, breaking two lines of the enemy and forcing them to abandon a battery and take shelter in the ravine north of the field. Three times the enemy tried to check the 5th Texas in the woods east of the cornfield, and each time broke and fled before their intrepid advance.

The Texas Brigade was now only a skirmish line; in fact, all of the Confederates on this portion of the field scarcely covered a fourth of the Federal front. It was yet early in the morning, although the battle had been hot and furious for some hours. In addition to the infantry and artillery on front and flanks, the heights above the Antietam were crowned with long-range batteries that poured a merciless fire; while the fresh troops of the Union forces seemed inexhaustible as they were thrown upon the fragments of the Confederate lines. The earth and sky seemed to be on fire, and it looked like here would be the Thermopylae of the Texas Brigade. With sublime courage the 1st Texas held their advanced position in the cornfield against overwhelming numbers, and retired only to escape annihilation. Unsupported and with both flanks uncovered, the 4th Texas, Hampton's Legion, and the 18th Georgia met the advancing enemy from across the pike and drove them back and held their line. Many of the men had exhausted their ammunition and supplied themselves from the cartridge boxes of the dead and wounded around them. They were holding a position they knew they could not maintain; yet men never fought better, and withdrew only to keep from being surrounded. Falling back slowly below the crest of the hill, the line moved through the field, crossed the pike, and took position in the woods near the church. The 4th Texas was then ordered up through the woods west of the pike near the edge of the field on the north, where they remained about an hour defiantly waving their flag over empty muskets, when they were ordered to rejoin the other regiments of the brigade. The 5th Texas, finding their ammunition exhausted and that they were being flanked, retired and also rejoined the brigade. By this time the morning was far gone, and the Federals had advanced down both sides of the pike to within a short distance of the line held by the remnants of Hood's Division, who stood facing them almost exhausted and practically without ammunition.

At last the long-looked-for reinforcements arrived, and again the enemy was driven back upon their reserves. The Texas Brigade was then ordered a short distance to the rear for a fresh supply of ammunition, and again returned to the front about noon and found the woods near the church, lately occupied by them, in possession of the enemy; but as our line advanced, the Federals fell back across the pike into the field, about three hundred yards beyond the church. We steadily held our line near the pike until about sunset, when we were moved a short distance to the right, where we remained in line of battle until the night of the 18th, when the entire army withdrew and recrossed the Potomac back into Virginia.

If the reinforcements had reached the firing line before the Texas Brigade and Law's Brigade were forced to abandon their advanced positions, the Federals would have been swept from the field and another triumph would have been added to the list of Confederate victories. Our dead lay in rows upon the ground, where they had fought a fruitless fight; and instead of a Confederate victory, it was an indecisive contest, giving hope and courage to the Federals and depressing in its effect upon the Confederates.

The battle of Sharpsburg was fought with desperate courage by both the gray and the blue, and the 17th of September, 1862, stands out conspicuously as the bloodiest day in American history. More men were killed and wounded that day than on any other one day during the War between the States, and I doubt if the dead and wounded ever lay thicker upon any field than was seen from the old Dunkard church north for more than half a mile. The action commenced about daybreak, and by sunset the bloody work had ended.

The 1st Texas went into the battle with 226 men, and lost in killed and wounded 186, a loss of eighty-two per cent. As one flag bearer would fall, another would seize the flag, until nine men had fallen beneath their colors. Official records show that the 1st Texas lost more men, killed and wounded, in the battle of Sharpsburg, in proportion to numbers engaged, than any other regiment, either Federal or Confederate, in any other battle of the war. The 4th Texas went into the fight with 200 men, and lost 107, the 5th Texas went into the fight with 175 men, and lost 86; the 18th Georgia went into the fight with 176 men, and lost 85; Hampton's Legion went into the fight with 77 men, and lost 55, including four flag bearers. In the aggregate the Texas Brigade went into the fight with 851, rank and file, and lost 519, killed and wounded, including sixteen flag bearers, a loss of over sixty per cent. This does not include the "missing," many of whom were no doubt killed or wounded.

On the field of Sharpsburg a monument should be erected to the memory of the dead of Hood's Texas Brigade. They were sacrificed for the want of proper support, but their spirits rise like white clouds in the sky and tell us that they died for a just cause. The cause for which they fought is not a "lost cause." I repudiate and condemn that phrase. They were not fighting to destroy the Union, but for the perpetuation of the principles upon which the Union was formed.

The right of local self-government, the sovereignty of the States, is the seed of the Union, and is steadily growing in strength and vigor. Their struggle was for constitutional government, the corner stone of national union. They were not rebels, nor were they traitors, they did not die for secession and slavery, but in vindication of constitutional sovereignty, without which constitutional liberty would be only a memory.

Many who once condemned the South and denounced us as rebels and traitors have raised the veil of prejudice, and now accord to us the highest tribute of patriotic courage and manly devotion to the great principle upon which this government was founded.

Looking back after the lapse of nearly half a century, the terrible losses sustained on all the red fields from Big Bethel to Appomattox throw a halo around a "just cause" which grows brighter as the years roll on, and which should nerve the heart and inflame the speech for the sovereign principle of "home rule."[29]

## Waco Evening News
## April 7, 1894

Captain W. C. Walsh has in his possession and exhibited to the soldiers yesterday the battle flag which was presented to the Fourth Texas regiment, Hood's brigade at Dumfries, Va., by Miss Louis Wigfall, daughter of Senator Wigfall, deceased.

This flag has sixty-nine bullet holes and was used by the regiment from the beginning of the war until the battle of Sharpsburg. It has been through close engagements at Second Manassas, Mechanicsville, Gaines' Mill, Sharpsburg and other battles, and although rent by bullet holes, not a star was touched or injured. It was kept buried until after the war.

TEXAS
Remembers the valor and devotion of her sons who served at Sharpsburg September 16–17, 1862. Here in the Cornfield early on the morning of September 17 the Texas Brigade helped blunt the attack of elements of Mansfield's Union Corps. Almost alone during this powerful Federal onslaught the Texas Brigade sealed a threatening gap in the Confederate line. In so doing the 1st Texas Infantry Regiment suffered a casualty rate of 82.3 percent, the greatest loss suffered by any

Texas Monument at Antietam National Battlefield. (*Antietam National Battlefield*)

infantry regiment, North or South, during the war. Of approximately 850 men engaged the Texas Brigade counted over 550 Casualties.

Texas troops at Sharpsburg were: 1st Texas Inf., Lt. Col. P. A. Work; 4th Texas Inf., Lt. Col. B. F. Carter; 5th Texas Inf., Capt. Ike N. M. Turner (Col. W. T. Wofford's Texas Brigade Hood's Division, Longstreet's Corps).

The Texas Brigade included the 18th Georgia Inf., Lt. Col. S. Z. Ruff, Hampton South Carolina Legion (Inf. Cos.) Lt. Col. M. W. Gary.

A Memorial to Texans Who served the Confederacy Erected: by the State of Texas 1964 No. 29-B.

# 5th Texas Infantry Regiment

The Regiment was authorized by the War Department of the Confederacy on October 1, 1861.

List of Companies and First Company Commanders:

Company A:   (Bayou City Guards) Harris County—W. B. Botts
Company B:   Colorado County—J. C. Upton
Company C:   (Leon Hunters) Leon County—D. M. Whaley
Company D:   (Waverly Confederates) Walker County—R. M. Powell
Company E:   (Dixie Blues) Washington County—J. D. Rogers
Company F:   (Invincibles No. 1) Washington County—King Bryan
Company G:   (Milam County Greys) Milam County—J. C. Rogers
Company H:   (Texas Polk Rifles) Polk County—J. S. Cleveland
Company I:   (Texas Aids) Washington County—J. B. Robertson
Company K:   (Polk County Flying Artillery) Polk County I. N. M. "Ike" Turner

## Fighting Through the Summer of 1862

The 5th Texas Regiment left Texas in 1861 with approximately 800 enlisted men and officers. During the winter of 1861–62, before the regiment's first engagement, the ranks of the 5th Texas shrank significantly as illnesses swept through the winter camps.

In order to bolster their strength, in early spring 1862, an officer and enlisted man from every company was sent back to Texas to recruit in their home counties. The large size of the 5th Texas during the first two major battles of the 1862 campaign reflected the success of this recruiting effort.

With addition of the newly recruited soldiers, the 5th Texas began its spring campaign with a strength of roughly 500 men. At the Battle of Gaines' Mill near Richmond in late June, thirteen men died in battle and sixty-three were wounded.[1]

5th Texas Infantry flag flown at Antietam. (*State of Texas Archives*)

The 5th Texas, as it marched to Manassas Junction in August, was comprised of somewhat over 400 troops. Fortunately, many of those wounded at Gaines' Mill had recovered well enough to continue campaigning. At the battle of Second Manassas, the 5th Texas was still a large regiment.

Their second day of combat at Second Manassas is recognized as the regiment's finest achievement. On that day, August 30, the 5th Texas routed the 5th New York Zouaves and the 10th New York Infantry. However, the cost was high, with 214 men killed, wounded, or captured—the most casualties of any regiment in Lee's army at the battle.[2]

## Leading the 5th Texas

Confederate regimental leaders led from the front and became battle casualties at an appalling rate. All three of the 5th Texas' regimental officers fell at Second Manassas. Colonel Jerome Robertson and Major King Bryan were wounded, while Lieutenant Colonel John Upton was killed.[3] Only one year before, all three men— Robertson, Bryan, and Upton—had been captains leading individual companies. At Second Manassas, when the trio of commanding officers fell in battle, command of the 5th Texas devolved to yet another company commander, twenty-three-year-old

Captain Ike Turner of Company "K."[4] Captain Turner continued to lead the 5th Texas two weeks later in mid-September as Lee's army marched into Maryland. After the regiment's dreadful losses at Second Manassas, the 5th Texas now fielded only 175 riflemen, substantially less than half the number who had filled the ranks on August 28.[5]

Even though only a captain in rank, the task of writing the official after-action report of the 5th Texas' participation in the Battle of Antietam belonged to Captain Turner as the regiment's senior line officer on the field. There is no better primary source to initiate the voices of the 5th Texas' soldiers at Antietam than Captain Turner's report.

## Isaac "Ike" Turner
## April 3, 1839–April 14, 1863

Ike Turner had come to Texas from Georgia before the war to manage new land holdings his father had bought. Aged twenty-two, he was elected captain of the "Polk County Flying Artillery," a band of volunteers who enlisted in Livingston, Texas.

Rather than enter the war as crewmen for an artillery battery, the eighty recruits from Polk County were attached to the 5th Texas Regiment as Company "K," the tenth and final company to be assigned to the 5th Texas. Turner participated in twenty-six engagements. He served as "acting major" of the regiment in the winter of 1861–62, but was never formally promoted. He received recognition from General Hood, who apparently intended to assign Turner to lead a battalion of sharpshooters. Ironically, on April 14, 1863, Turner was killed by a Union sharpshooter while the regiment was occupying fortifications on the banks of the Nansemond River near Suffolk, Virginia.[6]

**Captain Isaac N. M. Turner**
**Fifth Texas Infantry Regiment**
**Colonel W. T. Wofford,**
**Commanding Texas Brigade**

Camp near Martinsburg, W. VA.,
September 24, 1862
SIR:

I have the honor to submit the following report of the part taken by the Fifth Texas Regiment in the late engagements of the 16th and 17th instant, near Sharpsburg, Md.:

Late in the evening of the 16th instant our brigade was moved by the left flank from the position we had been occupying during the day to a field in front of a

Captain Isaac "Ike" Turner, 5th
Texas Infantry. (*Texas Heritage
Museum-Historical Research Center*)

church. We had not occupied our new position long before a brisk fire commenced
between our skirmishers and those of the enemy. The Fifth Texas Regiment was
ordered to the edge of the [east?] woods as a support for our skirmishers. On
arriving at the position assigned our skirmishers, being hard pressed, fell back and
passed to my right. I ordered the regiment to commence firing, which checked the
advance of the enemy.

About 8 o'clock at night we were relieved, and retired to the [west] woods in rear
of the [Dunker] church. Slept until about day, when firing commenced in front. We
were called to attention; thrown around the hill in line of battle to protect us from
grape and shell. We had not occupied this position more than half an hour before we
were ordered out as support for the Third Brigade. We caught up with said brigade
where our first line had been fighting. Here the Fifth was ordered to halt by Major
[Captain] Sellers, and allow the regiments on the right of the Third to advance.
While lying here, General Hood rode up, ordering me to incline to the right, press
forward, and drive the enemy out of the woods, which we did. The enemy twice
tried to regain their position in the woods by advancing a force through the lower
edge of the corn-field, which we repulsed. From a point of timber about 400 yards
to our front and left, I discovered strong re-enforcements marching out by the left
flank down a hollow, which protected them from our fire. Allowing them to get
within 75 yards of us with lines unbroken, I saw we would soon be hard pressed.

Sent four times to Major [Captain] Sellers for support, determined to hold my position as long as possible. My men, were out of ammunition, the enemy not more than 100 yards in my front, no support, no ammunition; all our troops had fallen back on my left; I deemed it prudent to fall back also.

Officers and men, with a few exceptions, behaved well.

The casualties of the regiment were 5 killed and 81 wounded, total 86. Of the wounded, 3 were mortally, and have died; 16 were not removed from the field, and 2 were left on the Maryland side in hospital for want of transportation.

All of which is respectfully submitted.

Ike N. Turner

Captain, Commanding Fifth Texas Regiment[7]

## James D. Roberdeau
## February 6, 1830–May 18, 1910

Another captain of the 5th Texas, James D. Roberdeau of Company "B," wrote a detailed and highly descriptive narrative of the battle. Roberdeau lists only eleven men fighting under his command during the battle of Antietam: one sergeant and ten privates—a very small company. Three Company B men had been sent to Sharpsburg to find food for the company and did not return in time for the fight. The company's lieutenant had taken sick and been left behind at South Mountain on the way to Sharpsburg. Two soldiers were detached as Company B's contribution to the regimental "picket and observation" detail, and Roberdeau says those men did not rejoin the company for the fighting on the 17th. He also mentions one man being very sick on the morning of the battle and sent to the rear area hospital.

Of the sixteen men on Company B's duty roster, a total of six riflemen and one officer were either sick at the last minute or on detached duty when the regiment marched into the East Woods. Roberdeau's memoir thus provides a fine example of how the paper strength of a regiment or company was routinely higher than the number of riflemen who were actually in the ranks, engaged in combat during a battle.

According to Roberdeau, of his ten privates who fought in the East Woods, four were killed, one went missing presumed killed, and two were wounded and captured. Roberdeau was wounded while the regiment was reforming in the latter stages of the battle, sending command of the tiny four-man remnant of his company to the only sergeant remaining on duty.

He initially served as 1st Lieutenant of Company B, serving under Captain John Upton, who was soon promoted to the regimental command staff. Roberdeau was sent back to Texas in the spring of 1862 as part of the 5th Texas' recruiting drive. He was promoted to captain of Company B in June, 1862, and was wounded in the right arm at the battle of Second Manassas on August 30, 1862. He was later wounded and captured at Little Round Top at Gettysburg on July 2, 1863. He remained a prisoner of war until March 14, 1865, when he was exchanged at Point Lookout, Virginia.[8] After the war, he first lived in Houston, then moved to Austin where he worked as a bookkeeper. In 1905, Roberdeau attended the annual reunion of the veterans of Hood's Texas Brigade. He was one of three survivors of Antietam who were given the task of revising the map of the Battle of Antietam showing where Hood's Brigade was at certain hours of the day. Presumably, the revised map was completed and accepted by the U.S. War Department, which had requested the revision.[9] Captain Roberdeau died on May 18, 1910, and is buried in the Weimar Masonic Cemetery in Weimar, Texas.

Captain James D. Roberdeau
5th Texas Infantry
*Colorado Citizen*
Austin, Texas, September 17, 1899

Editor Colorado Citizen:

In my last I announced the arrival of our command at Leesburg, Va., which was about 8 o'clock, p.m., and when and where I rejoined Co. "B" From here we moved towards the Potomac river, halting and bivouacking at the Big Springs, several miles distant. (Permit me to digress by saying that they duly entitled to the name, covering, as they did, a space equal to your public square, and furnishing water sufficient to run a mill, situated half a mile distant, the capacity of which had been several hundred barrels of flour daily.)

On the following morning's roll call, to the honor of Co. B be it said, developed the loss of only one man, and he left with a sick comrade, seventeen of eighteen remaining after the battle of Manassas answering to their names. Especial reference is made to this circumstance, since there was so much struggling reaching into the thousands—induced by hard marching, fighting and short rations. Halting one day and two nights, we again resumed the march, crossing the Potomac river at Edwards' ferry, by wading. You well know the pleasant sensation produced, after having marched long enough to warm the blood, and then plunge into a cold stream.

It was somewhat aggravated here by reason of a small island just large enough to conceal that other part, yet to be crossed. Here some religious services were had, winding up with a grand chorus, "Jordan is a hard road to travel!" You are also acquainted with the aftermath, or drying process, with the water sloshing out of your shoes, to be ruffled from the supply in your generous blanket, to continue until relieved by evaporation, heated words and vigorous sunshine.

We moved direct to Frederick City, Md., where another night and day were spent, variously; for instance, destroying the bridge over the Monocacy which the superstructure we were a success, but the stone piers withstood all assaults. I have since been told that, while we were engaged in the pastime, the railroad company in Baltimore were duplicating the bridge, and one day after we had departed they had put it up and were crossing McClellan's army in pursuit of us. There was another source of employment more generally indulged in, with better results, that of ridding ourselves of those friends who adhered to us under all circumstances, and which we so prodigally gathered in on march, here designated legion. Nor could we rightly be censured for the inhospitality, since, it must be remembered, that we had been marching and fighting since the 7th day of August without sufficient time for that sleep so necessary, much less sanitary care of person, or courtesies due an uninvited guest.

General Jackson left Frederick City on the day of our arrival, going on—then, we knew not where. We marched direct to Hagerstown, where we remained until Sunday, 14th inst. During the stay we had three days' rations issued on Friday, 12th. Just here it is proper to state that General Hood was placed under arrest and we turned over to General N. G. (Shank) Evans. You will remember that at Manassas, among other things captured by our command was a fine, officers' ambulance, which General Hood appropriated to his own use. This riled Shank, and upon refusal to deliver same to him, was placed under arrest. On the morning of the 14th we were put in motion and moved at quick-time to Boonsboro mountain, distant about twelve miles. It was a fearful march, all being sore-foot, tired and more or less suffering from disease incident to camp life. We arrived at the base of the mountain late in the evening and found General D. H. Hill busy entertaining the company which had arrived, and looking for others. Enthusiasm is what he needed, and we supplied the want. We here learned, for the first time since leaving Frederick City, the whereabouts of General Jackson. He had invested Harper's Ferry, and we were here to keep off McClellan until he captured the place, which he did, capturing 11,000 soldiers, 75 cannon, clothing, ordnance, commissariat, etc.

We were halted at the base of the mountain, preparatory to advancing, and for the first time in its history murmurs of insubordination were heard in the brigade— men asserting that, without Hood, they would not move. Of course the officers, while partaking, of the sentiment, employed themselves in allaying it. The situation was conveyed to General Lee, at whose request General Hood accepted a temporary release and rode to the head of the command. Never during my military experience had I witnessed such general satisfaction and for the first and only time did I doff my hat and yell! Soldiers are quick to discern a defect in an officer, and equally as prompt to resent an injury offered one of their officers. We were in a fix—led to the very verge of battle by one in whom we had no confidence, and stung by what we deemed an insult to our cherished leader, should and does command us. With that familiar command, "Tention!" we soon deployed and moved up the mountain, on the left of the pike, going east, under heavy cannonading, and pushing the enemy back.

While halting at base of mountain Lieut. Collier was taken seriously ill, and was sent to a private home, where he was captured. Dr. T. T. DeGraffenried was wounded while ascending the mountain, and sent to the rear. The command was transferred to the right of the pike, and after some skirmishing both armies rested in place.

During the night our army gradually withdrew for Sharpsburg, and, as usual, leaving our command the duty to bring up the rear, which we did, leaving just before daylight. It fell to my lot to be of the rear guard, and you well know what experience I had with those who had fallen out to take a nap—the officers being the more difficult to move. John B. Harvey, being bare-footed, was left to come at his opportunity. During our march to Sharpsburg we (rear guard) were at times closely pressed by cavalry, but the old Washington artillery, from eminences in our front, would soon relieve us by shelling them over our heads.

We arrived at Sharpsburg late in the evening of the 15th, bivouacked on the field, sleeping upon our arms. On the morning of the 16th we were moved north about one mile, where we remained during the day, supporting batteries, etc. The enemy having employed the day in disposing his forces, and having completed his alignments, threw forward the Fifth Pennsylvania reserve corps, when we were advanced, the 5th regiment deployed in front. Some desultory skirmishing was began about dark, resulting in a few casualties —among them Hardy Allen of Co. E, the color bearer. Then preparations for the morrow's strife were begun by throwing forward two men from each company for observation and picket, Hunt Terrell and Geo. Monroe were Co. B's detail and went forward. A detail to go to Sharpsburg for rations being ordered, Co. B named W. J. Sloneker, J. E. Obenhaus and Geo. Gegenworth. They did not return before the battle began. This was Tuesday night, 15th, the last rations issued having been on Friday, 13th. On taking position in the morning of the 16th in a field of Irish potatoes, plowed up for gardening, we secured a mess or two. The brigade was then (about 10 a.m.,) relieved by General Drayton's brigade, when we withdrew to a skirt of timber in the rear of the famous Dunkard's church, and lay down to sleep the last sleep for many. W. H. Carlton sent to the rear on surgeon's certificate, being quite sick.

The battlefield, as seen before the conflict, presented a scene of beauty to the lover of the beautiful and grand — surrounded by mountains and high ranges of hills, and dotted over with elegant farm-houses, barns, orchards, natural groves, of great beauty, and, with all in a high state of cultivation, rendering it not only pleasant to look upon, but remunerative. How changed the scene twenty-four hours later! You imagine shattered groves and orchards, burned houses and barns, lone chimneys, as sentinels on the ruins of man's wrath; the earth strewn with the dead and wounded dismantled batteries, and the debris peculiar to an army generally.

The battlefield proper lies west of South Mountain, running nearly north and south, at the base of which was formed the federal army, while ours occupied a high ridge immediately in their front and to the west, and between them flowed Antietam creek, spanned by a bridge, the subject of a heated discussion on the 17th, it being one of the main points of attack by the enemy. Our right rested on Antietam creek, and extending north some four or five miles, I suppose. On the 18th the view of the panorama spread before me was one to inspire admiration and delight, but for the purpose of assaulting; still it was grand to look upon. Bright uniforms, with dashing officers riding the lines, with bayonet and sword flashing in the sun, with cavalry and artillery flying hither and yon, made it a scene long to be remembered; all seen under a clear sky and just such weather as we have now, and equally as hot. Dotted along the slope and rising to the crest were many batteries, from which we suffered so much. To our rear was a succession of farms; the Potomac river, three miles distant, which here was shaped something like a horse-shoe. By critics the position was pronounced as well chosen, which was verified, since from the 16th to 18th, inclusive, Gen. Lee, with 35,000 soldiers, held it against 85,000 of the enemy. Of the battle, both sides named it as the bloodiest, since the percentage of losses, in proportion to the numbers engaged, was greater than any other of the war.

Here it is deemed proper to give the composition of our semi-division. That of Law's brigade was the 2d and 11th Mississippi, 6th North Carolina and 4th Alabama, commanded by General E. M. Law, a splendid gentleman and efficient officer. That of Hood's Texas brigade were the 1st, 4th and 5th Texas, Hampton's Legion and 18th Georgia regiment, and commanded by Colonel W. T. Wofford of the latter regiment. The Fifth regiment was commanded by Captain Ike Turner, Co. K, and the peer of any.

About 7 o'clock, a.m., while we were preparing to cook rations, we were startled by Drayton's brigade breaking in on us, having been driven in by the enemy. We were immediately formed and moved forward, Law's brigade on the right. As we moved forward Gen. Hood withdrew the 4th, placing it upon the extreme left and somewhat detached, as I learn, from the brigade. So impetuous was the enemy's charge on Drayton that we encountered him within a short distance of our camp, repulsing him and driving him into and beyond the skirt of woods from which he had emerged, but at fearful cost. From that time until relieved by Gen. T. S. Anderson's Georgia brigade it was a continuous "see-saw," the enemy renewing the charge and forcing us back, to be again repulsed and driven back. All this was over the dead and wounded of each army. At what time of day we were relieved there is a diversity of opinion, and I will say that it was far advanced, and after we had exhausted our ammunition and resorted to that of the dead and wounded, besides exchanging guns with them, those carried in being too hot to handle. You are aware that twenty rounds is considered quite a battle. Speaking of the duration of time we were engaged, a comrade of the 4th unites with me in saying, "It was the longest day ever made!"

Of the loss to our brigade, it was particularly severe, that of the 1st Texas being 82.3 percent, as gleaned from United States war department, and is given as the greatest of any regiment of either army during the war.

When it is remembered that, since the 7th of August we had marched from Richmond, Va., to Frederick City, Md., with counter marches, fought one of the greatest battles of the war at Manassas, with several skirmishes, without sufficient clothing or food, often bare-foot, the wonder is that we put up such a fight against an adversary generously equipped and daily receiving new acquisitions of men, and on his own territory. The conditions considered, stamp it not only the bloodiest, but place it in the fore front, in every particular, of conspicuous battles in modern history.

The following list comprises Co. B's strength on that occasion, as I find from my diary; Sergeant D. E. (Ellis) Putney, Privates A. Hicks Baker, W. J. Darden, W. S. Cherry, John Graf, John Hoffman, John Kolbo, John Morrissey, M. McNeilis, J. D. Roberdeau. Of the nine Baker, Hoffman, Kolbo and McNeillis were killed. Monroe, sent out the night before missing and supposed to be killed. Darden and Morrissey were wounded and captured, and the captain wounded while re-forming, after the battle was over. Of the four killed, three fell in the open field, and your brother Hicks just as we entered the woods, carrying the regimental flag. Here I shall speak of him only to say he possessed all the attributes of the soldier and genuine friend. Of those actively engaged in that battle, this writer only survives, save D. M. Currie, litter-bearer, who certainly was in it. Re-forming at the place from which we entered the woods, the command of the company devolved upon Sergeant Putney.

During the 18th the two armies, with few changes, occupied their respective original ground, busy burying the dead and caring for the wounded; and at night we recrossed the Potomac river at Sheperdstown—on the next day repulsing an effort of the enemy to pursue. General Lee then distributed his army between the river and Winchester, our command being at Baldwin's Spring, from which place I may renew and review in detail the incidents of the campaign.

The writer claims not to be correct in all the statements given, since a lapse of thirty-seven years of busy and varied pursuits have alike claimed a share of memory.

J. D. R.

## Watson Dugat Williams
## March 6, 1838–April 17, 1881

Watson Dugat Williams enlisted as a private in Company "F" in 1861 and rose to command of the company. He was one of eight men in Company "F" to surrender at Appomattox. After the war, he moved to Liberty, Texas, and was part owner of a steamship line. He also edited and published the *State Star* newspaper.[10] He died on April 17, 1881, and is buried in Liberty County Texas.

While many soldiers showed great restraint to not dwell on the grisly details of battle in their letters, Captain Watson Williams apparently felt no such compunction.

In his letter to a Miss Wilson, he was quite specific about battle casualties within his company, not only naming several men killed or wounded in action, but describing how each soldier was injured. Since his letter begins, "My Dear Laura," perhaps the recipient was a paramour. If so, it may be that the captain's candor was a factor in his after-war marriage to another woman.

Captain Watson Dugat Williams
5th Texas Infantry
Texas Depot Richmond
Oct. 2nd, 1862

My Dear Laura,

Perhaps the fate of this letter, like many other I sent you, is already sealed, but I have some hopes of you receiving it and with that hope will write. I have written numerous letters to you since I saw you last and how they could have been repeatedly lost is certainly a little strange. All the letters I have had from you more strange still, Dallis and I have frequently mailed letters together at the same time in this depot and his have been received while mine have not. I arrived in Richmond the night before last and I think I shall remain here for several days, at least I shall not start to join the regiment until I am a better able to "do duty." The last letter I wrote you, I think was dated about the 10th. Since then we have had hard times indeed and have been in two severe engagements in which the loss on our side has been very great. Since our Regiment left Richmond the last time we have been attached to Gen'l Longstreet's forces and still continue under his command. After the battle of Manassas No. 2 we followed the retreating enemy closely until after he evacuated Centerville then our direction was changed towards Leesburg. Our reception at that place was of the most cheerful kind. It was sometime after dark when we reached there and we searched through the city without halting. The houses were brilliantly lighted up with an extravagant number of candles in the windows and the sidewalks of the streets through which we passed were crowded with ladies and children and many a "God bless you all" was spoken out by the silvery voices on the sidewalks and more than once I heard the same voices say the words our boys so much love to hear of "Hurrah! For the Texas Brigade" and then what deafening cheers would go up from our ranks to answer the compliments.

We crossed the Potomac about noon on the 6th of Sept. at a place about 10 miles from Leesburg at a place called "Point of Rocks." Eight days after that (Sunday, 14th) we were fighting an overpowering number of the enemy with all the desperation that Southerners can fight. We were fighting only to hold them back while Jackson was maneuvering for the capture of Harper's Ferry which he accomplished the following day. We then fell back to Sharpsburg where on the 17th (Wednesday) another terrible battle was fought. Our loss there was great but

I have no idea it is near so great as the enemy. In my company I don't know but two that were killed. Viz. 2nd Lt. Mack Strickland was shot down in the forenoon on Wednesday but did not die until Thursday night. McCall, I think died in a few minutes after being shot. Pinkney was wounded in the forehead by a ball striking him obliquely which most fortunately did not kill him. Hall Johnston was shot through the arm but did not hurt his bone. Whelon (recruit) had the little finger of his left hand carried away by a piece of shell. Jeff Chaison and Joe Spencer of Beaumont are both missing. I am very much afraid Mr. Spencer is wounded but I'm pretty sure Jeff is not. They both fell into the hands of the Yankees and very likely, before now have been paroled and are on their way to this place. Neither the Major or Dallis were in these fights nor Milam nor Henry Whitlock so they are all safe. This leaves at 5 o'clock in the mail and as it is almost dark now, I must close. Tomorrow I will write again to both yourself and Sis. I have not time to write to Sis just now. I was wounded slightly in the engagement of Sunday, 14th and on that account I am here now. I am improving though, very fast in the course of a week I think I shall be fully able to rejoin the Company. Now Lollie, don't think hard of me for sending this short note, for it is now really too dark and I had only a few minutes notice of an opportunity of writing. So Goodbye for a very short time—My kindest regards to Mr. Bryan, Aunt Martha and Florence.

Yours as Ever,

Dugat[11]

## Campbell Wood
### December 5, 1842–October 28, 1914

Campbell Wood enlisted on August 2, 1861, near Harrisburg, after withdrawing from the Texas Monumental and Military Institute at the direction of his father. Woods was elected third lieutenant of Company "D." In June, 1862, he was appointed to the position of regimental adjutant and was wounded at Gettysburg, losing three toes. Wood survived the war and became a physician in San Saba County.[12] He died on October 28, 1914, and is buried at Sunset Memorial Park in San Antonio, Texas.

While the following memoir appeared in the San Antonio *Daily Express* in a column written by J. B. Polley of the 4th Texas Infantry Regiment, Polley's recollection came from a post-war letter written by Lieutenant Campbell Wood, who was the adjutant of the 5th Texas. It is a fascinating memory that focuses on two aspects of soldiering in the 1860s. First, soldiers had to cope with gruesome deaths while continuing to carry on with the basic chores of a soldier—like cooking the first rations received in a couple of days, regardless of being cannonaded, and then being forced to abandoned their half-cooked breakfasts to return to battle, as the 5th Texas did at Antietam. Second, Wood's story touches on the other side of the religious fervor that swept through the armies—the popularity and belief in non-religious spiritualism and the carrying of charms or talismans.

Lieutenant Campbell Wood
5th Texas Infantry
San Antonio *Daily Express*
April 17, 1910

On the morning of the second day's fighting at Sharpsburg, Private T. J. Edwards—a member of Company D of the Fifth Texas—was one of the detail sent back to cook for the regiment. The fires were made and preparations for the cooking under way, but the smoke from the fires revealed the position of the detail, the Federal artillery caught range and shells from their guns soon extinguished them. It was then that Edwards was killed. A ball struck him about the height of his elbows severing both arms and cutting his body into two separate parts. The detail sought another location, but had sooner built new fires than those that were extinguished by the artillery and the cooking abandoned, the men of the Fifth Texas fought the second day at Sharpsburg with empty stomachs.

By the little town of Danville, Montgomery County Texas, where Company D of the Fifth Texas was organized, lived in 1861 an old German known as Jack Hostetter but was familiarly known as Uncle Jack. But the old man and the town exist now only in memory. The morning we were leaving and bidding goodbye to the people of the little town, Uncle Jack came out of his front gate, holding in his hand some bits of paper which he handed one to each of them to Capt. R. M. Powell, W. B. Campbell, R. C. Stanton, T. J. Edwards and myself. They appeared to be strips of Bristol board an inch in width, folded longitudinally and glued tightly, and then doubled once making them each three fourths of an inch long and half an inch wide.

The old man explained that they were 'charms' and that as long as carried would protect the bearer from leaden balls, but not from a cannon ball or any missile made of iron. "You may be struck by a spent ball," said he, "but no leaden ball will kill you while you carry this charm." Noticing an incredulous smile on my face as he tendered one to me, he remarked, "You may laugh but it will not take up much space in your purse, so take it to please an old man."

Of course each of us accepted a charm, and naturally, we joked each other often about them. Holding them to the light we could see writing inside of the glued fold, but could not decipher it.

While wading the Rappahannock River at Freeman's Ford the contents of my purse became saturated with water. Examining the charm I discovered that after its wetting it could be easily opened and pulling its folds apart, I read the words "max fax du max," A few days later, at the battle of Second Manassas I was struck just below the belt by the fragment of a shell, which I accepted as a punishment for my audacity in tampering with Uncle Jack's charm. However, I had restored it to its original condition, and still carried it on my person.

Of the five persons to which Uncle Jack gave charms, R. C. Stanton was slightly wounded at Second Manassas, Colenel R. M. Powell then Capt. Powell of the Fifth Texas and myself were wounded at Gettysburg, and W. B. Campbell although never missed a battle, was never wounded. As for the fifth man, T. J. Edwards, he was never struck by a leaden bullet, but his body was cut in two by an iron shell at Sharpsburg.

Old Jack Hostetter was a "forty-niner," in the gold mines of California. I have often seen him relieve the toothache by a process he called "coning." He would place the sufferer behind a door, and with a hatchet in one hand and a nail in the other, he would make four strokes on the door facing the wall and inquire, "How does it feel now?" The usual reply in the first inquiry was: "It hurts like the devil." Four more strokes and another familiar inquiry would elicit the reply, "It feels a little better." Again Uncle Jack would make four strokes with the nail and told in reply to his third inquiry how the tooth felt that it did not hurt at all he would drive the nail into the door facing and assure the patient that as long as the nail remained there the tooth would never ache again. And never did ache, so far as I could learn. I always believed that with each stroke of the nail he uttered one of the mysterious words: "max fax du-max," that was concealed in the folds of the charm he gave me. I give no opinion as to the virtue of that charm. I have stated the facts—your readers may draw their conclusions.

Campbell Wood

## John W. Stevens
### February 22, 1832–August 24, 1919

John W. Stevens enlisted in Company "K" in the spring of 1862. At Antietam, John Stevens served as a private in Company "K." He was appointed fourth corporal in October, 1862, then second corporal in June, 1863. Stevens was among the 112 men of the 5th Texas who were captured during the assault of Little Round Top at Gettysburg in 1863, and he spent four months as a prisoner of war until he was exchanged in November, 1863, in ill health. He was promoted to first corporal in May, 1864. Around 1872, Stevens moved to Hill County, where he served as the county judge for several years. After 1878, Stevens returned to East Texas and devoted himself to the Methodist ministry.[13] He was one of the last surviving soldiers of Hood's Texas Brigade when he died on August 24, 1919, and is buried at the Forest Hill Cemetary in Seymour, Texas.

### Condensed from the *Polk County Enterprise*, Dec. 18, 2003

John W. Stevens walked nearly 2,000 miles back home from the Civil War and ruined his feet for life. Stevens was a late-comer to one of the companies that originated in Polk County and were already in battle when he enlisted. According to Stevens' diary, during his imprisonment, his diet consisted of rats, rotten potatoes and, sometimes, cornbread. He recalled the journey from prison in Maryland to the exchange point in Georgia by steamer. "We were weary and hungry, some unable to stand on their feet. My weight was reduced from 222 to 141 pounds—81 pounds of pure Rebel flesh left behind."

### Surgeon A. H. Scott

A. H. Scott was the regimental surgeon of the 4th Texas Regiment during the Maryland Campaign in September, 1862. In May, 1863, he was transferred to the Richmond Hospital, where John Stevens probably met the doctor, who he refers to has "John" Scott.[14]

### Private John W. Stevens
### 5th Texas Infantry

Just before daylight on the morning of the 17th· we cooked some meat and flour issued to us with orders to cook it at once. No such order was necessary, as we had been practically without rations for three days; hence the starting of the fires and wetting up of the flour in any way we could was started at once. Some of us used an old scrap of oil cloth or one corner of our blankets as bread trays. We all understood that we must work in a hurry or go into battle with very empty craws. But daylight came to soon, the smoke of our fires proving a good mark to indicate to the Federals where our lines were. They began to shell us with their canister shot and at the same time to advance their lines. The falling shot raked our bread pans, skillets and fires right and left, putting a complete check to all preparations for the much needed breakfast. Simultaneously with this our commanders came in dashing down the line ordering us to fall in, load and prepare for action, and in less time than it takes to pen these lines we were in line and moving out in battle array to play our part in what is said to be the hardest fought battle of the war. It is about 600 yards across an open field to the point at which we had been relieved the night before by a command of Georgia troops.

They are now hotly engaged and we are moving on to support them. The enemy is pressing them back and at the same time raining a terrible shower of shell and shrapnel on us as we advance. We are suffering greatly and our men are falling all along the line. The Georgians are being cut to pieces badly by overpowering numbers who are pressing them back. We advance at double-quick and cheer the Georgians. More than half their numbers lie stretched upon the ground. As they close up their ranks to the left an opening is made which admits our brigade; we cheer our friends and raise the rebel yell as we take positions in line, now sixty or seventy yards of the enemies line. We charge them with a yell, and not only check their advance but push them back some 400 or 500 yards, but at a most terrible cost.

At this point this writer received a terrible wound that left him flat of his back on the ground, where in a few minutes he received second wound that for some time left him unconscious on the field. Upon recovering consciousness, to his horror, our lines were falling back. The idea of falling into the hands of the enemy was too horrible to be considered, so, making an effort to stand up, I found that I was not disabled so badly that I could not walk. Therefore I determined to make my exit to the field hospital, some 700 yards to the rear in an old barn. As I passed off the field I found one of our line officers, who had the reputation of being the bravest man in the brigade, lying behind a large rock. As I passed him he pulled his hat over his face, but I knew him as well as I knew any man in the command. He was a bully at home in private life and assumed to be a brave man in battle, but like all bullies in private life he was a most consummate coward, and I never knew an exception to this rule.

As I saw no more of the battle, I will let Dr. Jno. [a common old abbreviation for John] O. Scott, of Sherman, Texas, tell you about this day's work.

Dr. Scott says:

Here on the morning of Sept. 17th, 1862, at sunrise when the red haze of early morning was mantling the eastern skies, all nature arrayed in gorgeous beauty seemed standing on tiptoe silently waiting the coming contest. The Texas brigade, led by Hood and Col. Wofford (Col. Wofford of the 18th Georgia was in command of the brigade, Hood in command of the division) using Hood's own language, went gallantly in the fight. The firing of the artillery was so terrific that the very earth shook beneath the detonations. The batteries belched forth such a volley of sulphurous smoke and hurricane of fire that it appeared doomsday had come; the blue ridge in sight seemed to quake in fear and the clear water of the Antietam ran red with blood. The 1st Texas lost its flag and two-thirds of its members in this conflict, exhibiting, in the language of Jackson, "Almost matchless display of daring and desperate valor." "A brigade of men," writes Hood, "whose achievements have never been surpassed in the history of nations." Hood and his Texans held the gap like Marshall Lannes at Friedland, 26,060 Frenchmen against 80,000 Russians. It was the contest in the lane and cornfield that Lee said was the hottest on any battlefield. When the 1st Texas flag made from Mrs. Wigfall's bridal dress, was found by the enemy in the cornfield thirteen dead Texans were stretched over its tattered shreds—immortal names on the escutcheon of fame, bright stars in the galaxy of glory. No wonder Lee wrote to Hood: "I rely much on you; I always have you in my eye and thoughts." It was paying him a debt of gratitude after helping him so often that Jackson should say of Hood: "I regard him as one of the most promising officers in the army." It was after this battle that Lee, appreciating the sacrifices of the Texans, wrote to Wigfall, "They have fought grandly and bravely," and Hood tells them officially: "You have justly entitled yourselves to the proud distinction of being the bravest soldier in the army."

In after years when rosy spring comes with fragrant flowers, the fair maidens of Maryland will assemble on the banks of the clear sparkling waters of the Antietam and shroud the graves of the soldier dead, with garlands of nature's most loving offerings. Their fair hands will bedeck the little mounds with the gorgeous rose, the queenly tulip, the sweet scented pink, the beautiful purple tinted heliotrope and the fair majestic lily. The orator of the day will tell in in thrilling language how Hood with his two brigades held the gap and drove the enemy in front until McLaws came to Johnson's aid (Bushrod Johnson.) The chorus of lovely daughters of old Maryland—a state which through all time been an asylum for religious liberty and has sent brave men to battle by sea and by land—will make the woods melodious with the ever memorable song "Stonewall Jackson is on Your Shore, My Maryland, My Maryland." The old Maryland battery will be brought out, manned and planted in position and will make the hills resound with its thundering salutes in honor of the distinguished dead.

I suppose it was about 8 'o'clock in the morning when I reached the field hospital. Dr. Breckenridge, our regimental surgeon, after examining my wound, said to me if I was able to walk to try to cross the Potomac River, three miles distant, at Shepherdstown. So on I moved, weak and faint from loss of blood and the pain I was suffering. Just at sundown that evening I got into the town, on the south side of the river. There I met Major Littlefield, who gave me three army biscuits—more than I had to eat in three days previously. I thought it was the sweetest morsel of bread I had ever tasted. A bed was provided for me and there I remained until the morning of the 10th, when I was sent to the hospital at Winchester, some thirty miles away.

On the 16th we buried our dead. This don't look like a defeat, but when we call the roll and find that two-thirds of our brave Texas boys have gone down in battle and that their remains now lie buried in soldiers graves on the field of Sharpsburg, we are hardly to boast of it as a victory. Less than three weeks before we had lost two-thirds at Manassas, and now the same proportion of the remainder is gone, leaving us but a very insignificant number the captain of my company and his entire command, cook and eat out of one skillet—five men—just five, (The company is entirely annihilated, not a man left in it.) O, what sad letters we have to write home to the bereaved loved ones in Texas. On the night of the 18th Lee begins to move his worn out and sesterce army across the Potomac. McClellan follows, pressing hard, but our old general moves grandly along sending all his foot-sore and wounded ahead of the army and finally lands them all safely on the south side of the river. As the Federal Gen. Heckman—the same man we drove out of Thoroughfare Gap—attempts to follow us. We wait until they are at the south bank and then charge them—killing and drowning in the river some 2000 or more. This ends McClellan's pursuit of our army and he remains at Antietam until the 7th of October when he is relieved of his command in the army for all time to come, and General Burnside is put in command. McClellan's loss in this battle was 14790 men killed, which was largely in excess of our loss. I do not remember what our loss was, but it was 8,000 or 10,000 men killed and wounded. This is regarded as the severest of the war for the numbers engaged. McClellan when ordered by his government to follow Lee acknowledged he was too badly crippled. Lee had all told 32,000—the Federals nearly or quite double our numbers, yet some school histories will tell our children that we were badly whipped. Lee went in with 32,000 effective men.[15]

## Abner Hinson
## 1839–1926

Abner Hinson was first corporal of Company "D" during the Battle of Antietam. He was promoted to first sergeant in April, 1863. However, on February 1, 1864, Hinson went AWOL from the regiment's winter camp near Morristown, TN, along with the company's Third Lieutenant O. P. Caldwell. Hinson later returned to camp and was reduced in rank to private. He was wounded in the shoulder at Cold Harbor on June 3, 1864, and wounded again at Darbytown Road on October 7, 1864, the regiment's last major engagement of the war. He was paroled at Appomattox on April 12, 1865. After the war, he farmed in Walker and Coryell Counties in Texas.[16]

### First Corporal Abner M. Hinson
### 5th Texas Infantry

At the battle of Sharpsburg we went in with eighty rounds of ammunition to the man. When we had used up all our ammunition we were ordered to hold our position at all hazards. My Captain came to me and asked if I had any ammunition and I told him yes that I had just taken some from a dead man's cartridge box. He asked who else had any and I told him Parker as I had just divided with him. He said he wanted me to go to that big tree in front and shoot all the officers and color bearers. We agreed to go, but asked him not to go off and leave us, he agreed to call us when he went to leave.

In a little while Parker looked around and said, "They are all gone." I looked and said that Capt. Turner was there yet as he promised to call us if he went to leave. Presently we looked around and sure enough they were all gone and Parker wanted to know what we would do and I said, "Run."

We were very nearly surrounded and we ran nearly half a mile across an open field to our regiment which we found in a grove of timber and neither of us was hurt. The boys gave us all a hearty cheer and Capt. Turner complimented us very highly in our escape.[17]

## John N. Henderson
## February 26, 1843–December 22, 1907

John Henderson was promoted to third corporal of Company "E" in May, 1862. He was wounded twice that year, first during the fighting around Richmond, then again at Antietam, where his left arm was severely injured, resulting in amputation. He returned to Texas, was meritoriously promoted to lieutenant, and, after he recovered from the amputation, he returned to the Brigade and served on the staff of General Jerome Robertson during 1864–65.[18] After the war, Henderson became a well-known and respected judge along the Texas Circuit. He died on December 22, 1907, and is buried at Oakland Cemetery in Dallas, Texas.

### 3rd Corporal John N. Henderson
### 5th Texas Infantry
### *Dallas Morning News*
### June 29, 1901

On the occasion of the thirty-first annual reunion of Hood's Texas Brigade at Galveston Judge John N. Henderson of Bryan, a former member of Company E, Fifth Texas, Hood's Brigade, made the response to the address of welcome of Major Hume. He spoke as follows:

At Antietam or Sharpsburg, 17 days later, the Texas Brigade materially aided Lee to repulse and hold the enemy at bay, thus winning another victory. At this time, by the long marches of the campaign and by the casualties of battles, the effective force of the three regiments, all told, was about 850. On our part of the field, which was the left, we constituted both support and reserve.

On this battle ground about 35,000 Confederate troops confronted about 140,000 Federals under General McClellan, who had again resumed command of the Army of the Potomac. The conflict on our part of the field began about sunrise, and soon raged fiercely in our immediate front. The word came that the Brigades of Lawton, Trimble and Hays were being hard pressed and Hood's Division composed

Captain John N. Henderson, 5th Texas Infantry. (*Tennessee State Library and Archives*)

of an Alabama Brigade under Law, and the Texas Brigade, under Colonel Wofford of the Eighteenth Georgia, were ordered forward. When the troops emerged from the timber and passed the old church and into the open corn field a herculean task lay before them. Down the slant of the hill stood the remnant of the division before mentioned. They still held their position, but were unable to advance. Beyond them in the open and in the timber stood a solid field of blue, at least three columns deep. To an observer it looked as if the whole of Hooker's Corps was there. As we occupied a position on the hill and above the Confederate line in front, the fire of the enemy played havoc in the ranks of the supporting column. In vain did the officers in charge of Hays and Trimble's urge them to charge; and in vain did the Texas Brigade add its entreaties to theirs. The line would neither advance nor retreat. Its ranks were decimated, and its fire was ineffective. Suddenly, as if moved by a single impulse, the Texans, unable to be restrained longer by their commanding officers, charged over the line of our own troops and swept upon the advancing foe like an irresistible avalanche. In the twinkling of an eye, the enemy wavered, turned and fled—still the Brigade pressed forward until two other lines of the enemy were broken and driven from the field and through the wood and were routed from behind a stone wall, where they sought shelter. Not receiving an expected support, it was beyond human endurance to advance further: but here the line rested, and was held through that bloody day, resisting assault after assault of the enemy. But for this terrific and successful assault on the part of Hood's Division, our left center would have been broken, the left wing of the army turned, and the fords on the Potomac captured the army and Lee's army shut in between the Antietam and the Potomac. By members of the Brigade who were engaged in nearly every battle in Virginia and Maryland, Sharpsburg, on the account of its sanguinary and protracted character, has been characterized as the hardest fought battle of the war.

General Hood, who won his rank of Major General for gallantry on that day, speaks of this charge in the following language: "Here I witnessed the most terrible clash of arms by far that has occurred during the war. Two little giant Brigades of my command wrestled with the mighty force, and although they lost hundreds of their officers and men, they drove them from their position and forced them to abandon their guns on our left."

This battle completed the campaign of 1862, and established for the Texas Brigade a reputation for bravery and courage, which was not excelled by that of any troops in General Lee's army.

## William L. Barnes Campbell
### *Circa* 1834–between 1884 and 1890

William "Bose" Campbell enlisted in August, 1861, and was elected first corporal in Company "D." He was wounded in the abdomen at Second Manassas in August, 1862, while serving as Color Bearer. Campbell was promoted to fifth sergeant in April, 1863. He was taken prisoner at Gettysburg and remained a prisoner of war until June, 1865.

Below are excerpts of two letters that Campbell wrote to his Aunt Wood, the mother of Lieutenant Campbell Wood, who was William Campbell's first cousin and adjutant of the 5th Texas Regiment. The first letter is Campbell's military reflection on the recently fought Battle at Antietam, Maryland.

The second letter is included to illustrate through this primary source that the soldiers of the Texas Brigade devoutly maintained their pre-war friendships, regardless of the respective ranks of two friends. In Sergeant Campbell's letter, he tells his aunt that upon his return to the regiment from a furlough in Texas, he is tenting temporarily with his old friend "Mike," who is now the commanding colonel of the regiment. Mike would have been Colonel Robert M. Powell, the first captain of Campbell's company from Walker County.

Second Sergeant William L. Barnes "Bose" Campbell, 5th Texas Infantry. (*Elsa Vorwerk*)

## Second Sergeant William L. Barnes Campbell
## 5th Texas Infantry
## Near Winchester

Sept. 30

Aunt Wood

We have stopped marching for a short time and I write to let you know of our whereabouts. After a short and unfortunate trip through Maryland we are again camped on Virginia soil six miles east of Winchester. The trip was a very severe one and proved fatal to many. I suppose you have heard ere this of the battle of Manassas and the part played by our brigade. The battle was most terrific and the loss in our regiment was very severe....

We passed over the battle field next day and the sight was really sickening. We made forced marches across the Potomac and had a quiet time until we got to Hagerstown where we rested two days. And then we were sent back sixteen miles to Gen. Hills relief, who was fighting the whole of McClelland's army. We got up just in time to save our receiving a terrible defeat. It was bad enough however as it was our army fell back during the night in the direction of Shepherdstown.

When we were met by a courier from Gen. Jackson saying that he had captured Harpers Ferry and eleven thousand prisoners and that he would join us [the] next day. Gen. Lee at once halted and determined to have the fight out, which they did on the 17th. It is considered the biggest battle of the war. Neither side claims a victory. Pirtle of Waverly and Tom Edwards was killed in our company and Ridgway wounded and in the hands of the enemy. Peter Williamson received a slight wound in the arm. I had been sick for some time and was not in the fight but was close enough to get an awful shelling. Campbell had also gone to the rear sick and tired down by incessant marching. The position of the two armies at present is this. The enemy are scattered from opposite Shepherdstown to Harpers ferry threatening to cross the Potomac. And our army is stationed between Martinsburg and Winchester waiting for something to turn up. It is generally believed that there will be no more big fighting this winter. There is no prospect of Peace yet. We found very few secessionists in Maryland. And our whole forces are opposed to going into it again.[19]

## Second Sergeant Bose Campbell
## 5th Texas Infantry
## Near Richmond Feb. 26, 1863

Aunt Wood

After many ups and downs though without any very serious accident, I arrived at Richmond on the 11th of this month. Where I met with Campbell on his way home. I was very glad to find him looking so well. I suppose he is home by this time and enjoying himself finely. I joined the regiment on the 12th just one month from the time I left home. I found Mike looking very well and is exceedingly popular as a Col. his honors rest very easy upon his shoulders. I have been staying in the same tent with Mike since I returned. Col Bryan his mess mate is in town sick. As soon as he comes out I will return to my company.[20]

## C. J. Jackson

C. J. Jackson was a private in Company "G." He was wounded at Gaines' Mill on June 27, 1862, and captured at Raccoon Mountain, TN, on October 28, 1863. He was paroled on June 9, 1865, from Fort Delaware.[21]

Private C. J. Jackson
5th Texas Infantry
*Temple Daily Telegram*
May 20, 1913
Hood's Brigade Reminiscences
Nolanville, Tex. May 19, 1913


To the Telegram

As the survivors of Hood's Texas Brigade are to hold a reunion in Temple in a few days, June 27, it might be well to summarize some of the things that they will talk about to each other. Then, I will suggest that Sharpsburg may be talked about, the bloodiest and games from a viewpoint from both sides, the most terrible battle that was fought during the four long years of the war. Gen. McClellan discovered the fact that Gen. Lee's forces were divided. Harper's Ferry some distance away and on the opposite side of the Potomac. Gen. McClellan determined to march upon Lee and defeat him before Gen. Jackson could rejoin him. So this was an accident battle and a surprise to the Confederates. Gen. Lee formed his lines behind a creek called Antietam, a strong position, behind which lay the village of Sharpsburg. Gen. McClellan began his advance early in the day and pressed this advance with great vigor, at the same time extending his lines so that extent weakened the Confederate lines, which forced the Confederate line to gradually give way from this terrible onslaught of the Federals. But remember that only a few yards given up at a time. By noon the Confederates had lost considerable ground, while the Yankees had paid dearly for the ground they had gained, as their losses were terrible; and just at this time, high noon, when it looked bad for the Confederates. Jackson appeared on the scene with his heroes from Harper's Ferry, and within two hours' time after Jackson began his advance these Yankees were driven back to where they had started in the morning. Gen. Lee's lines were re-established and the Yankees didn't seem to be hard to make go, either, for the reason that they had taken some good medicine before that noon hour arrived. But sunset all firing had ceased and everything was quiet and the great battle was over.

McClellan had failed to do just what Lee failed to do at Gettysburg, that is, to drive the others from the field.

At about 9.30 Lee took his stand on "Traveler," about midway and to the rear of his lines and sent for all his division commanders. As they arrived Gen. Lee would speak to them calling them by name and ask the question, "How is it along your line general?"

The officers would reply, "Bad, bad enough," and would go into details of his terrible losses, and would wind up by saying that he thought the army should cross the river before morning.

This continued for quite a while, all having suffered terrible losses. Finally Gen. Hood rode up who seems to have been a little late, and when Gen. Lee spoke to him, calling him by name and asking him the same question, "How is it along your lines general?" Gen. Hood for a moment could not speak a word. Gen. Lee noticed this and said to Gen. Hood, "Why general where is that splendid division I saw you in command of this morning?"

"They are lying upon the field where you sent them this morning general," replied Gen. Hood pointing to the field.

After Gen. Lee had all the information he desired he said to these officers, "Our men have been well fed tonight and we have plenty of ammunition. If Gen. McClellan wants to battle tomorrow we will give it to him. Gentlemen, go to your commands."

The next day the two armies remained confronting each other the whole livelong day and not a gun was fired. The following night the Confederates crossed the Potomac into Grand Old Virginia.

C. J. Jackson
One of Hood's Men


## Madison Ross
## September 20, 1840–August 7, 1924

Madison Ross was promoted to third sergeant, then second sergeant of Company "H" sometime prior to his being captured at Bunker Hill, VA, on July 17, 1863, shortly after the Battle at Gettysburg and nearly a year after Antietam. He was exchanged at an unrecorded date and place and went AWOL in Texas on February 29, 1864. He was dropped from the rolls of the 5th Texas "for prolonged absence from his command."[22] That Ross submitted the following article for publication in 1920 at the age of eighty, and refers to himself as "Captain" Ross, is curious at best. Nonetheless, his memoir has interesting information that appears in accord with the memories of other veterans. He died on August 7, 1924, and is buried at Forest Park Cemetery in Houston, Texas.


**3rd Sergeant Madison Ross**
**5th Texas Infantry**
**The *Daily Express***
**December 20, 1920**
**Houston, Texas**

We went to Centerville near Washington. From Centerville we crossed the Potomac River above Washington and went into Maryland. While in Maryland, we fought the Battle of Finktown and Boonsborough Gap. The Texas Brigade held Boonsborough Gap after several divisions had been forced back. We held it all night and when daylight came, we were compelled to follow the Army which was then on the way to Sharpsburg. The Yankee Historians pronounce the name Antietam. The next morning we fought the Battle. I will never forget it because it was on my birthday in September. General Jackson was gone with half the Army to capture Harper's Ferry, which left General Lee with a small Army to hold the whole army of Meade which was over 100,000 men, leaving Lee with less than 25,000 to hold them until Jackson returned with his Army from taking Harper's Ferry. In this battle, I was commander of my company. I was wounded and fell between the lines. Both Armies passed over me; did not offer to hurt me. I regard this battle as one of the worst fights, if not the worst fight of the war...

   Madison Ross

December 20, 1920

   Editor of the *Daily Express* Note: ...Captain Ross was born on September 20, 1840 and says that the battle of Sharpsburg was fought on his birthday, actually the battle was fought on September 17, 1862. His great-great grandson makes a valid point that Captain Ross's letter was written 58 years after the battle so the error is forgiven.

## Quartermaster Sergeant J. B. Polley
## 4th Texas Infantry

Joseph B. Polley was a quartermaster sergeant in the 4th Texas Regiment, but this article involves two members of the 5th Texas, and is well worth reading for its human interest, if not its military value.

## Robert A. Brantley
## June 3, 1838–August 3, 1911

Robert Brantley was first corporal of Company "D" and served as the regimental color bearer in the summer of 1862 and was wounded at Second Manassas. He was promoted to fifth sergeant in April, 1863. He was captured at Gettysburg on July 2, 1863, and paroled from Fort Delaware on June 5, 1865. After the war, Brantley operated a mercantile store in Burleson County, dying on August 3, 1911.[23] He is buried at Oaklawn Cemetery in Somerville, Texas.

## Robert E. Mitchell
## 5th Texas Infantry

Robert E. Mitchell was a musician in Company "D" of the 4th Texas Regiment.[24]

## Charles F. Hume
## 1843–1920

Charles F. Hume was a fourth corporal in Company "D" of the 5th Texas Regiment. In 1862, he was wounded in the fighting near Richmond and at Second Manassas as a regimental color bearer. In December, 1862, he was transferred to the 32nd Virginia Cavalry to serve as the regiment's adjutant. He survived the war to practice law in Walker County and Galveston, Texas, dying in 1920.[25]

Fourth Corporal Charles Hume
5th Texas Infantry
The *Daily Express*
November 15, 1905
A Review of Times that are Past but Live in History—
Prepared by J. B. Polley, Floresville, Texas

While the Fifth Texas was in camp near Richmond Corporal R. E. Mitchell met and fell desperately in love with a young lady living in the vicinity. She was handsome and highly accomplished, and Mitchell resolved if it were possible he would win her for a wife, and when the regiment was ordered to the Potomac arranged for correspondence with her. But though a soldier of merit and good standing enough to take the fancy of the most fastidious lady, Mitchell's penmanship was illegible to himself when the ink got cold. Well-read and having knocked about the world a great deal, his conversation was always entertaining, but writing the hand he did it was impossible to make his letters a charm. So when the time came for the first he persuaded Charlie Hume—now Major F. C. Hume of Houston—to do both the writing and the composing of all the missives mailed from camp.

The novelty of the situation inspired Hume to do his best, and that best resulted in a series of letters that were marvels of the epistolary art and so gratifying to the lady that in return she did her best, and the correspondence rapidly changed from that of simple friendship to one where sentiment bore a large part, culminating finally in a declaration of love by Mitchell and an acknowledgement of its reciprocation by the lady. After the retreat from Yorktown, and later after the seven days' battles, his regiment was in the vicinity of Richmond. Mitchell managed to visit his betrothed and presumably received proof stronger than mere profession that she loved him. Just after the battle of Sharpsburg, and before he could write the letter for Mitchell that would announce his escape from the bullets of the enemy, Hume was transferred to another command and immediately joined it.

This put Mitchell in the middle of a bad fix. It was utterly impossible for him to write such letters as Hume had been writing over his (Mitchell's) name, and nobody in his company could do it. Heroic measures his only recourse; he called to his assistance another messmate, Bob Brantley, now living in Somerville. Under his instructions Brantley wrote as follows:

In Camp near Shepherdstown,
Va., Sept. 25, 1862
Miss ----, Richmond Va.

Dear Miss: Your letter of recent date addressed to my late comrade and friend, Robert E. Mitchell enabled me to secure your address, and makes it my painful duty to inform you that my comrade and your lover was killed on the 17th of September 1862, while far to the front most gallantly fighting for his beloved South. He was shot through the heart and fell with his face to the foe. We buried him on the field of battle with your letter resting on his heart. Words are powerless to express the deep sorrow we feel over his untimely death, or the sympathy that wells up in the hours of your grief, and therefore I make no attempt to console with you. With assurance of my sympathy, I am, dear miss, yours most respectfully,

R. L. Brantley

"What the mischief do you want to send such a letter as that for?" inquired a comrade, cognizant of all the circumstances. "Why do you not write to her yourself, tell her of the deception you have practiced, ask her forgiveness and forever after be happy?"

"What!" exclaimed Mitchell, "put down in my scrawling handwriting that for more than a year, I have been making her the victim of a fraud? No, sir, I'd rather be dead to her than to let her know either by letter or by a face-to-face confession that I'm as d----d a humbug as I really have been."

The letter was mailed, and although often in Richmond afterward Mitchell never met the lady again, if yet living she no doubt still believes he was killed at Sharpsburg. In truth, though, he survived the war, came back to Texas and died some ten years ago.

## P. P.
### nom de plume

P. P. is the penname for a soldier in the 5th Texas who wrote the following letter for publication in the Houston newspaper and chose to remain anonymous. P. P. appears to be writing while recuperating from illness or injury, and devotes much attention to the treatment of other recently exchanged soldiers who were captured after the Battle of Antietam.

*Tri-Weekly Telegraph*
November 7, 1862
Letter from Richmond
Richmond Oct. 9, 1862

Ed. *Telegraph*—The storm of battle for a time has lulled and a brief rest, after their arduous duties, has been allowed our brave soldiers. With the exception of the daily skirmishes between scouting parties, nothing arises to excite the mind. Our division is stationed near Martinsburg, and the convalescents are coming in fast. The army is pronounced, by the commanding General, Lee, to be in better condition than at any former period, and the fact will re-assure the timid, as Gen. Lee speaks nothing but the truth. The enemy is beginning to realize the fact their success at Sharpsburg was not so great as the first flaming bulletins of McClellan announced. Their loss was fully five to one, and they were opposed to our forces with immensely superior numbers. We certainly did not have 50,000 men engaged in the battle, and those that were present, were almost utterly exhausted, and yet, notwithstanding this fact, the enemy received the worst drubbing that they have met with since the inauguration of the war. The captures they made consisted of those who were so worn out as to be altogether unable to proceed with our forces. Among the number, 7 of the Bayou City Guards—James Welch, Pat Burns, Adam Beasly, Chas. Stevens, George Miller, Thos. Bigbee, and Wm. Clark. Of this number, J. Welch, Stevens and Brady took the oath of allegiance, and remained with the enemy. Geo. Miller, Bigbee and Burns, were paroled, but prevented by sickness from returning.

Wm. Clark has just arrived and I have been enabled to learn from him interesting accounts of his treatment while in the hands of the Federals. While the prisoners were under charge of the fighting men of the enemy, they faced not admirable, but as well as they desired, being prisoners; and their ears were saluted by no jests or mockeries from those over them; but after they were handled over to the raw recruits, to the men who have never smelt powder, the abuse was heaped upon them; and while on the march a guard of two men to a prisoner was kept around them; they had to endure all insults, not being allowed to reply, but occasionally the desire to answer could not be withheld, and a retort would come forth. On one occasion, while passing a little village, a strapping fellow of six feet stepped up and in a jeering, sarcastic manner asked, "Where's Jackson now?" Before the guard could prevent it, one of the Fifth replied: "Shoulder your gun and go to the front, you *contemptible scoundrel* and you will find out." And he added, by way of parenthesis: "It is not for a base wretch like you to taunt prisoners that your coward heart would not assist you in taking." The officers seemed to appreciate it, and the fellow slunk back in the crowd and had no more to say about Jackson. Many inquiries were put to our boys, to all of which they returned prompt replies—that is, when not prevented by the guard. "You are a nice specimen of Southern chivalry," said a splendidly dressed young lady to one of our boys as he trudged along, barefooted, hatless, and his garments in rags. With a toss of his head he answered:

"Pshaw! Miss; if you knew how many niggers and what a plantation I own, you would be following me now. I am awful pretty when dressed." This young miss was one of the few—for the majority of the gentler sex treated our men with the greatest kindness and attention; and many a slay look sent a thrill of joy to the bosoms of our brave boys. Cakes were not unfrequently handed to them, which on being opened, were found to contain various amounts of Federal money, which proved extremely serviceable. Many signs and tokens of sympathy were exhibited by the ladies wherever met, but it was especially the case in Baltimore. The ladies in a number of cases stood a piece from their windows, and when the wondering eye of one of the prisoners could be caught, the stars and bars, though diminutive would be exposed to his view. Whenever this happened, the Texans would set up an old "Comanche" yell, and "Hurrah for Jeff!" would fill the air, while the discomforted officers in vain attempted to discover the cause for the uproar. Many foolish questions were asked, and if reasonable, were properly replied to. They endeavored by every possible means to obtain a list of all the officers in the service, hoping thereby to estimate our real force. One of the 5th was called upon to answer inquiries, and after the usual amount of small talk, the court of interrogation commenced:

"You belong to Hood's brigade?"

"Yes, sir."

"How many men were in your regiment?"

"There was 1000, and it was the smallest in the brigade."

"How many brigades attacked the 5th New York brigade at Manassas?"

"They were attacked sir, by 500 of the 5th Texas regiment, and were whipped in ten minutes after the first fire."

"Were you there?"

"Well, I reckon."

"What do you suppose is the number of men in your Virginia army?"

"Well, I could not tell the exact number; but there is always enough to whip every fight, and some to spare."

"How do you account for the number of men that have taken the oath of allegiance during the last two months?" (Some 200)

"I can only account for it by their having a diseased taste; and I am glad to know that they are gone, as it was a waste of rations to keep them. Now, if I may be allowed to ask how do you account for the thousands who don't take the oath?"

When the questions were being turned the court adjourned, and the witness was released. Every inducement was held out to remain in the North, but he replied—"I am a true Southerner, fighting for the country that gave me birth; and I live or die North, it would be only as a prisoner." Such an answer was truly commendable.

For twelve days they were confined in Fort Delaware, and were subject to the most inhuman treatment at the hands of the Hessian hirelings, in whose custody they were placed; many articles of food and clothing were sent to them by the ladies, but the luxuries were never allowed to cross the threshold of the prison, and a cup of bean soup and a slice of bread, were the weak rations upon which they were fed; the parole should have been extended upon the battlefield, but were set aside for flimsy reason. One reason, however, advanced seemed very probable, namely—that they had rather feed the rebels than fight them. Of those from the "Bayou City Guards" that took the oath of allegiance, two had families in the North, and one was a German with, as he said, "No interest anywhere, North or South"—they had been with the company but a short time, having come out with the recruits. One of our boys asked what they were going to do with such men, and the answer was: "Nothing, for they are much detested here, having played the traitor as they would be down South. We do not place the least confidence in them." After calling out the black sheep, the remainder of the prisoners were started home, and reached this city after a voyage of two days.

In connection with prisoners and captures, there is another circumstance that requires mentioning. Some seven days ago, the Yankee cavalry made a raid upon Warrenton, and succeeded in capturing some 700 sick and wounded, that had been placed there after the battle of Manassas; the enemy merely paroled them and left. Among the captured and paroled, the following were from Company A, Lieut. Ed Noble, Serg't John A. McMurtry, Serg't B. C. Simpson, S. Watkins, J. O. Norton, Jas. Landers, S. D. Howes, W. J. Patton, Owen O'Mally, Robert Campbell, Sam Bailey, and Jas. Netherly.

All of the wounded were doing well, and were pronounced out of danger. Three of the company have died of their wounds since the fight: John DeYoung, P. Hefforn and John W. Delesdernier. This makes a total of seven killed at the battle of 30 August; the other four being Dempsey Walker, John H. Bell, A. Angell, and J. Massenburg. Three of the wounded now in the hospital in all probability be discharged, having been rendered unfit for military duty.

The news of the battle of Corinth has just been received, though nothing can be learned regarding it. The notorious Dr. Ruckor has been turned over to the civil authorities of Virginia for trial. The city is filled with provost guards who are daily becoming more obnoxious to the citizen and soldiers. The position of the forces indicate a battle before long. I will probably leave for the lines in a few days, from where, if nothing happens, I will write—as so I remain,

Yours,

P. P.


## Rufus K. Felder
## September 2, 1840–September 6, 1922

Rufus K. Felder was a student in the Soule University in Chappell Hill, Texas, in 1861 when the war began. He enlisted and became a private in Company "E."

Privates Rufus K. Felder and Miers
Felder, 5th Texas Infantry.
(*Thomas Hughes*)

Felder was sick in the spring and summer of 1862, but was present for all the battles. He was paroled at Appomattox on April 12, 1865. After the war he became a prominent merchant in Brenham, Texas.[26] He died on September 6, 1922, and is buried at Atkinson Cemetery in Chappell Hill, Texas.

### Private Rufus K. Felder
### 5th Texas Infantry
### September 23, 1862

Dear Mother

I suppose ere this you have heard of our departure from Richmond, of our hard campaign, of our brilliant victories at Manassas & other places & also of our entrance into Maryland. We arrived here today after a hard march of about two hundred miles & of still harder fighting all along the route.

This has been a hard campaign unequaled by anything of the war & which has added great gain & renown to our arms by another complete route of the Yankees and our capture of Harper's Ferry with 15 thousand prisoners, four thousand stolen negroes & an immense amount of arms & ammunition. I passed through it all like a hero, went through the fight of Manassas besides several others of less importance without a scratch. Miers, I suppose you have heard, was wounded at M. in the arm & foot. I have not seen him as he was sent to Warrington & we had to renew our march the next day. The boys that have seen him say his are only flesh wounds and is doing well. I wish I could give you full details. I was told only a few minutes ago that a man would start to Texas tomorrow. This is the first chance I have had to write since I left Kentucky. I rec. two letters today; one from yourself & the other from Kate. They have made a quick trip considering the distance we are from Richmond. We crossed the river into Maryland at Leesburg & crossed at Shepherdstown. We went six miles of the Pennsylvania line.

I must close in haste as the man is packing up the letters. I only scribble these few lines to let you know that I am still alive, notwithstanding the severe march & shower of bullets.

My love to all

Your Son

R. Felder

P.S. I wish I could give a list of the killed and wounded in the camp, but I have not time to think them up. They have all left except twenty. Bob Toland, Hardy Allen & Heart were killed in the Maryland fight. Those killed at Manassas were orderly Sergeant Petty, Moncires, Nute Mullins & Jim Hutchenson missing.[27]

**Private Rufus K. Felder**
**5th Texas Infantry**
**Camp near Winchester**
**Oct. 1, 1862**

Dear Sister,

Once more I have an opportunity of writing. I have received two letters from you since I left Rich. & this is the first chance I have had of answering them, as we have been on the go ever since the first of August, never camping two nights at the same place until we came out of Maryland, then we halted a few days at Martinsburg where I dropped a few lines to Mother…

We remained on the field a day to cook, bury the dead & then took up march for Maryland. Had it not been for the hard marches we would have had a pleasant trip. The country was beautiful & fruit plentiful. I have heard a great deal of southern feeling in Ma, but found it a mistake. There are some trusted men there, but the majority are Union. We have had a very hard fought battle at Sharpsburg before we left. M. The enemy greatly outnumbered us. The battle raged furiously the whole day commencing early in the morning & ceasing only at night. The slaughter on both sides was terrible; there was very little ground gained on either side. Both sides were too exhausted to renew the fight next day & a flag of truce was agree upon to bury the dead. This occupied all day & that night our forces fell back across the river. Next morning the Yankees thinking we were retreating crossed over a brigade which was immediately attacked & the whole except a hundred was killed & taken. They have not attempted to cross into Va. since. We rested at Martinsburg a few days & then came here, six miles from Winchester where we will remain for several days. I do not know where we will go from here, but think we will feel our way back down the valley where we can get supplies from R. It is rumored that our Congressmen are trying to get us removed south to winter. I have no idea it will succeed, as I think another big battle is pending and we have gained too great a reputation to be sent off. Since I wrote to Mother two more boys from our company died from their wounds. Sam Dean & Julian Hutchinson. Jim has not been heard from yet. I am afraid he was killed. What a shock it will be to the family, two sons in one fight. I have not heard from Miers in some time. His wounds were light & I suppose by this time he has recovered sufficiently to go home. My health has been remarkably good on this trip.

I must close as the ink is out. Love to all and with a petition that you will write soon.
Your affectionate brother
R. Felder
P. S. John Roberts is well & with the company.[28]

## Rufus King Felder
## 5th Texas Infantry Regiment

We had a very hard fought battle at Sharpsburg before we left M (Maryland). The enemy greatly outnumbered us. The battle raged furiously the whole day commencing early in the morning & ceasing only at night. The slaughter on both sides was terrible; there was very little ground gained on either side. Both sides were too exhausted to renew the fight next day & a flag of truce was agreed to bury the dead. This occupied all day & that night our forces fell back across the river. Next morning the Yankees thinking we were retreating crossed over a brigade which was immediately attacked & the whole except about a hundred was killed and taken.

October 1
You said in your last letter that you hoped the Texians thirst for Yankee blood had partly been quenched. I can speak for the three reg. in Va. Their thirst has not only been partially quenched, they have been in so many fights and have suffered so much they would be willing never to go in another fight.[29]

## Arthur H. Edey (Eddy)
## May 18, 1830–October 5, 1873

Arthur H. Edey served on detached duty as the regiment's agent for the Texas Depository Depot in Richmond in the fall of 1861. He returned to the ranks and was wounded in the hip at Gettysburg and was captured. He remained a prisoner of war until the final surrender.

In this account published just a month after Antietam, and most likely penned by Edey just days after the battle, Edey puts the number of 5th Texas casualties at Antietam at thirteen killed and sixty-three wounded—seventy-six casualties out of the 175 men engaged.

### Captain Thomas Baber
### March 19, 1833–1888

Thomas Baber was the initial first lieutenant of Company "E." He was promoted to captain in July, 1862, and wounded in the arm at Antietam. He was detailed to recruiting duty in Texas in the fall of 1862. Baber returned to the regiment, and on October 7, 1864, was wounded at Darbytown Road. He was retired for disability in December, 1864.[30]

### Private John Randle
### 1832–June 6, 1909

John Randle was a member of Company "E." He was granted sick leave in October, 1862. He was recorded as AWOL in November, 1862, and never returned to the company.[31]

### Private Arthur H. Edey
### 5th Texas Infantry
### *Tri-Weekly Telegraph*
### October 15, 1862
### The Battle of Sharpsburg
### Etc., Etc., Etc.

Agency 5th Tex. Vols
Richmond, Sept 25, 1862

Editor *Telegraph*, Dear Sir:

By the arrival of Capt. Baber and Private Julius A. Randle, Co. E. 5th Tex., from Maryland, I have the honor of giving you some general ideas of the terrific series of battles, which lasted, ant intervals, one week. Beginning at Manassas on the 29th and 30th Aug., we go onto the 13th and 14th of Sept at South Mountain, near Boonesboro' Maryland—D. Hill's division engaged—the Texas Brigade under the fire, but not in action. Withdraw from there at 1 p.m. 14th to Sharpsburg, about 6 miles. On Tuesday, 16th, heavy cannonading and skirmishing. About 1 o'clock a.m., on the 17th the battle commenced by starlight on an open field, similar to the prairies in Texas. It raged terrifically for 13 hours, commencing on the left wing (Jackson's corps).

We drove the enemy about a mile and a half, with great slaughter. About 10 a.m., they were strongly reinforced and drove us back to about where we started from. We then received reinforcements from the left, and drove them back again, and then the battle became general from one end of the line to the other—the left wing wavering all day long, first on one side, then on the other, often locking bayonets. Upon the right and center our forces drove the enemy, and held the ground about two hours before sun down, when A. P. Hill arrived with his division from Harper's Ferry, and then the slaughter of the Yankees was terrible. Both parties slept on their arms that night—pickets within 50 yards of each other. Remained in that position all day, 18th. At night the enemy commenced moving. Gen. Lee gave orders to cross the Potomac at Shepardstown, thus saving his whole army and trains without molestation, except some wounded whom he could not remove from hospital. Friday, 19th, one division of Burnside's corps attempted to pursue our forces this side of the river, which division was entirely annihilated—not more than 200 escaping—300 prisoners, and the balance killed. The wounded were drowned, almost damning the river. This force is estimated carefully at 6000. This brilliant feat was accomplished by A. P. Hill, by placing one brigade on a hill in fair view of the enemy with a battery with instructions when the enemy arrived on the opposite bank, to fire on them, throw down their arms, and scatter to the woods. As he anticipated, the enemy charged on the hill, with a yell, thinking we were routed. Hill had other batteries arranged, raking the river, with the men concealed, which the enemy had not discovered. After they were well across, he opened his batteries loaded with grape and shell, causing great destruction. As they reached the top of the hill, he charged them with bayonet and drove them into the river. Another Leesburg affair, only magnified in importance, thus chewing up an entire division.

...To recur to the part that the Texans played, the 5th Texas was commanded by Capt. J. N. M. Turner, whose gallantry was the admiration of the regiment, and all the Generals who witnessed his movements, Col. Robinson being sick. The Texas brigade was commanded by Col. Warfield, of the 18th Ga., (a general favorite) Hood acting as Major General. As the brigade entered the fight, supporting Ewell's Division, marching one mile under a tremendous fire of grape and shell, arriving at the line of battle of Gen. Lawton's (Ga.) brigade which was lying down, fighting with great spirit; when the Texans came within fifty yards of this Georgia brigade, they shouted to them "charge"—when our line, becoming entangled in theirs. Major Sellers, like magic appeared in front between two fires and commanded the Texas brigade to halt and lie down, for the Texians started to pass them; and he with the assistance of the other officers, and the encouraging shouts of our boys, succeeded in bringing on the charge. After they had advanced fifty yards, we were ordered forward again. We then joined them in the charge, and drove the enemy back. As the rumors of the killed and wounded are so conflicting, I deem it advisable to wait a day or so, until an official list arrives, (which is now on the way) which I will forward with dispatch. The following names Capt. Baber can vouch for:

Killed. 1st Texas—Maj. Dale, Capt. Bedell, Co. L 5th Texas—Lt. Strickland, Co. F; Lt. Drake, Co. I; Sergeant major Hardy Allen, Jas. Hart and Robert Toland, Co. E.

Wounded. 5th Texas—Lt. Boyd, Col. C, severely in side. Lt. New, Co. H, arm broken. Lt. Alexander, Co. K, severely. Capt. Baber, Co. E, slightly in the arm. Serg't Thomas Murray, Co. D.; Ord. Serg't Park, Co. I, shoulder; Ord. Serg't Williamson, Co. E. slightly; Ord. Serg't Joseph Tulmer, Co. K, hip; 2d Serg't Mc -, Co. H, hand; Privates in Co. E, J. Henderson, left arm amputated; Thos. Mullins, shoulder. T. Newman, Co. I, arm amputated; Deen Morgan, Co. I, slightly in side; B. Dyer, Co. A, right leg amputated at the thigh.

There were 13 killed and 63 wounded belonging to the 5th Texas. The 1st and 4th Texas lost very heavily. It is almost superfluous for me to say that the Brigade fully sustained the reputation required at Gaines' Mill.

Yours truly, A. H. Edey

## Nicholas Pomeroy
### 1835–1919

Nicholas Pomeroy was a private in Company "A." Pomeroy was born in Ireland and returned there after the war, where he married and farmed. He is buried in Millstreet, County Cork, where his membership in Company "A," 5th Texas, CSA is inscribed on his tombstone. Pomeroy was wounded in the hand and side at Gettysburg, where he was also taken prisoner. He was exchanged on July 31, 1863.[32]

Of all the primary source documents about Antietam, this author found that the unpublished memoir of Nicholas Pomeroy best describes the daily interests of soldiers in the ranks. He compares the difficulty of seeking food from farms in Maryland and Virginia to supplement their ever-short issued rations. He writes of the important and often dangerous task of canteen details. His narrative of combat is succinct and rather breathtaking.

## Private Nicholas Pomeroy
### 5th Texas Infantry
### Crossing the Potomac

It was on the following day Sept. 3rd that our picket guard was withdrawn, and we started to join our command that was now crossing the Potomac. Entering

Maryland we went by twos or threes just for company, and I think it took us about 6 days before we reached our commands. We followed the tracks of the army, crossed the Blue Ridge Mountain at Snicker's Gap and into the Valley of the Shenandoah. The weather was beautiful and the country we marched through was delightful, lots of fruit everywhere, and though not yet quite ripe we nearly lived on them. We passed great numbers of stragglers on our way, many of them footsore and many barefoot. These poor fellows could not help being in this plight as we had been marching for weeks, more of them being forced marches like the present one, and as I have related we had hard fighting on the way, and we were everyday going farther from our base of supplies (Richmond). After we crossed the ford at the Potomac River, and entered Maryland, being in need of food, a comrade and I went to a nice looking farm house to buy some bread. The young woman who furnished us with it refused to take our money and better still she gave us some cider and filled our canteens with milk. We went off under the shade of some trees and made a splendid meal. I still picture that woman's face. Kind actions like this were quite common in old Virginia where every house was a soldier's home. The trouble there, then was that people were on short rations themselves being overrun by both armies. In Maryland, the people were about equally divided in sympathy between the north and south.

We had some regiments of them in our army at the time, and splendid soldiers they proved to be. Next day I joined my regiment and was pleased to be with my comrades again. They were bivouacked on the bank of a fine stream of water and resting (near Hagerstown). On the 14th of September our army was again in motion, a portion of Jackson's and Longstreet's Corps had been sent to Harper's Ferry, where they captured that garrison and all it contained comprising several cannon, thousands of small arms, and about 8000 prisoners. The rest of our army was now moving toward Sharpsburg where the Federal Commander was now concentrating all his army. On this day our division (Hood's) which was marching in the lead of Longstreet's Corps had a sharp fight in forcing our way through a pass at South Mountain. We had a few casualties in the Texas Brigade, but we cleared the way for the rest of the army. On our march on the 15th nothing of any importance happened.

# Battle of Sharpsburgh or Antietam September 16, 1862

About 5 o'clock on the 16th September our division at the head of Longstreet's Corps after a hard days marching arrived close to the town of Sharpsburgh, and formed in line of battle off the road. The position of the 5th Texas was along the edge of some woods. Not far to our left and out in an open field was a little framed church, which was now to become historical from the position it occupied in the great battle before us, and how many narrow escapes it had from the numerous shells that were falling and exploding around it that evening and next day. The Federal batteries were posted on the hill in a semi-circular line in our front. Their shells were dropping and exploding all round us whilst taking up our position. About dusk the Federal batteries on the surrounding hills opened up with still grater violence. At the same time our pickets in front were now falling back to take their places with the regiment. The enemy were now advancing in a heavy line of battle and our division was immediately under arms and moved forward to meet them. The 5th Texas passed through the wood, met the enemy in an open field in front— we got the order to charge and then fell back before us into the opposite wood. We followed up the retreating enemy almost to the other side of the woods when our line was halted. It was now dark. We held this position till we were relieved about 10 o'clock that night by another troops. We then fell back a short distance to the rear. We were without rations, and had not partaken of any food since morning and were now anxiously waiting for it to come. The flour we generally made into biscuits, and baked in pans but the bacon for economy we ate raw. I recall taking half a dozen canteens (my own and comrades) to procure some water to wet the flour whilst the others were starting fires to cook. I went round to the rear and turned to the left searching for the water, when I met one of our men coming against me with a number of canteens filled, and he directed me to a good spring, but cautioned me to be very careful as there were stray bullets dropping about it. I soon found the water, and when in the act of filling the canteens, a number of stray bullets struck the ground near me, showing that the enemy was not far off. I hastened back to camp, and just as I was in the act of reaching it, shells from the Federal batteries were exploding in our midst. Cooking utensils and rations were now abandoned and immediately the Texas Brigade were under arms. It was broad daylight now.

## Battle of Sharpsburg (Sept. 17, 1862)

The Texas Brigade moved out of the woods we occupied during the past night and entered the same open field, and immediately shells from the Federal Batteries on the surrounding hills began to fall and burst around us, and right in our front emerging from the opposite woods was a heavy line of the enemy with a line of skirmishers in front advancing against us. Firing from both sides commenced, the 5th Texas advancing and firing. We got orders to charge and then our men rushed forward with loud cheers and the Federal line fell back into the woods. The 5th Texas following up entered the woods after some distance and then halted. There was silence for a little while in our front, and then we were assailed by a heavy fire of artillery and our men sought shelter as best they could and lay down flat on the ground. This continued for some time when it suddenly ceased, and then a heavy line of the enemy's infantry advanced rapidly on our line, cheering as they came on, and the men of the 5th Texas with steady cool aim kept firing into their midst and at last they broke in disorder and fled. Desultory firing was then kept up for some time, and occasionally some shelling and then it ceased, and again we were charged by a second line of the enemy, but they were repulsed and driven back in disorder as before.

Desultory firing and some shelling again for a time and then silence for a few minutes. Then we were charged for a third time by a third line of the enemy, and they again in their turn were driving back and repulsed in disorder. Some firing and shelling, and after a while firing not only came from our front, but also from our right and left, showing that we were about to be surrounded. On our side nearly every man had expended his last cartridge, besides rifling our dead and wounded comrades cartridge boxes. It was then well into the afternoon, when the 5th Texas, now only a mere skirmish line (having lost about 60 percent of their number, killed our wounded got the order to fall back and be relieved and replenish their ammunition.

Since early morning, General McClellan, who had all the men and means he needed at his command, was hurling his divisions into our thin gray line, only to be time and again driven back in disorder, leaving their dead and wounded on the ground after them. But could that thin gray line, now reduced to a mere skirmish line, hold out against such fearful odds, in what every man in that devoted rank thought at that hour of the day, and it looked as if before another hour had passed, that these men, who had only a short time before crossed the Federal breastworks in front of Richmond would be driven into the Potomac, which was only about a mile in our rear. The 5th Texas fell back through the woods and entered the field where we first met the Federals in the early morning. Shot and shell were now falling over it and tearing up the ground and we moved in open formation, and with a rapid pace through it. Here I mention an incident—when we were about half way across I met one of our wounded men lying on the ground, and was in the act of passing on with my Company, when he called me by name. He was Lieut. Boyd of Company C, of my regiment. He said he was shot through the leg and could not move, and feared he would be killed at any moment by the shelling now going on, and he therefore begged me to try and take him out to some safe place. I could not refuse his appeal, although it was a trying one for me to undertake. However, he was rather a slight man, and I was fasting since the previous morning but had forgotten that I was hungry in the excitement of battle, still I was young and strong, and I managed to get him on my back, and in the act of starting—bullets began to whiz around us I turned round and saw a line of Federals just coming out of the woods we left behind us, they were firing on my retreating comrades that were now in front of me. I did not believe that there were any American soldiers on either side who would deliberately fire on a wounded man, but there was many a foreigner in the Federal Army whom I knew had no such scruple, and we were in front of the line of fire, and it was a very critical position. I moved on as quickly as I could. I met another man of my regiment—he was lying on his back with his blanket roll under his head reading his pocket Testament and seemed resigned to die at any moment.

It was a sublime spectacle. The 5th Texas had now disappeared in the woods at the end of the field, and I was about 300 yards in their rear. I knew if we could reach the woods we would be safe from the enemy's fire, as the ground on the other side sloped down to a hollow. I knew this because it was about there we started to meet the Federal line in the morning, I kept moving on. A shell struck the ground near us, throwing the earth on us, and at the same time the force of the wind of it threw me on my knees. My wounded comrade at the same time begged me not to abandon him, and I did not, I reached the edge of the woods and as I now moved down in safety on the other side, I heard loud cheering, it was Jackson's division coming to the rescue. After capturing Harper's Ferry he made forced marches, and arrived in time to save the day. I had not far to go now, I moved down the wooded slope, and came to the open piece of ground at the bottom, and here I met my good old friend Dr. Roberts of the 5th Texas, with the litter men and a number of our wounded. He rushed towards me and held me up whilst they tenderly lifted my wounded comrade off my back, and I then dropped to the ground completely exhausted. I rested for a few minutes and then bade my wounded comrade goodbye. He thanked me over and over again for endangering my own life to save that of another, and he said he would always remember me as his truest bosom friend, and that was the last I saw of him; his thigh-bone being badly shattered, he succumbed shortly after the operation of cutting off his leg. When I joined my regiment immediately afterwards, we were all supplied with as much ammunition as we could conveniently carry, we also got a little rations, our teamsters having cooked it in the rear. Never was food so badly needed by soldiers. We were then about 30 hours fasting, but the terrible excitement of the battle kept us up. The whole of our division after suffering frightful losses, and expending all their ammunition, fell back about the same time to replenish their cartridge boxes and fill their pockets also with cartridges, and it was very fortunate for us that the long expected relief arrived at that moment, otherwise our situation would be critical indeed. These troops were now keeping the enemy that followed us up in check from advancing any further. It was now early afternoon and when the 5th Texas with the rest of the Texas Brigade, and what was left of Hood's division, now a mere skirmish line, charged the enemy's lines; drove them back and recovered the same ground that we left when we started to fall back. We held this position till nightfall, and I think we were then moved to the right where we remained in a line of battle with the rest of the army all that night. Our lines were so close to the Federals that we could hear the words of command of their officers, showing they were maneuvering, probably bringing in fresh troops to relieve those in our front. We all expected that the battle would be renewed next morning, but it was not. About the middle of the forenoon General Lee ordered that one of his big guns be fired, and after firing there was no response from the Federals. I do not think any shot was fired on that day the 18th September, in the meantime all our wounded were safely taken across the Potomac, as well as our wagon trains and supplies, and on that night our army also crossed the Potomac, we were in dear Old Virginia again, and thus ended the bloodiest and hardest contested battles of the war. Our army then marched to Martinsburg where we all stayed for some time. In a short time all our stragglers came up, many of them in pitiful condition—some without shoes—footsore and lame. We had some habitual stragglers in all our regiments, but the majority of these poor fellows could not help it, and were good soldiers. These men increased our army considerably .We then got some clothes and shoes.[33]

## William T. Wofford
## June 28, 1824–May 22, 1884

Perhaps heroic acts of personal sacrifice are the "silver lining" that rim the dark cloud of battle. Since men started writing about war, acts of personal sacrifice and heroism have been included in the accounts of great battles. Thankfully, it appears to be a human condition that, when placed in dire circumstances, some soldiers will perform unexpected selfless acts to save others.

To close this chapter about the 5th Texas at Antietam, such a tale is appropriate. It is written by Colonel W. T. Wofford, commander of the Texas Brigade at Antietam.

While this memoir by Colonel Wofford contradicts an account written by a soldier in the 4th Texas Regiment and reminds us that memories fade over time, the two versions of who saved the flag in no way diminish the brave acts of Captain Darden of the 4th Texas Regiment or Private Monroe of the 5th Texas.

Wofford was the first colonel of the 18th Georgia Infantry Regiment, which was assigned to the brigade commanded by General John Bell Hood. In mid-September, 1862, just before Antietam, Wofford assumed command of Hood's Brigade. In January, 1863, he was promoted to the rank of brigadier general and became the commander of the Department of Georgia. He was paroled at Resaca, Georgia, in June, 1865. John Monroe enlisted in Company "G" in Milam County, Texas, in March, 1862. He died of "pleurisy" on December 22, 1862.[34]

## Colonel William T. Wofford
*Weekly Times-Democrat*
## March 30, 1894
## Told by Col. W. T. Wofford

Before writing my story, I have read over with care all the "Bravest Deeds" so far published, and I note that without exception the writers declare it is most difficult to recall some one man or act and point to it as exceptional. Speaking for myself, and I am sure it is the experience of other officers, valor was so usual that it was only an act of cowardice that impressed one, and of this, I must confess, I saw but little. In bodies men would undertake things that could not be thought of by smaller numbers, and then again field officers did not have an opportunity to note individual acts.

From the many rushing through my mind I select one, not because I think the hero was the bravest man I ever saw, but because this act was uncalled for and showed indifference during where there was a duty or a great principle involved.

It was at the battle of Sharpsburg, where I had the honor to command a brigade under Gen. Hood. I need not remind any of the survivors North or South that Sharpsburg, or Antietam as our Yankee friends call it, was for the numbers engaged in the bloodiest battle of the war.

We had been fighting all day near or about a building known as Mumma Church. Sometimes we were in the advance of this building, and again the terrific firing would force us to seek shelter places in the woods, where there were a few pieces of almost useless artillery. As we had done again and again during the day, we drove the enemy back and were again subjected to a perfect rain of shells. The Fifth Texas on the right of the brigade was commanded by the gallant Capt. Turner, and as I rode in his direction I noticed that an enlisted man, whose name I learned was Monroe, was engaging him in earnest conversation.

Before I came up Monroe had left the captain and was running like a deer in the direction of the enemy, who were quick to fire on any moving things. "Captain, what does this mean?" I asked, as I looked after the flying figure.

Pointing to the tramped cornfield in which so many men, friends and foes lay, the captain said: "Monroe, one of my men saw a flag rising and falling a bit ago, over near that burned stump, and he asked for leave to go out and get it."

"Has your regiment lost its flag?" I asked, "No," he replied with pride, "what's left of the colors of the Fifth Texas is still in our possession and we'll keep it while there's a man to carry it," and he pointed down the line to where a lot of blood-stained tatters flapped about a bullet-scarred staff.

"It must be a Yankee flag," I said, "and if so, I hardly think it prudent to risk a man on such a venture."

Capt. Turner made no reply, but meanwhile my attention was drawn to Monroe, for I was now intensely interested in the outcome of this adventure.

He reached the black stump about two hundred yards away and dropped so suddenly that at first we thought he was shot. Soon, to our great relief, Monroe rose to his knees. We saw him lifting a man on his back and that the man clung to a flag.

Monroe straightened up, took a quick glance about him, and then started for our lines. He was a young, athletic fellow, but he had no child's burden. Men were falling back in the line, and how he escaped is one of those wonders that can never be explained, though he was slightly wounded in the shoulder.

He brought back with him not a Yankee and his colors, but the color bearer and flag of the Fourth Texas, lost in our retreat. Every man in the brigade saw this exploit and greeted it with a ringing cheer. The colors were saved, and I may add the color bearer got well. Had it not been for Monroe the flag would have fallen into the hands of the enemy, and so I cannot count his act as sheer rashness. W. T. Wofford.

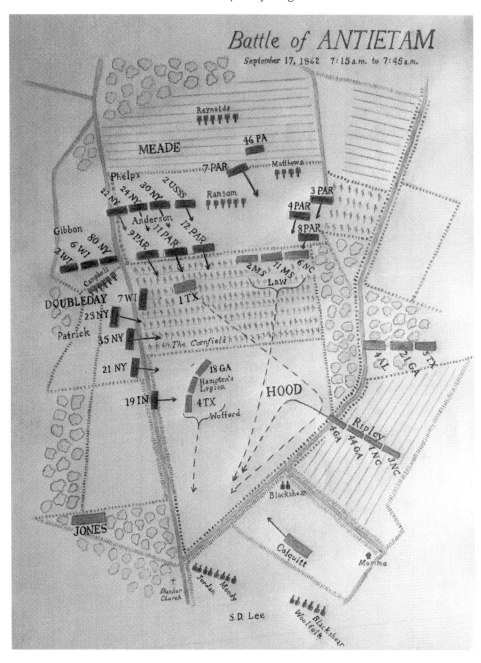

Battle of Antietam, 7.15 a.m. to 7.45 a.m., Hood's Texas Brigade locations against the Army of the Potomac—September 17, 1862. (*Natalie Wolchover*)

# 4

# 18th Georgia Infantry Regiment

The 18th Georgia Infantry Regiment was composed of ten companies, mostly from central counties in Georgia.

List of Companies and First Commanding Officers:

Company A:  (Acworth Infantry) Cobb County—J. L. Lemon
Company B:  (Newton Rifles) Newton County—J. A. Stuart
Company C:  (Jackson County Volunteers) Jackson County—D. L. Jarrett
Company D:  (Davis Invincibles) Dougherty County—S. D. Irvin
Company E:  (Stephens Infantry) Gordon County—E. L. Starr
Company F:  (Davis Guards) Bartow County—J. C. Roper
Company G:  (Lewis Volunteers) Bartow County—J. C. Maddox
Company H:  (Rowland Highlanders) Bartow County—F. M. Ford
Company I:  (Dooly Light Infantry) Dooly County—R. T. Coley
Company K:  (Rowland Infantry)—Bartow County—J. A. Crawford

The 18th Georgia Infantry Regiment was organized at Camp Brown, Cobb County, Georgia, on April 22, 1861, under a special act of the Georgia legislature and was originally designated 1st Regiment, 4th Brigade, State Troops commanded by Colonel William T. Wofford and Lieutenant Colonel Solon Z. Ruff.[1]

After drilling at Camp McDonald, Georgia, the regiment was ordered to the Confederate capital Richmond, Virginia, arriving on August 8, 1861. Upon arriving, the regiment's primary duty was guarding Union prisoners captured at the battle of First Manassas, fought on July 21, 1861. On November 20, 1861, the regiment was assigned as the 4th Regiment to the Texas Brigade, thus bringing the Brigade to full strength under Commanding General Louis T. Wigfall.[2]

The 18th Georgia remained assigned to the Texas Brigade, under the command of Brigadier General John Bell Hood, and fought alongside the Texans in some of the bloodiest battles of the war—Gaines' Mill, Second Manassas (Bull Run), and Antietam (Sharpsburg). During the Battle of Antietam, the 18th Georgia was heavily

18th Georgia Infantry flag flown at Antietam. (*JackMelton.com, Collection of Beverly Dubose III*)

engaged in the northern part of Miller's Cornfield when most of the unit's casualties were taken in repeated assaults of the guns of Federal Battery "B," 4th US Artillery. When the Army of Northern Virginia was reorganized in November, 1862, the 18th was reassigned to the Georgia Brigade commanded by Brigadier General T. R. R. Cobb. The 18th would fight in the Army of Northern Virginia for the entirety of the war. Following Wofford's promotion to brigadier general, the 18th Georgia was commanded by Lieutenant Colonel S. Z. Ruff.

By April, 1865, the regiment was decimated, and it was commanded by Lieutenant G. I. Lasseter after the death of Lieutenant Colonel Ruff at the Battle of Knoxville. By the time of General Robert E. Lee's surrender at Appomattox Courthouse on April 9, 1865, only forty-eight men were present for duty.[3]

From the beginning of the annual reunions of Hood's Texas Brigade Association in 1877 to the last reunion held in 1932, the veterans of the Brigade were always welcomed. The veterans of Hood's Texas Brigade always considered the 18th Georgia an integral part of the brigade.

## Solon Zachariah "S. Z." Ruff
## 1837–November 29, 1863

S. Z. Ruff was born in Smyrna, Georgia, in 1837. He graduated second in his class from Georgia Military Institute in 1856. After graduation, he taught mathematics and drill at the institute. On April 18, 1861, he was appointed lieutenant colonel of the 18th Georgia Infantry, after the promotion of its previous commanding officer, William T. Wofford, to brigadier general. By this time, Lt. Col. Ruff had already gained the attention of General Longstreet and others. He led his regiment during the successful charge against Union fortifications at the Battle of Gaines' Mill on June 27, 1862, and was hailed by *The Richmond Campaign* as the "hero of the battle of Gaines Mill."[4] Lt. Col. Ruff continued to lead the 18th Georgia, when the regiment was attached to Hood's Texas Brigade, and after the Battle of Antietam, when the 18th Georgia was transferred to Cobb's Georgia Brigade. Lieutenant Colonel Ruff was killed on the assault of Fort Saunders at the Battle of Knoxville on November 29, 1863, and is buried at the Gibson Family Cemetery, near Knoxville, Tennessee.[5]

## Lieutenant Colonel S. Z. Ruff
## 18th Georgia Infantry
## Colonel W. T. Wofford,
## Commanding Texas Brigade
## September 23, 1862

Sir: I have the honor to report that this regiment was drawn up in line of battle, late in the evening on the 16th instant, to the left of the position it had occupied during the day and previous night, which was north of the town of Sharpsburg and parallel to the Antietam River. On our left was the Hampton Legion, commanded by Lieutenant-Colonel Gary, and on our right, the First Texas commanded by Lieutenant-Colonel Work.

Just at dark, the enemy advanced and attacked the brigade on our right, when we received orders to advance to a piece of corn a short distance in front, where we remained without firing a gun until about midnight. The brigade was then withdrawn to a piece of woods, to cook rations.

The next morning, 17th instant, just after daylight, the brigade was drawn up in line of battle, and ordered to lie down under cover of the hill from a terrible storm

Lieutenant Colonel S. Z. Ruff,
18th Georgia Infantry. (*Lucile
Woods Hardwick Lind*)

of shell that the enemy's batteries were at that time pouring into the woods. A heavy firing of musketry had been going on in our front for some time.

About 7 a.m., the brigade was ordered to move forward in the direction of the firing. Advancing about a quarter of a mile through the timber, we came upon the enemy posted in front of a piece of corn, and immediately opened fire upon them. After one or two rounds they gave way, and fell back to a considerable distance in the corn. Advancing, with the left of the regiment resting on the right of the legion, which had its left upon the turnpike, we drove the enemy in fine style out of the corn and back upon their supports. At the far edge of the corn, the ranks of the retreating line of the enemy unmasked a battery, which poured a round or two of grape into our ranks with terrible effect; but it was soon silenced by our riflemen, and the gunners ran away. At this moment we discovered a fresh line of the enemy advancing on our left flank in an oblique direction, threatening to cut us off, and our ranks being reduced to less than one-third their original strength, we found it necessary to fall back. At the edge of the woods we met supports and rallied on them a part of our men, but the regiment was too much cut up for further action, and in a short time, in connection with the whole brigade, was taken from the field.

We carried 176 men into the action, and lost 101 in killed, wounded and missing; most of the missing are either killed or wounded.

All the men and officers, so far as I was able to observe, acted with the most desperate coolness and gallantry. Not one showed any disposition, notwithstanding their terrible loss, to fall back or flinch from the enemy until they received orders to do so.

I regret exceedingly to report that Lieuts. T. C. Underwood and J. M. D. Cleveland of Company K, are among the missing. They are known to be wounded and it is feared they are dead. I regret also to be obliged to record among the wounded the names of Capts. J. A. Crawford and G. W. Maddox and Lieuts. J. F. Maddox, O. W. Putman, W. G. Calahan, J. Grant, and D. B. Williams.

Very respectfully, your obedient servant,

S. Z. Ruff,

Lieutenant Colonel, Commanding Regiment.[6]


## James Lile Lemon
## 18th Georgia Infantry
## October 25, 1835–June 12, 1907

James Lile Lemon was born on October 25, 1835, in Decatur, Georgia. Aged eighteen, he joined his brother in the banking business. In 1853, Lemon and his brother formed the first bank in Cobb County, Georgia. He was a soldier in the "Acworth Infantry" militia in Acworth, Georgia.[7] He joined the 18th Georgia Infantry Regiment as a second lieutenant and was promoted to first lieutenant on June 5, 1862. He would fight in the major battles of Gaines' Mill, Second Bull Run (Manassas), Antietam (Sharpsburg), Fredericksburg, Chancellorsville, Gettysburg, and Knoxville.

He was promoted to captain on March 5, 1863, and was captured during the Battle of Knoxville on November 29, 1863, and was first sent to POW Camp Chase, Ohio.[8] Lieutenant Lemon was then transferred to the POW Camp at Fort Delaware and arrived at the camp on March 27, 1864. Afterwards, he was sent to various POW Camps throughout the South and would become a member of the "Immortal 600." He ended up at Fort Delaware and was paroled on June 12, 1865.

After the war, he returned home to Acworth, Georgia, where he slowly recovered from deteriorated health from being a prisoner of war. He was elected in 1870 to the board of commissioners in Acworth and was also a founding member of the Acworth Presbyterian Church. He and his wife, Eliza, raised seven children.[9] He died on June 12, 1907, and is buried at Mars Hill Cemetery in Acworth, Georgia.

On July 21, 1995, the Sons of Confederate Veterans awarded Captain James Lile Lemon the Confederate Medal of Honor for his valor under fire at an extreme peril of his life at the Battle of Fort Sanders in Knoxville, TN, on November 29, 1863. Captain Lemon's great-great-grandson, Mark H. Lemon, accepted the Confederate Medal of Honor in Captain Lemon's name.[10]

Captain James Lile Lemon, 18th Georgia Infantry. (*Mark Lemon*)

## Second Lieutenant James Lile Lemon
## 18th Georgia Infantry
## Battle of Sharpsburg

Upon reaching the town, our brigade was ordered to the left of our lines, where we lay tired & hungry all day on the 16th, while under fire of the enemy's long-range guns. Our haversacks were empty & our rations had not arrived, causing much grumbling among the men, as we had not eaten in several days. On the evening of the 16th our brigade was ordered to form line of battle & we advanced into a cornfield & into a piece of timber where we met almost by accident a force of the enemy. We drove them with style back through the woods, capturing some Yanks from the 1st and 3rd Penn'a Reserves. Among this bunch were a couple of drummer boys, about 12 or 13 years old who were trying hard to "put on a brave face," but who were clearly terrified. Col. Ruff ordered their drums confiscated & then released as we were not equipped or inclined to care for children. Our drum had been damaged & thrown away at Groveton, so we took theirs as "spoils of war." Private Boring captured the boys. As he was driving them to the rear at point of bayonet they heaped so much abuse upon him—out of their fear or nervousness—that he had to be restrained from striking them with a club musket. Of course, he instantly the target of many wags among our company who joked with him about "scaring little boys" & etc. He replied that he would be d***d if he'd take such abuse from "d***d Yankee whelps." The boys were release & "beat a hasty retreat" back to their lines, with Boring giving them a rite hard look as they went. The other prisoners were sent to the rear to cook rations, which, it was said, had finally arrived. We were literally famished having marched hard, fought battles & marched again on nothing but green corn in the last 3 days. We formed in the rear & waited, but the promised wagons & rations had not arrived. Thus, we lay our arms suffering from the most severe hunger, with no recompense. The wagons did not reach us until just before dawn & were almost assaulted by the men, wild as they were in their hunger. Calm was quickly restored however & rations were drawn, & cook-fires started. To our everlasting dismay, the firing from the field from which we had withdrawn had greatly intensified & we were ordered back to the front at once. Our men went almost wild with anger & furiously threw their rations to the ground & poured out their coffee as they moved into line. Gen'l Wofford had ridden up & was among us as we formed, calling out "Never mind boys, there will be plenty to eat soon enough. It is the Yankees who have taken your breakfast. Make them pay for it!" A savage yell went up in response & the men's faces I shall never forget. Wild eyed and furious clenched teeth & oaths from every man, from the most savage to the most mild-hearted, all were as one in their wrath.　They were like savage Devils from the infernal regions, howling madly & looking for a fight. Off we stepped at the shift, passing at length up a hill & out of the timber near the little Dunker church. We crossed a pike into a field of clover where we formed into a line of battle & loaded our rifles. Our order of advance was as follows—Hampton's Legion on our left & next to the pike, 18th Geo., 1st Texas, 4th Texas & 5th Texas on the right. The Yanks, Wisconsin men, were about this time emerging in force from the large piece of corn to our front. Out in front of them & coming towards us were hundreds of our own troops of Gen'l Lawton's command who had been repulsed. Once again, as at Coal Harbor, we heard the command "Trail arms!" & knew what that meant. It was to be an advance without perceptible halt on our part. Do or die, victory or death! At "Forward, quick-time, march!", we stepped off again in perfect unison, a thousand Confederates, bone tired & starving but with a burning fury for the hated Yankees. The fugitives to our front had just passed through or around our advancing lines, & now we saw the black-hatted Yanks coming on in style. Ruff, his fighting blood up, called out "Looky there boys, at them black hats! Let's go knock them off!" Wild laughter & the piercing "Rebel-Yell," is heard again & at the command "Fire!" a rolling volley blasted forth, delivered from the hip—as at Coal Harbor—instantly killing scores of the enemy & halting his advance. In an instant came the command "Fix bayonets!" & this was, again done without halting. All knew what would come next. "Double-time, March" came the command & a yell, more like a tortured scream bellowed forth from every throat. Off we went at charge bayonet & at the double-quick. The ranks of the Yanks, men of the most-vaunted Wisconsin Black Hat Brigade, shuddered & broke, turning at once & flying through the corn. On we swept like a cyclone driving them before us in demoniacal fury. As we reached the ground where they had briefly stood, about 70 or so Yankee bodies lay on the ground, some writhing, some still. I clearly remember the ground being litter with dozens of black hats, & then also remembering Ruff's words with grim amusement. After entering the corn for some distance, which was already choked with bodies both blue & gray, we perceived several regiments of the enemy, about 200 yards distant on the far side of the pike, moving by the flank towards our left with the intention of turning our flank. At this point Col Ruff & everyone else, also became aware of a battery of guns placed obliquely in the road ahead & to our left which, if we had advanced as planned, would have taken our left flank in enfilade fire. Ruff accordingly obliqued us, to the left (along with the gallant Hampton Legion) directly towards the guns & their infantry supports. As we advanced, these guns began to do terrible work among us. With guns double-shotted with canister, they blew gaps in our lines. We halted by sheer necessity by the fence among the pike & began to concentrate our fire on the gunners, whose guns were now about 70 yards away. When at one point we had momentarily silenced the guns by shooting down every man who approached them, we quickly formed & made at them at the double-quick. In the intervening moments, however, more men had manned the guns & when we approached within about 40 yards the most horrible blasts belched forth from the pieces which killed and maimed dozens of our boys. It was on this first charge that my beloved friends & brothers in law, my wife's only dear brothers, Wm & Marcus Davenport were cut down while running side by side, united in death as in life. We reluctantly fell back to the dubious shelter of the fence, where we continued our fire on the gunners. We had killed at least 4 complete crews it seemed to me, yet more men, perhaps artillery men, or from the infantry supports, had stepped up to replace them. Twice more we attacked each time coming closer than before, & each time taking horrific casualties before being forced back for lack of support. At this point we were decimated. Fully half our men were down, yet we were forming for another go at the guns, whose fire had slackened somewhat. Before we set forth on what surely would have been a forlorn hope, we were ordered by Col Ruff, who had been so ordered by Gen'l Wofford, to disengage & withdraw, as we were receiving front & left flank fire & were in danger of being cut to pieces & annihilated. We formed & moved at a trot, but in fairly good order by the left flank down the fence-line to the Dunker church, being shot at all the way back. I had the queer notion that we were human participants in a "shooting gallery". Bullets kicked up dust & splintered fence rails as we ran. At length, we reached the area of the church & formed in defensive positions nearby, where we replenished our cartridge boxes & prepared for another fight. We were mere shadows of our former strength, & due to lack of support at the most crucial moment of our victory, we were almost completely destroyed. Col Ruff, Gen'l Wofford & I am told, Gen'l Hood, were livid in their wrath at our not being supported. We had done all that was humanly possible & more, but alone as we were & against massed regiments & batteries of guns so were arrayed against us, no more could possibly be achieved. When we were able to account for our losses, we had, it was seen, only 75 men fit for duty in the entire regiment. Our losses were 16 killed 72 wounded, 20 missing, meaning more than one-half, and then some, of our regiment was killed or wounded. We took no further part of the fight owing to our butchered condition. Later in the evening we were moved closer to town where we bivouacked, & at last were able to draw & cook rations.

The next day no fighting of any consequence occurred & our two armies remained on the field each watching the other warily as if not wanting to be the first to withdraw. From what I saw & experienced, & what I have been told occurred elsewhere on the field, the fight was a "draw" more or less. During the lull in the fighting many flags of truce were seen, while we went about gathering the dead & wounded. I therefore took the opportunity, under one such flag of truce, to seek out & recover the bodies of William & Marcus, which I did with the aid of J. J. O'Neill & a few of our boys from home. We carried them back to a spot near the church, where we buried them side by side. From my Testament I read a Psalms over them & they were covered over. Marking the spot in my diary, I resolved to return one day, if I survived the war, to recover them & carry them home.[11]

Private Chester Pearce
18th Georgia Infantry
*Galveston Daily News*
July 1, 1894
A Story of the War
How a Wounded "Boy Solider" is found in After Years by an Old Friend

The following story is taken from a recent issue of the Macon, Ga., *Telegraph*. It will be read with special interest by the friends of Mrs. Rosenberg of this city. The story follows:

"A few evenings since I was at the Tuttle house in Perry, along with Chester Pearce and General C. D. Anderson. These gentlemen were old soldiers, and the conversation drifted into experiences in camp and field.

"Chester Pearce, one of Houston's noblest citizens, had just received a letter which filled his mind and heart with reminiscences tender and romantic. To appreciate the letter a brief history of Chester Pearce's life is necessary.

"In common with the young men of the south, Chester Pearce, when about 19 years of age, answered his country's call and went to the front in 1861. He was a member of the Eighteenth Georgia and belonged to Hood's Texas brigade. In the terrible battle of Sharpsburg he was badly wounded, a minie ball passing entirely through his body. He laid on the battlefield for many hours in great agony, bleeding most profusely. He was taken prisoner and taken to Hagerstown, some miles distant. Here the doctors held consultation over him and declined to even dress his wound, as death would soon come. For two days he was left in that condition, without nourishment, no one so much as bathing his face or speaking a kind word, as the hospital was filled with federal wounded, who claimed the attention of the doctors and nurses.

"A committee of ladies visited the hospital and finding him in his forlorn and wretched condition, gave him nourishment. Among these were the daughters of Dr. McGill, who was surgeon on General Lee's staff and was absent from home, having cast his fortunes with the confederacy. These daughters of Dr. McGill, ministering angels indeed, gave guarantee bond for the return of the young soldier should he recover, and took him to their elegant and palatial home. Here for the first time he received medical attention, and Dr. McGill, Jr., took him in charge and dressed his wounds. Miss Millie McGill, a beautiful young lady of culture, and just 18, became his charming nurse. When taken to the McGill residence Chester was introduced to Colonel Nisbet of the Third Georgia, who was wounded six times in the same battle. This young colonel is the now well-known Dr. R. B. Nisbet of Eatonton.

"Chester Pearce remained with the McGill's for two months and, under their gentle treatment, recovered sufficiently to go to Baltimore, the military post. Mr. James Carroll, a friend to southern soldiers, gave guarantee bond for his safe keeping and took young Pearce to his home, where he remained for six weeks. He then succeeded in getting exchanged. In the course of years Miss Mollie McGill, who had so tenderly nursed back to life the boy soldier, married a Mr. Rosenberg, a wealthy banker of Galveston, Tex. There she met Mr. and Mrs. Dan Henderson, formerly of Camilla, Ga., and she told them the story of the handsome young soldier she had nursed and requested them to discover the whereabouts, if possible, of Chester Pearce.

"Not long since Mr. Henderson read in the *Macon Telegraph* that a Chester Pearce was candidate for the legislature from Houston County. Mrs. Rosenberg wrote to the candidate to know if he could be the Chester Pearce whom she had cared for: sending her kindest remembrances and expressing joy that she had found the soldier boy. And this was the letter that brought forth the war record of Chester Pearce—this is the letter of which he so fondly spoke—a letter that girdled his memory with tender thoughts which, recalled, were as delicious to the senses as music softly played. It goes without saying that Chester Pearce's heart was filled with gladness on the receipt of the letter, and his expressions of gratitude to the McGill's for rescuing him from an untimely grave did credit to his noble nature and manly heart.

"Though having been shot 'through and through,' yet Chester Pearce make what the doctors called a 'good recovery', and, irrepressible, he plunged again into the confederate army after his exchange. He was in the heroic battle of Gettysburg, rushed on in the murderous charge of Round Top, where he was captured and sent to Fort Delaware. He escaped, was recaptured, placed in a dungeon at Fort Henry among criminals and in time sent to Point Lookout, and was exchanged and was with Lee at the sad surrender at Appomattox.

"Though so long ago, yet now the friends of Chester Pearce join him in the pleasurable emotions of renewing his friendship with Miss Mille McGill, now Mrs. Rosenberg, and returning thanks to her and her family for their tender care of him when so much in need of help. God bless the women! Theirs is a ministry of love; theirs is to inspire within us noble emotions, lofty thoughts; to soothe the fevered brow, make strong the fainting heart, and from the purity and loveliness of their own characters to impart a beautiful romance to the lives of men, making them more perfect in the sight of God."

*Atlanta Constitution*
June 28, 1887
The Flag of the Eighteenth Georgia
T. Warren Akin in Cartersville *Courant-American*

Let the nation preserve her heroic Confederate children's battle flags. We would like to see the flag of the glorious old Eighteenth Georgia tendered to the government that it may be preserved in the capitol forever. We would have it bear this inscription, "This is the flag of the Eighteenth Georgia Regiment, Confederate States Volunteers, of the army of northern Virginia. Robert E. Lee bared his illustrious head and saluted it on the field as it was borne past him in a charge which cleared the foe as the whirlwind sweeps the chaff away. The fair lock of hair which binds the remnants of this tattered flag was cut from temple of a New York Zouave. A shell tore through the flag, when the color bearer stooped and cutting this lock from the Zouave's brow, tied up the flag and lifted it again in the hell storm of battle, the long lock gleaming like gold above the men who cheered again and again at this most glorious amendment.

The survivors of the Eighteenth Georgia Regiment Confederate States Volunteers of the army of northern Virginia, present this flag to the nation, that it may be preserved at the capitol, where the citizens of the entire country may view it, and pilgrim from every laud through all coming years behold the battle flag of that regiment whose glorious achievements on the field of battle its surviving member look to history to record and the love of liberty to perpetuate in the minds of men forever.

The survivors of the Eighteenth Georgia Regiment Confederate States Volunteers of the army of northern Virginia present this flag to the nation, conscious that American valor so the common property of the whole people. As citizens of a united country, we rejoice in the heroism of the gallant men against whom we contended. We salute their memory. They were worthy of our steel.

"Glory to God in the highest." Peace on earth; goodwill to men."

**North Platte Semi-Weekly Tribune**
January 11, 1898

Two weeks after Manassas Hood's division, together with Stonewall Jackson's old command, bore the brunt of the fighting between the east and west woods at Antietam. The space between these two pieces of woods in front of Dunker church was partly pasture covered with tall standing corn—that is the corn was standing when the battle raged. Wofford's brigade of Texans led the charge, coming from the west wood toward the east reckless or ignorant of the fact that the open field north of them was filled with Federal cannon and men.

As Wofford marched into the cornfield from the west, two Federal divisions under Williams and Crawford started in from the north side of the field. The leading Federals bent around the left or rear flank of Wofford, completely cutting off from the retreat while his right flank was rushing ahead to the east wood. Gordon's Federal division lay ahead in the open field adjoining the east wood on the north end Green's division at the moment of collision charged from the east wood westward, meeting Hood's dauntless soldiers at arms' length. Hood's line facing north was buffeted back by Williams, Crawford and the batteries and that portion moving east was broken into fragments by Greens resistless masses.

Although it was a hopeless fight the Texans, Georgians and others that had followed turned upon the enemy, first one way and then another, wherever a shower of grape mowing a swath of cornstalks gave sign of the enemy's presence. The Union artillerists, having a clear sweep of the cornfield, held their fire until the awful harvest was ready for the sickle. Slaughter so sudden and terrible as that visited upon Hood's men, and Wofford's Texans in particular, was never known. In the First Texas, which formed Wofford's center on the flank of the Eighteenth, 186 men were shot down out of 226 in the ranks. The Eighteenth lost 90 killed and wounded. The cornfield had proved a trap to both sides alike, but in the end the Confederates got the worst of it. Hood's men left a row of dead along the east wood and upon the northern border of the field.[12]

**Privates Marcus Lafayette Davenport and William Alexander Davenport**
**18th Georgia Infantry**
*Marietta Journal*
January 24, 1992
**Graves of Civil War Casualties Discovered**

The recently rediscovered and marked graves of two Cobb County brothers will be rededicated Saturday—129 years after they were killed by the same artillery shell at the Battle of Sharpsburg during the Civil War.

"Neither of them knew his brother had been killed," said Larry Blair of Marietta, one of three members of the Sons of Confederate Veterans (SCV) who cleaned and marked the family cemetery where Marcus Lafayette Davenport and William Alexander Davenport are buried.

Marcus, 28, and William, 23, were privates in Company A of the 18th Georgia Volunteer Regiment known as "The Acworth Infantry," part of Gen. John Bell Hood's division of Gen. Robert E. Lee's Army of Northern Virginia.

The Davenports were killed Sept 17, 1862, in Maryland in the Battle of Sharpsburg (known in the North as the Battle of Antietam), the bloodiest one-day battle of the war. The 18th had the dubious distinction of having the highest proportion of casualties in one-day battle—57.3 percent—of any unit on either side during the war, according to Marcus Thayer III, of the Kennesaw Battlefield Camp No. 700 of the SCV. Some 101 of the regiment's 176 officers and men were casualties that day, he said.

"I assume (Lemon) felt protective of them," Blair said "They probably had never been more than five or 10 miles from their homes (before the war).[13]

Lemon made a mental note of where the two were hastily buried on the battlefield, and after the war—and after spending time in a Union prisoner of war camp, returned to Sharpsburg with a wagon and several other relatives and brought the two bodies back to Georgia.

"The same kind of story can be found all over the South, where families gave sons and fathers and brothers," Thayer said, "If a soldier fell away from home, he just hoped someone would care enough to put a marker of some kind and say a prayer for him. Usually, they were just wrapped in a blanket (and buried)."

"In the pre-dog tag era, soldiers scratched their names on their rifles or other equipment with the hope they wouldn't be buried in unmarked graves," Thayer said.

The Davenport brothers were reinterred in the Davenport family cemetery off MacLand Road in west Cobb, and their names were added to a small headstone marking the grave of an older brother Frances Marion Davenport who died in 1849. But the unfenced graveyard contained only one other marble headstone, the 20 or so others consisting only of rough fieldstone markers—and its location gradually faded from memory as the years went by and the county grew.

That changed after Caroline Ferguson of Keith Drive called Thayer about an old headstone that had the names of two Confederate veterans on it.

Thayer and SCV friends Blair and Michael Taylor cleared the underbrush from the graveyard.

"We made it a project to take care of that cemetery from now on," Blair said.

The three on Dec. 2 erected two new marble headstones for the Davenports provided by the U. S. Veterans Administration.

"The SCV is duty-bound to put up markers for those who deserve them," Blair said. "They fought for what they believed in. They weren't trying to overthrow the United States. They were trying to protect their own country."

"The rediscovery of the graves floored Marcus Davenport's great granddaughter former Cobb resident Dorothy Davenport Brazelton 74 now of Virginia Blair said her husband had looked for that cemetery all his life but couldn't find it," Blair said. Mrs. Brazelton and other family members plan to be on hand at 3 p.m. Saturday for a rededication ceremony that will also feature SCV women in Civil War era mourning dress and members of the 35th Tennessee Volunteer Infantry and Company F of the Mountain Rifles Civil War reenactment groups. Participants will march the 100 yards or so from the intersection of Keith Drave and Clay Road to the cemetery.

Mrs. Brazelton told Thayer she plans to bring a photograph of Marcus Davenport, as well as some Confederate money he had set aside in a thwarted attempt to help his family.

"He had a feeling he might not survive the war so to try to provide for his wife and children he sold his farm for $2,000 after he enlisted" Thayer said.

Unfortunately for his family the transaction was in Confederate money which by the middle of the war was useless.

"The family had just lost their bread winner," Thayer said. They had some money but it wasn't worth anything. But somehow they survived.

The unspent money was kept in an old coffee tin and handed down from generation to generation, Mrs. Brazelton told Thayer.

Saturday's ceremony will include wreath laying remarks by Thayer and a musket salute.

"The war has been over all these years but it still has an effect on people," Thayer said.

"You don't forget your heritage no matter what it was, just because they didn't prevail it doesn't mean it should be forgotten," Thayer said.


*Atlanta Constitution*
**February 6, 1910**
**To Raise Monument to Hood's Brigade**
**Governor and His Staff Invited to Participate in the Ceremonies**


Governor Brown and his staff have received from William R. Hamby, of Austin, Texas, president of Hood's Texas Brigade, an invitation to be present and participate in the ceremonies incident to the unveiling on May 7 next to the monument to be erected in Austin.

This monument is to be built of Georgia granite, besides which the Eighteenth Georgia regiment was a part of this famous command, so that Georgia is doubly interested in the occasion. Hood's Brigade participated in many of the bloody battles in Virginia and lost 80 percent of its men in killed and wounded.

Governor Brown replied, thanking President Hamby for the invitation, but expressing doubt as to whether it would be possible for him to attend at that time. His attendance, he said, would depend upon the status of business in the executive office.

Hood's Texas Brigade Monument, State of Texas Capital Grounds. (*Diane Kirkendall*)

Brigadier General John Bell Hood
Headquarters Hood's Division
Near Fredericksburg
November 27, 1862

General Order
No. 32.

It is with unfeigned regret that the Major General commanding announces to his command the departure of the 18th Ga. Regiment; they have been ordered to report to General Cobb. The 18th Ga. was one of the original members of the Texas Brigade, having served with that command for more than a year, and leaving it causes a void difficult to fill. In the battles of West Point, Seven Pines, Gaines' Farm, Malvern Hill, Freeman's Ford, Manassas No. 2, Boonsboro Gap, and Sharpsburg, this regiment has shown itself unsurpassed for gallantry, and both officers and men on all occasions exhibited the highest regard for discipline and unwavering devotion to duty. In parting with them the General commanding hopes their future may be as honorable to themselves and useful to their country as their past has been.

By command of

J. B. Hood,

Major General Commanding[14]

# Hampton's Legion

The Hampton's Legion (Infantry) consisted of eight companies from the Charleston and Columbia, South Carolina areas.

List of Companies and First Commanding Officers:

Company A:  (Washington Light Infantry Volunteers) Charleston, SC—J. Conner
Company B:  (Watson Guards) Charleston, SC—M. W. Gary
Company C:  (Manning Guards) Columbia, SC—B. Manning
Company D:  (Gist Rifles) Columbia, SC—H. J. Smith
Company E:  (Bozeman Guards) Columbia, SC—T. L. Bozeman
Company F:  (Davis Guards) Columbia, SC—W. L. M. Austin
Company G:  (Claremont Rifles) Columbia, SC—J. G. Spann
Company H:  (South Carolina Zouave Volunteers) Charleston, SC—L. C. McCord

Hampton's Legion was originally organized and partially financed by wealthy plantation owner Wade Hampton. The legion would have a number of wealthy and well-known South Carolinians such as future generals J. Johnston Pettigrew, Stephen D. Lee, Martin W. Gary, and Matthew C. Butler. The legion was composed of six infantry companies, four cavalry companies, and a battery of artillery.[1]

The infantry and cavalry companies fought together at the Battle of First Bull Run (First Manassas) on July 16, 1861, where Colonel Hampton would suffer his first of several battlefield injuries.[2] With the reorganization of the ANV in mid-1862, the legion was broken up and reassigned. The infantry component of the legion would be reassigned to Hood's Texas Brigade in June, 1862. During the Battle of Second Bull Run (Second Manassas) on August 30, 1862, the legion along with the 5th Texas Infantry inflicted heavy casualties on the 5th New York Infantry (Duryea's Zouaves) and the 10th New York Infantry during their successful charge against the ill-fated New Yorkers.

At Antietam (Sharpsburg), according to the legion's historian O. Lee Sturkey, the legion suffered an 85.7 percent casualty rate, which is higher than the 82.3 percent

Image of Hampton's Legion flag flown at Antietam. (*Cynthia Dorminey*)

casualty rate of the 1st Texas Infantry.[3] The legion carried seventy-seven officers and men into the action at Antietam and suffered a total of sixty-six casualties: ten killed on the field, seven mortally wounded, fifty-one wounded (not mortally), and six prisoners of war (four of them wounded as well).[4]

In mid-November, 1862, the legion was reassigned to Micah Jenkin's South Carolina Brigade, and in the spring of 1864, the legion became mounted and was transferred to the cavalry service. The legion was paroled at Appomattox, April 12, 1865, as "Hampton's Legion Mounted Infantry, South Carolina Volunteers."[5]

## Martin "Mart" W. Gary
## March 25, 1831–April 9, 1881

Martin W. Gary was born in Cokesbury, South Carolina, on March 25, 1831, and graduated from Harvard University in 1854. He became a highly successful criminal lawyer, and a member of the South Carolina legislature.

He entered the Confederate Army as a captain in Hampton's Legion, and he commanded the legion at the Battle of First Bull Run (First Manassas), after the death of Lt. Col. Johnson and the wounding of General Wade Hampton. He led the legion (infantry) as a colonel when it became attached to Hood's Texas Brigade.

Colonel Gary was promoted to brigadier general on May 19, 1864, and commanded the last Confederate troops to leave Richmond in April, 1865.

He escorted President Jefferson Davis and his cabinet south as they tried to evade the Union Army. After the war, he ran two unsuccessful campaigns for the U.S. Senate; however, he was a state senator for four years.

He died on April 9, 1881, and is buried at Tabernacle Cemetery in Cokesbury, South Carolina.[6]

Lieutenant Colonel Martin W. Gary
Hampton's Legion
Camp near Martinsburg, W.V.A.
September 23, 1862
Colonel W. T. Wofford
Commanding Texas Brigade

Colonel: I have the honor to submit the following report of the infantry battalion of the Hampton Legion in the battle of the 17th at Sharpsburg, Md.

The battle opened about day-break along the whole line. The legion was placed to the left of the brigade, the Eighteenth Georgia being to its right. We began to

Lieutenant Colonel Martin W. Gary, Hampton's Legion. (*Library of Congress*)

advance from under cover of [the West] woods in rear of a church, and engaged the enemy so soon as we emerged from them, the enemy being in line of battle near the edge of the corn-field immediately in our front. We advanced steadily upon them, under a heavy fire, and had not gone far when Herod Wilson, of Company F, the bearer of the colors, was shot down. They were raised by James Esters, of Company E, and he was shot down. They were then taken up by C. P. Poppenheim, of Company A, and he, too, was shot down. Major J. H. Dingle, Jr., then caught them and began to advance with them, exclaiming, "Legion, follow your colors!" The words had an inspiring effect, and the men rallied bravely under their flag, fighting desperately at every step. He bore the colors to the edge of the corn near the [Hagerstown] turnpike road, on our left, and, while bravely upholding them within 50 yards of the enemy and three Federal flags, was shot dead. I immediately raised the colors and again unfurled them amid the enemy's deadly fire, when Marion Walton, of Company B, volunteered to bear them. I resigned them into his hands, and he carried them gallantly and safely through the battle. Soon after the death of Major Dingle, I discovered, about 200 yards distant, a brigade of the enemy in line of battle, covering our entire left flank. I immediately ordered the men to fall back under the crest of the hill. I then rallied them and reformed them, and remained with the brigade the remainder of the day.

I have to record the death of many of my best officers. The brave, modest, and energetic Major J. H. Dingle, Jr., fell, among the foremost in battle, and died with the colors in his hands; Captain R. W. Tompkins, who was killed near where Major Dingle fell, and was conspicuous in the fight, for his gallantry and efficiency; Lieutenant J. J. Exum was killed near the same place, heroically leading his men; Captain H. J. Smith was mortally wounded, in the same charge, while bravely leading his men (he has since died); Lieutenant W. A. B. Davenport was wounded at the head of his company; Lieutenant W. E. O'Connor, acting adjutant, was wounded in the engagement the evening before. I have but to mention my four remaining officers-Captain T. M. Logan, Lieuts. B. E. Nicholson, J. H. M. James, and J. J. Cleveland-all of them in command of their companies, and bearing themselves with great bravery, having shared the same dangers of their less fortunate comrades. The number of the legion was reduced more than one-half by the numerous details for skirmishers, scouts, cooks, and men barefooted, unfit for duty.

The following is a list of the casualties. Strength of battalion in action, officers and men.

I have the honor to be, your obedient servant,

M. W. Gary

Lieutenant Colonel—Commanding Hampton's Legion.[7]

Lieutenant Colonel Martin W. Gary
Hampton's Legion
*Daily Phoenix*
July 24, 1875
Hampton Legion Reunion—Remarks of Gen. Gary

At the collation served to the Hampton Legion, Lieutenant McElroy read the following toast sent by telegram by Dr. F. L. Parker: "Honor to the dead of the Hampton Legion." Gen. M. W. Gary was at once unanimously called to respond to it, and spoke as follows:

Fellow Comrades: I have endeavored in the past to respond, to the best of my humble ability, to every demand that has been made upon me by the Hampton Legion. During my long connection and association with it, whether in the bivouac in the field, no duty was ever discharged with a more sad yet ready response than the one of speaking for the dead of the Legion. I can scarcely realize that fourteen years have passed since that flag was first baptized in blood upon the field of Manassas, and that the first life that was offered up in its defense was that of the gallant Lieutenant-Colonel B. F. Johnson, who fell so soon after entering the battle, that he scarcely had time to draw his maiden sword; and close by his side fell Lieut. Yerger, with the beauty of youth upon his heroic brow. The modest but chivalrous Major J. H. Dingle fell in the bloody charge at Sharpsburg, in which that flag was shot down five different times, and when it fell the fifth time, it was being born to the front by the brave Dingle. I was a few paces to his front, when I cast an eager eye upon the three stand on colors of the enemy, who were huddled in the corner, near the stone fence hard by, and was in the act of charging again, when the intrepid Dingle was shot down; he fell with the flag on his hand, and when I stooped down over him to raise it again, it was with difficulty that I wrenched it from the hand that fondly clutched it in death.

Fifty-six out of the seventy-seven, rank and file, of our comrades who participated in that battle, had fallen under the folds of our flag in that memorable charge. In the bloody track of the Legion, lay the brave Capt. Smith, who was shot so near me that his life-blood spattered on my sash; there too, fell Capt. R. W. Thompkins, covered with glory; Lieut. Axton, in the bloom of manhood lay among the bravest of the brave; the non-commissioned officers and privates lay wounded, dying and dead—were stretched side by side—the peers in courage of any soldiers that ever fell in battle. It was amidst such havoc and death that while unfurling that flag again to the storm of battle, its staff was struck by musket balls, and its beautiful folds sent by a shot of cannon. It was there, too, I hoped to find a soldier's grave, but the talisman that I wore gave me a "charmed life," and I passed the terrific danger unharmed, and I am here tonight to give this feeble tribute to their imperishable fame. "Brief, brave and glorious was their young career."

Lt. Col. Martin W. Gary
Hampton's Legion
*Times and Democrat*
August 25, 1910

Another thrilling incident: We go now to the 17th of September, 1862, when Mart Gary was leading the Hampton legion, then infantry, in a charge, at the battle of Sharpsburg. Capt. Smith of the same legion, being shot down right by Gen. Gary and the blood was spattered all over Gary's shirt bosom. Capt. Smith was the father of W. G. Smith, the cotton manufacturer of Orangeburg, also the first cousin of R. W. Shand, of Columbia.

Lieutenant Colonel Martin W. Gary
Hampton's Legion
*Cherokee Times*
December 14, 1925

General Gary went out with the Edgefield company, which was received into the Hampton Legion and right gallantly they did their duty to the Confederacy. Gary rose to the command of the legion and fought it magnificently. He was a born fighter. It is related that at Sharpsburg, the legion, commanded by Lieut. M. W. Gary, went into the fight on the left of Hood's brigade. It had, by previous losses, been reduced to a skeleton, in fact it had only 77 men and lost in the battle 55. As they advanced Hood Williams, the color bearer, was shot down, then James Estes, then C. P. Poppenheim and finally Major Dingle fell within 50 yards of the enemy's line. Lieutenant Colonel Gary seized the colors and gallantly bore them until relieved by Marion Walton. Just to think 22 men left out of the 1,000 who volunteered.

Lieutenant Colonel Martin W. Gary
Hampton's Legion
*Edgefield Advertiser*
April 21, 1881

At Sharpsburg, Capt. R. W. Tompkins (another most Gallant officer) was killed. The officer—commanding the company after his death—requested permission of Col. Gary to have his body carried to the rear. We had just been relieved by fresh troops. He replied: "Yes, take poor Bob back to the woods and bury him, we can scarcely do more than care for our dead and wounded now." We had lost two thirds of the men whom we carried into the action. He felt sadly the loss of his men.[8]

James Harvey Dingle Jr.
1824 (?)–September 17, 1862

Harvey Dingle was registered in the 1860 census as being from Clarendon, South Carolina, and being a married farmer. He joined Hampton's Legion as a lieutenant on June 12, 1861. He was promoted to major on June 20, 1862. Dingle was noted for his bravery at Second Bull Run (Manassas). Major Dingle was killed at the Battle of Antietam "with the flag of the Legion in hand."[9]

Major Harvey Dingle
Hampton's Legion
*The Manning Times*
July 29, 1914
Historical Fact

In naming Clarendon's heroes who so gloriously laid down their lives on the field of battle that of Maj. Harvey Dingle was strangely omitted. None was so conspicuously heroic as his. It was at Sharpsburg in a crisis of the battle when our lines were heavily and repeatedly assaulted by the enemy that Major Dingle commanding the Hampton Legion caught the flag from the dying color-bearer and waving it high in the air shouted, "Legion follow your flag," and rushed forward, falling pieced by many balls. General Gary who was acting as brigadier general but in view of the Legion during the action, said it was the most bloody and desperate ever fought by that command and the conduct of Major Dingle both in deed and language surpassed any act of desperate courage he witnessed during the war.

I am unwilling that such an act of superb courage should be passed into oblivion, but would have it engraved beneath the photograph of this hero and placed upon the wall of every academy in Clarendon. It would teach a lesson to the rising generation greater and grander than ever taught by books.

T. W. Brailsford

Major Harvey Dingle
Hampton's Legion
*Charlotte Democrat*
September 30, 1862

Killed—Major Dingle, Captains Tompkins and Exum, of the Hampton Legion. Major Dingle fell with the flag of the Legion in his hand. The last words on his lips were "Legion, follow your flag."

Captain Smith of the Legion, is also supposed to be mortally wounded. Generals Starke and Branch are also killed.

## William F. Lee
## 1845 (?)–August 20, 1925

William F. Lee enlisted in Williamston, SC, on March 13, 1862. At the Battle of Antietam, he was on a cooking detail. In late December, 1862, he caught pneumonia and was sent to the hospital in Richmond, VA. He returned to the legion in March, 1863, and was captured at the Battle of Farmville, VA, on April 7, 1865; he was paroled on April 13, 1865. After the war, he settled in Pendleton, SC, and held various jobs as a farmer, construction superintendent, civil engineer, and a surveyor. He was married twice and died on August 20, 1925. He is buried at Shiloh Methodist Cemetery near Piedmont, SC.[10]

Major William F. Lee
Hampton's Legion
*The Intelligencer*
June 5, 1914
Anderson Man Saw Belle Boyd the Confederate Spy

Maj. Wm. F. Lee of Co. D., Hampton Legion says that Belle Boyd, the sixteen year old girl, was an interesting mounted figure by the side of Gen. Lee the day after the great battle of Sharpsburg. The army was assembled at Winchester for general review and her healthy and pretty face of light complexion with dark hair, while she enjoyed the splendid scene upon her prancing steed and in the protection of the great commander of Southern forces was an inspiration to the soldier boys.

Miss Boyd was born and reared somewhere in that valley.

She became a spy through having been driven from her home in fright by bodies of Yankee soldiers, one of home she shot dead in her home when he entered in assault, then after the killing she fled for refuge to her countrymen and remained with the army during the war.

## Stephen Elliot Welch
## January 12, 1843–December 19, 1938

Stephen Elliot Welch was born in Philadelphia, Pennsylvania, on January 12, 1843; his parents were visiting Philadelphia at that time, and after his birth, they decided to take up residence in the city.[11] The Welch family returned to live in Charleston, South Carolina, in 1848.

He enlisted in the Confederate Army in January, 1861, with the rank of second sergeant in the South Carolina Zouaves, which was being formed to augment the Hampton Legion, where he became first sergeant of Company "H."

He was wounded in the head at the Battle of Antietam, and rejoined his company on December 13. 1862.[12] Welch was elected by his company to second lieutenant on January 31, 1863, and was promoted to first lieutenant on January 17, 1864. He was paroled at Appomattox on April 12, 1865.[13] Soon afterwards, he rejoined his family in Charleston and was in the wholesale marketing of produce and fruit. He was married in 1871 to Laura Speer, who, in 1886, gave birth to twins. He would live for another sixty-five years after the war and died on December 19, 1938, at the age of ninety-five. He is buried at Magnolia Cemetery in Charleston, SC.[14]


## Lieutenant Stephen Elliot Welch
## Hampton's Legion
## Winchester, Va.


[Monday] Sept. 22nd 1862

My dear Parents,

Doubtless you have seen by the papers that I am among the wounded of the battle fought in Maryland. I believe I wrote you last just before crossing the Potomac into Maryland. We travelled on and were near Hagerstown, when we learned of the approach of the enemy. As they were between the rivers & ourselves we had to meet them.

Sunday, the 14th, we marched back and filled into a cross road [at Boonsboro, Maryland] where one of our batteries was firing on the Yankees but a battery of the enemy's obtained our range & we had to move. Our next position was at the foot of a deep mountain [South Mountain] and then we had to march to the top. A call was then made for 3 volunteer skirmishers & [Henry] Brandes, [George B.] Gelling & I slept out. Under one of the Lts. We pushed ahead and on reaching the crest of the mountain we saw a line of blue coats [51st Pennsylvania] not 30 yards from us. Fortunately they did not see us, so taking deliberate aim we fired & withdrew; it had the effect of astonishing them and as soon as possible they fired upon us in return, doing no damage, however. Not being ranked [in line of battle] we [four] lay down& the Yanks fired over us. During the night we retired & I was nearly captured, being only a qtr. of a mile off asleep.

I escaped and Monday & Tuesday we were in line of battle. Tuesday night we were under a terrific fire of shot & shell, but only a few were wounded, among them [Henry] Brandes, his wound is not serious but is quite painful.

Wednesday the 17th, the day opened with a hail storm of shell, grape & canister shot and until 8 A. M. we had to submit to it, but we heard the order to forward and off we went. Coming to a fence we had to climb it and then additionally expose ourselves but once over and like a hurricane we swept over the land. I stood near the flag and saw it fall but being hard at work loading I did not pick it up though it was raised by a color corporal [James E. Estes, Company "F"] before I was ready. Seeing it float again I pressed on.

The first gun I had wouldn't go off; throwing it down I found another when, like the first, [it] wouldn't shoot so I had to get a third, which [at] last fired well. After firing five or six shots I fell, doubled up & lay insensible for a while; as soon as my senses returned I felt a queer sensation on my head & found my right eye closed & ear full of blood & a pool of blood by my side, my rifle was thrown one way & hat another. Picking up my cap it bore no trace of a cut on the outside but the inside was much torn. It is really a mercy I was not torn to pieces for it appeared I never saw rain fall faster than the bullets around us.

I fired every shot at the U.S. flags and as fast as [they were] raised they fell again. We rushed to within 50 or 60 yards of their battery and the grape & canister tore immense holes through our ranks. Our reinforcements did not come up, but theirs did & on both flanks and in front we had one continued sheet of flame. All around me the bullets whistled and from a battery far on our right the shells burst upon us. A piece of shell struck me and knocked me stupid.

Never have I seen men fall so fast and thick and in about one hour's time our whole division was almost annihilated. The order was given for us to retreat and slowly, sullenly we fell back but as soon as our reinforcements arrived we forwarded up again and drove them back. As an evidence of that fire we had six color bearers shot down: the major [J. Harvey Dingle] was killed holding them up and the others were wounded.

I had to get off the field the best way I could and after hunting for several hours found the hospital where I had my head dressed. We were then sent across the Potomac to Shepherdstown [Virginia] where we almost starved but for the kindness of a lady and a gentleman whom we asked to cook a little meat for us; not content with cooking the meat she had some nice bread and preserves set out for us. On leaving we requested to call again and we did so until orders for moving to this town came. Enclosed are the names of our kind friends Mr. [John] & Mrs. [Sallie] Criswell. Save the card for me.

Winchester is quite a nice town and the people are very kind to us. In the hospital our accommodations are very scant and provisions are rather scarce but some better arrangements will be made in a day or two for us. So many soldiers have passed through the various towns in Va. & Md., that the wounded cannot by anything but we manage now & then to get something.

Our army retreated from Maryland but has again crossed into it. The Yankees did not get much of a victory. With nearly six times our force they had us almost entirely surrounded but we drove them back on the left & center and slept on the field.

I should like to see a copy of the telegraphic news; if you can get it please send it in a letter. Direct as formerly to Richmond. I have [not] received a letterform home since early August, but the movements of the army are so varied that we do not know one day where we shall be the next. I love the looks of Maryland and it was a pity to desolate such a beautiful country. After we left Frederick City [on the National Pike] we marched up the valley and climbed the Blue Ridge Mts. [at Turner's Gap] from the top of which we had a magnificent view of the vale for miles.

Such a sight, I never saw in any state. The beauty of the scenery charmed me & if I live till after the War I should like to have a farm & settle down there.

We obtained a quantity of apples of the finest sort, which were very nice indeed; we miss them now.

I am anxious to hear something of Geo. [Gelling], I have not seen anything of him or the Legion since I was wounded. I am quite well, and suffer from my head to the right. The wound is more than an inch long, on the scalp, and just touching the bone. I am thankful my life is spared, for surely it seems no one had a more narrow escape than myself. My spirits are up at high water mark.

Give my love to Sammie, Carrie, Henry, Theo & kiss Robbie for me. My love to Aunt Emily, Uncle William & family as well as Mr. & Mrs. Inness. Write whenever you have a chance & I shall do the same. God bless you my dear parents is my daily pray.

Your Affectionate Son

Elliot

Excuse errors & c.[15]


## E. Scott Carson
## September 2, 1842–October 11, 1923

E. Scott Larson enlisted as a first corporal on July 15, 1861. He was promoted quickly to third lieutenant at the Battle of Antietam, and then to captain on April 1, 1864. He led the rear guard of the legion back to Virginia. He became a POW at Appomattox on April 8, 1865, and was paroled in Farmsville, Virginia, a few weeks later. His first wife, Anne, died on November 30, 1868, and soon afterwards, he married her sister, Harriet. After the war, Carson became a farmer and later a merchant and Sheriff of Sumter County, South Carolina. He died on October 11, 1923, and is buried at Sumter Cemetery in Sumter, South Carolina.[16]


3rd Lieutenant E. Scott Carson
Hampton's Legion
*Confederate Veteran*
July, 1908
Hampton's Legion and Hood's Brigade, By E. Scott Carson, Sumter, SC

To avoid apparent egotism I have refrained from writing some things for the *Veteran*; but after reading the statement of a Federal officer, who says. "The only criticism I have to make is that there is not enough of personal experience of the boys from your side," I feel impelled to lay aside my modesty. I had the honor of being a member of the Hampton Legion in Hood's Texas Brigade, and was present at the battle of Sharpsburg. My senior officer having been killed in the early part of the engagement, the command of my company fell upon me. I have often wished that some dear comrade who was present would write some account of the part taken by the Hampton Legion, but I have seen none. While in the Texas Brigade our regiment did its hardest fighting, having been with them at Second Manassas, Boonsboro, Sharpsburg, and elsewhere, and I have no hesitancy in saying that no troops ever exhibited such bravery as did the Texas Brigade at Sharpsburg. In referring to my regiment, in our immediate front there came up three successive lines of Federal troops. We repulsed the first two; and as the third came on, being reinforced with those who had fallen back, it seemed that the whole world was in arms against us. A grander sight I never witnessed. Their new, bright flags were waving in every direction. They had, as I then thought, massed in our front. The firing was fast and furious at very close range; a gun becoming too hot or a ramrod lodging in a foul barrel, the gun was thrown down and replaced with one that had fallen from the hands of a comrade either killed or wounded. Our regiment, like the Texans, was thinned down to a mere skirmish line. Officers and men fought with the rifle, and the dead and wounded lay in heaps. The sun was obscured by the smoke that hung over us, and partly hid the horrible sight from view. Our flag fell time and again until the entire color guard was swept away, when our gallant Maj. Harvey Dingle took it up and was instantly killed, the flag falling over him. Immediately the order to "fall hack and take care of the colors" was given by our Col. Mart Gary, and with a few others I brought out the dear old flag. I heard Colonel Gary ask General Hood if we would get reinforcements. The reply was. "I have sent for them, but they are not to be had;" and General Hood wiped his eyes as the tears ran down his cheeks. I thought the day had gone against us, for we fell back, passing through the woods by Dunkard church. Coming into a field, we made another stand in the edge of the woods, awaiting the Federals, who were following us up not far off. When we fell back again, my heart leaped with joy, for I beheld the field full of fresh troops—the long-looked-for reinforcements. Kershaw's South Carolina Brigade was at hand marching in column of regiments, their brave old general at their head. They had come from Harper's Ferry; and as we passed his brigade to the rear, the General waved his hat and said: "Cheer up, men! South Carolina is not whipped yet; here are more of her boys." I thanked God and felt like a new man. They had not gone far when they wheeled into line and drove the Federals beyond Dunkard church. The Hampton Legion when halted made four or five stacks of arms and had saved the colors of their regiment. The Legion resembled an ordinary company, and did not regain its regimental appearance until we recrossed the Potomac and went into camp at Winchester, Va. The Hampton Legion was sometime afterwards placed in Jenkins's South Carolina Brigade. Think of it! six regiments of South Carolinians, the flower of the old Palmetto State, a noble and brave body of young men with as fine a man as gallant an officer to command them as ever lived. While in East Tennessee, after our failure to capture Knoxville, Colonel Gary received orders to have his regiment mounted. In the meantime he was promoted to brigadier general. Leaving Jenkins's Brigade and marching across the Blue Ridge Mountains, we came to Greenville, S.C. and received twenty days' furlough to visit home, get horses, and report back mounted to Columbia. The Legion then went to Virginia and was brigaded with Haskell's South Carolina Cavalry and the 24th Virginia Cavalry, all under the command of Gen. Mart Gary. He had the implicit confidence of his old regiment, who had served under him from the time he was made colonel, at the reorganization of the army at Yorktown, Va. He was a brave and fearless officer with a heart full of love for his old regiment, an officer who always studied the comforts and wants of his men, and did not hesitate to show by promotion his high appreciation of gallantry on the part of an officer or the most humble private in his command. Such was Gen. Mart Gary, and his blessed memory follows me through life. During our stay in Hood's Texas Brigade there had sprung-up a feeling of brotherly love between the Hampton Legion and the Texans. We placed great confidence in our Texas brothers that lasted through the war. On more than one occasion I heard the question, "What troops on our right or left?" and when the reply would come. "The Texans!" a feeling of delight and confidence would thrill the breasts of the entire regiment. I have mentioned only a few facts in connection with my old regiment, trusting they may reach the eyes of some of my comrades. 1 was taken prisoner a night or two before the surrender and after the surrender was taken in a box car to Farmville, Va. To my old comrades I would say: "When thinking of friends and loved ones whom death claimed on many hard-fought battlefields and your eyes moisten with tears, harbor no feeling of resentment, but add a fervent prayer for the good of our common country and teach our children to love it and our flag!"[17]


## Joseph D. Pinson
## February 4, 1842–May 2, 1915

Joseph D. Pinson was born on February 4, 1842. He originally enlisted in the "Bozeman Guards," which became Company "E" of Hampton's Legion, Infantry. He was promoted to third sergeant in the spring of 1863, but was shown absent in the ranks in December, 1864.[18] He and his wife, Mary, raised seven children. Pinson died on May 2, 1915, and is buried at Shady Grove Baptist Church Cemetery in Belton, South Carolina.

Private Joseph D. Pinson
Hampton's Legion
*The Intelligencer*
May 28, 1914
Battle at Sharpsburg
By Jos. D. Pinson, Company E, Hampton Legion

It was my fortune during the war to be with Gen. Lee in his Maryland campaign opposing General McClelland, who was the most able general that Gen. Lee ever fought against. After our stay in Maryland for several weeks, Gen. Lee saw that he could not transport rations for his army and not wanting to forage on the country for rations for his army, he decided to return to Virginia, crossing the Potomac river.

When he commenced his return to Virginia, the Yankees were in close pursuit and as we marched in column, men were frequently wounded while in line. Gen. Lee not wanting to be pushed on too hard decided to give them battle, then making us a short speech said: "Soldiers we will have to give them battle again and I hope you will treat them as you have always done."

Then there was a detail of men from each company for the skirmish line. As the orderly of my company was calling over the names alphabetically the captain said to me: "Pinson, you had as well volunteer they are sure to get you anyways." Then we were ordered to report to Lieut. Fields in front. This we did, but were told to wait until the others came, then we were ordered to deploy saying "now men hump yourselves and go at double quick with trail arms and get to that rock fence in front."

We gained the fence and gave a whoop as much as to say "we mean to stay here." Now Gen. Lee had formed his line of battle as he supposed facing the enemy, but was mistaken, then had to reform his lines another way that was facing them.

Then the battle commenced. Lee with his 40,000 men and McClellan with his splendid army of 87,000. The fighting was desperate and the grandeur of the sight was beyond description, as our pickets gazed upon the scene, we looked over the plain and could see the pickets on the Yankee side were doing the same as well as I can remember. Lee's line fell back some fifty yards then they faced about, reformed and fought on, in the mean time I was uneasy for field that they might force Lee back. I began to think of myself, just how I would get away in safety from that picket line. When the fight had commenced the men on the picket line quit firing at each other and stood gazing at the battle as it was going on. This fight was a drawn battle and many killed on both sides.

Then the battle closed for the night, both armies lying on their arms. All this was near the Potomac river.

General Lee that night called the generals together and consulted as best what to do. Gen. Jackson advised him to cross the river that night but Gen. Lee replied,

"No, we will fight them again tomorrow." Everything was quiet next morning. Gen. Lee sent Gen. Jackson and his chief engineer, Col Lee to a certain place, Indian Mound, telling them they could ride so far and they would have to dismount, walk and crawl to reach this place, then took observations with their field glasses. Lee remarking to Jackson: "Why General Jackson a chicken rooster could not live in front of that line," meaning the Infantry and Artillery being so well located and covering the entire front. The next day the two armies lay fronting each other all day, no fighting at all that night.

Gen. Lee had moved a part of his artillery across the river to use in case the enemy followed him in crossing the river. After we crossed the soldiers seemed as game as ever. Glad to get back into Virginia, glad to rest a while, but still willing to do our best. Willing yea, more than willing to do anything on the face of the earth that "Marse" Robert would have us do.

## The Intelligencer
## February 22, 1883

Following the lead of the new idolized Lee, the Legion with the army crossed the Potomac River near Leesburg, engaging with the enemy at Boonsboro and South Mountain, but it was at Sharpsburg on the 16th and 17th of September that death with a relentless hand decimated the ranks of this dauntless and intrepid regiment. Thinned by previous losses it went into this battle with nine commissioned officers and seventy-five rank and file. Of this number fifty privates and non-commissioned officers were killed or wounded, five commissioned officers were killed and two wounded. No single company could muster a corporal's guard, and thus dwindled a once strong regiment was for the time formed into two sparse companies. By an impetuous advance the Legion had penetrated the enemy's lines, and being flanked on each side and opposed by reinforcements in front was compelled to retreat to escape complete annihilation from the deadly concentrated fire of the foe. It was during this

Rain of Leaden Hail
That the color bearers were killed in such quick succession that the flag fell to the ground and the men hesitated to lift it; seeing it lying in the dust, Major Dingle seized it and held it aloft to seal the gallant act with his life. With devoted fortitude Private Marion Walton, of Edgefield, next rescued it and bore it safely out of sight. For this brave deed he was appointed color-sergeant. Fearing the loss of the colors under similar circumstances it was deemed best to return them to the State for safe keeping, and the Legion after this fought under a small battle flag, presented by the ladies of Lieut-Col. Logan's family. This flag was received while the Legion, on its return from Maryland, was at Charlottesville, Va.

The fruitless victory of Sharpsburg caused the return of the army and after a few weeks of camp life in the Valley of Virginia, the Legion marched to Fredericksburg and went into winter quarters.

*Edgefield Advertiser*
May 6, 1863
Our Dead in Maryland

The following is a list of the South Carolina soldiers who died in action or from disease during the Maryland campaign, and were buried near Frederick City, Md. Relatives and friends desiring information as to the removal of remains should address W. G. Harrison, Baltimore, or Lewis Cruger, Esq., Richmond:

*No Regiments Named*—F. M. Tuck, Joseph Jeringham.

*Hampton Legion*—Joseph Budd, Company K; A. V. Kennerly.[19]

*The Intelligencer*
July 8, 1869
Dead Confederate Soldiers

The following soldiers from South Carolina are buried in the Confederate Cemetery at Shepherdstown, Virginia:

S. L. Robinson, Brooks' Artillery; Samuel Canty, Company D, 16th Regiment; M. Banks, Hampton's Legion; E. J. Rogers, Spartanburg; Captain H. J. Smith, Company D, Hampton's Legion; J. E. Dawkins, Union District.

The cemetery is now under the exclusive control of the Memorial Association, composed of the surviving Confederate soldiers, and efforts are making to raise funds to erect a handsome monument over the dead, and to remove those who fell at Sharpsburg to this cemetery.

Persons who wish to learn anything about Confederate graves at this place or Sharpsburg, or who may wish to contribute their mite to the "Monument Fund," will have their letters promptly answered by addressing,

Joseph McMurran

*Daily Phoenix*
July 22, 1875
Houston, Texas, July 12, 1875

Gen. Wade Hampton, President Hampton Legion Reunion—My Dear Sir: I see by the papers that you are to have a reunion of your old and glorious Legion survivors on the 21st, and I have the pleasure to herewith send a portion of the proceedings of our reunion, had at Huntrodon, Texas; and as we do, and always have, at all of our meetings, considered the Hampton Legion a part and parcel of the Texas Brigade, I trust you will appoint a Committee on Statistics, to act in conjunction with a like committee of our association of which Gen. J. P. Robinson, of Austin is Chairman, and Gen. M. W. Gary having been appointed by us on said committee.

Our next annual meeting will be held at Bryant, Texas, on the second Wednesday in July, 1876; and you and each and every member of your glorious command are most cordially invited to attend. We assure you that you will all be most heartily welcomed to Texas. All transportation companies will pass you in Texas at half rates; and in addition, the people will not allow any of us to pay any bills. Every town is, and always will be free, in Texas, to the Hampton Legion; so come along, as many as you can. Nothing would give us greater pleasure that to take you all by the hand and welcome you to Texas.[20] Our hearts reach out to you as to brothers, and God knows we would be delighted to see you, and have you meet with us. May the blessing of God rest upon you all, as it should upon such glorious men as compose the Hampton Legion; and may your meeting be the result of much good; and if we should never meet again upon this earthly camping ground, may we all meet "over the river," in that eternal camping ground, where all true soldiers have a right to go. I am, with great respect, very truly, your comrade, Robert Burns, Sec. Hood's Texas Brigade Association.

# Generals and Commanders Correspondence

## John Bell Hood
### June 29, 1831–August 30, 1879

John Bell Hood was born in Owingsville, Kentucky, on June 29, 1831. He graduated from West Point in 1853, and served in California and in the famous 2nd U.S. Cavalry Regiment in Texas under Colonel Albert Sidney Johnston and Lt. Colonel Robert E. Lee. He immediately resigned his commission in the U.S. Army after the firing upon Ft. Sumter and cast lot with the Confederate Army.

He rapidly advanced in rank and distinguished himself in the Confederate Army as a regimental, brigade, and division commander within the ANV.

At the Battle of Gaines' Mill, Brigadier General Hood led his old regiment, the 4th Texas Infantry, on a successful charge against Union fortifications. As division commander under General James Longstreet, he again distinguished himself in the battles of Second Bull Run (Second Manassas), Antietam (Sharpsburg), and Fredericksburg. During the Battle of Gettysburg on July 2, 1863, Major General Hood was severely wounded in the left arm by an exploding artillery shell above his head while leading his brigade in the assault of the Devil's Den and Little Round Top.

At the Battle of Chickamauga on September 20, 1863, he was again severely wounded, this time in the right leg by a Minié ball, and was reported dead on the field. However, the doctors were able to save him with the cost of amputating his leg.

He was appointed lieutenant general on February 1, 1864, and full general with temporary rank on July 18, 1864. His corps was repulsed in the battles of Peachtree Creek, Atlanta, Ezra Church, and Jonesboro. He led his corps that was defeated at the battle of Franklin on November 30, 1864, and six of his generals would be killed in action on the same day. He reverted back to his rank of lieutenant general and surrendered himself in Natchez, Mississippi, where he was paroled on May 31, 1865. After the war, Hood and his family resided in New Orleans, where, on August

General John Bell Hood, photograph taken when he was the commanding colonel of the 4th Texas Infantry, *c.* 1861–1862. (*Library of Congress*)

30, 1879, he died from yellow fever along with his wife and one of their children.[1] He is buried at Metairie Cemetery in New Orleans, Louisiana.

General Hood was beloved within the Texas Brigade, where the men would remember his gallant leadership within the Army of Northern Virginia.

**Brigadier General John Bell Hood**
**Senior Brigade Commander**
**Division Headquarters**
**September 27, 1862**

Maj. G. Moxley Sorrell,
Assistant Adjutant General,

Sir: I have the honor to submit the following report of the operations of this division, composed of two brigades—Fourth Alabama, Second and Eleventh Mississippi, and Sixth North Carolina, Col. E. M. Law commanding; my own brigade, First Fourth, and Fifth Texas, Eighteenth Georgia, and Hampton Legion, and Reilly's, Bachman's, and Garden's batteries, Maj. B. W. Frobel commanding—in the engagements at Freeman's Ford, on the Rappahannock River, August 22; plains of Manassas, August 29 and 30; Boonsborough Gap, Md., September 14, and Sharpsburg, Md., September 16 and 17.

The next day [September 1], after burying the dead, the march was continued [from vicinity of Smiley Ford, Va.] to Sudley Ford and from thence to Hagerstown, Md., via Frederick City, crossing the Potomac at White's Ford, near Leesburg.

On the morning of September 14, we marched back to Boonsborough Gap, a distance of some 13 miles. This division, arriving between 3 and 4 p.m., found the troops of General D. H. Hill engaged with a large force of the enemy. By direction of the general commanding, I took up my position immediately on the left of the pike. Soon, orders came to change over to the right, I met General Drayton's brigade coming out, saving the enemy had succeeded in passing to their rear. I at once inclined more to the right over a very rugged country and succeeded in getting in a position to receive the enemy. I at once ordered the Texas Brigade, Col. W. T. Wofford commanding, and the Third Brigade, Col. E. M. Law commanding, to move forward with bayonets fixed, which they did with their usual gallantry, driving the enemy and regaining all of our lost ground, when night came on and further pursuit ceased. On the field, fell, mortally wounded, Lieut. Col. O. K. McLemore, of the Fourth Alabama, a most efficient, gallant, and valuable officer.

Soon after night, orders were received to withdraw and for this division to constitute the rear guard of the army. The march was accordingly taken up in the direction of Sharpsburg. Arriving on the heights across the Antietam River near the town, about 12 m. on the 15th instant, I was ordered to take position in line of battle on the right of the road leading to Boonsborough, but soon received orders to move to the extreme left, near Saint Mumma Church, on the Hagerstown pike, remaining in this position, under fire of the shells from the enemy, until early sunset on the evening of the 16th. The enemy, having crossed higher up the Antietam, made an attack upon the left flank of our line of battle, the troops of this division being the only forces, on our side, engaged. We succeeded in check and driving back the enemy a short distance, when night came on, and soon firing ceased. During the engagement, the brave and efficient Col. P. F. Liddell, Eleventh Mississippi, fell, mortally wounded. The officers and men of my command having been without food for three days, except half a ration of beef for one day, and green corn, General Lawton, with two brigades, was directed to take my position, to enable my men to cook.

On the morning of the 17th instant, about 3 o'clock, the firing commenced along the line occupied by General Lawton. At 6 o'clock I received a notice from him that he would require all the assistance I could give him. A few minutes after, a member of his staff reported to me that he was wounded and wished me to come forward as soon as possible. Being in readiness, I at once marched out on the field in line of battle and soon became engaged with an immense force of the enemy, consisting of not less than two corps of their army. It was here I witnessed the most terrible clash of arms, by far, that has occurred during the war. The two little giant brigades of this division wrestled with this mighty force, losing hundreds of their gallant officers and men but driving the enemy from his position and forcing him to abandon his guns on our left. The battle raged with the greatest fury until about 9 o'clock, the enemy being driven from 400 to 500 yards. Fighting, as we were, at right angles with the general line of battle, and General Ripley's brigade being the extreme left of General D. H. Hill's forces and continuing to hold their ground, caused the enemy to pour in a heavy fire upon the rear and right flank of Colonel Law's brigade, rendering it necessary to move the division to the left and rear into the woods near the Saint Mumma church, which we continued to hold until 10 a.m., when General McLaws arrived with his command, which at once was formed in line and moved forward, engaging the enemy. My command was marched to the rear, ammunition replenished, and return at 12 m., talking position, by direction of the general commanding, in rear of the church, with orders to hold it. About 4 p.m., by order, the division moved to the right, near the center, and remained there until the night of the 18th instant, when orders were received to recross the Potomac.

I would respectfully state that in the morning about 4 a.m. I sent Major Blanton, aide-de-camp, to Maj. Gen. D. H. Hill to know if he could furnish any troops to assist in holding the left of our position. He replied that he could not; and the major-general command is aware of the number of messages received from me asking for reinforcements, which I felt were absolutely required after seeing the great strength of the enemy in my front, and I am thoroughly of the opinion had General McLaws arrived by 8.30 a.m. our victory on the left would have been as thorough, quick, and complete as upon the plains of Manassas on August 30.

During the engagement, Major [J. H.] Dingle, Jr., of Hampton's Legion, gallantly bearing the colors of his regiment; Major [Matt.] Dale, First Texas, and Major [T. S.] Evans, Eleventh Mississippi, fell, while leading their brave regiments against ten times their numbers.

Colonel [J. M.] Stone, Lieutenant-Colonel [D. W.] Humphreys, and Major [J. A.] Blair, Second Mississippi; Lieutenant-Colonel [S. F.] Butler. Eleventh Mississippi; Captain [L. H.] Scruggs, Fourth Alabama, and Major [R. F.] Webb, Sixth North Carolina, also received severe wounds.

Conspicuous were Colonel Law and Wofford, commanding brigades. Lieutenant-Colonel Gary, commanding Hampton's Legion; Lieut. Col. P. A. Work, commanding First Texas; Lieut. Col. B. F. Carter, commanding Fourth Texas; Captain Turner, commanding Fifth Texas, although not wounded, deserve great credit for their skillful management and coolness during the battle.

It is but justice to Col. J. C. G. Key, Fourth Texas, to state that he was present at the battles of Boonsborough Gap and Sharpsburg, although unable to take command of his regiment, in consequence of a severe wound received at the battle of Gaines' Farm, June 27.

During this engagement and that of the battle of Manassas, Reilly's, Bachman's, and Garden's batteries were admirably handled by the battery commanders; Maj. B. W. Frobel commanding, acting with great coolness of my staff, the chief,

Maj. W. H. Sellers, having his horse shot while ably directing the Texas brigade at the battle of Manassas during the time of my being sent for by the general commanding to receive additional orders. He has proven himself competent to command a brigade under all circumstances. This distinguished officer, together with my two aides (Maj. B. H. Blanton and Lieut. James Hamilton) had their horses shot during the battle of Sharpsburg while most gallantly pushing forward the troops and transmitting orders, Major Blanton, Lieutenant Hamilton, Lieut. Joseph Phillips, C.S. Army, of General Magruder's staff, and Capt. C. S. Mills, assistant quartermaster First Texas Regiment, rendered invaluable service during the battle of Manassas in bringing forward and placing in position additional brigades upon the long to be remembered heights around the Chinn House.

Lieut. D. L. Sublett, acting division ordinance officer, was prompt in bringing forward ammunition, and otherwise efficiently performed the duties pertaining to his department.

All praise is due Dr. [John T.] Darby, chief surgeon of this division, for his untiring efforts and skillful manner in caring for the numerous wounded.

Dr. [E. J.] Roach, senior surgeon Texas Brigade, and Dr. [H. H.] Hubbard, senior surgeon Law's brigade, Dr. Breckinridge, and all other surgeons and assistant surgeons of this command, have my heartfelt thanks for their valuable services.

I would be wrong in not acknowledging the valuable services rendered during the several engagements, in transmitting orders, of the following couriers of this command: M. M. Templeman, T. W. C. Lake, J. P. Mahoney, James Malone, W. E. Duncan, J. A. Mann, W. J. Barbee, W. G. Jesse, J. I. Haggerty, and J. H. Drake.

For additional particulars, reference is made to the reports of brigade and regimental commanders, herewith respectfully submitted.

Below will be found a report of casualties.

I am, sir, very respectfully, your obedient servant,

J. B. Hood

Brigadier-General, Commanding Division.[2]

## Lieutenant General John Bell Hood

The morning of the 15th our forces were again in motion in the direction of the Antietam; the cavalry and my two brigades, in addition to Major Frobel's artillery, formed the rear guard to hold our opponents in check, whilst the Army marched quietly to its destination. My troops, at this period, were sorely in need of shoes, clothing and food. We had issued to us no meat for several days, and little or no bread; the men had been forced to subsist principally on green corn and green apples. Nevertheless, they were in high spirits and defiant, as we contended with the advanced guard of McClellan the 15th and forenoon of the 16th. During the afternoon of this day I was ordered, after great fatigue and hunger endured by my soldiers, to take position near the

Hagerstown pike, in an open field in front of Dunkard Church. General Hooker's Corps crossed the Antietam, swung round with its right on the pike, and, about an hour before sunset, encountered my division.

I had stationed one or two batteries upon a hillock, in a meadow, near the edge of a corn field and just by the pike. The Texas brigade had been disposed on the left, and that of Law on the right. We opened fire, and a spirited action ensued, which lasted till a late hour in the night. When the firing had in a great measure ceased, we were so close to the enemy that we could distinctly hear him massing his heavy bodies in our immediate front.

The extreme suffering of my troops for want of food induced me to ride back to General Lee, and request him to send two or more brigades to our relief, at least for the night, in order that the soldiers might have a chance to cook their meagre rations. He said that he would cheerfully do so, but he knew of no command which could be spared for the purpose; he, however, suggested I should see General Jackson and endeavor to obtain assistance from him. After riding a long time in search of the latter, I finally discovered him alone, lying upon the ground, asleep by the root of a tree. I aroused him and made known the half-starved condition of my troops; he immediately ordered Lawton's, Trimble's and Hays's brigades to our relief He exacted of me, however, a promise that I would come to the support of these forces the moment I was called upon. I quickly rode off in search of my wagons, that the men might prepare and cook their flour, as we were still without meat; unfortunately the night was then far advanced, and, although every effort was made amid the darkness to get the wagons forward, dawn of the morning of the 17th broke upon us before many of the men had had time to do more than prepare the dough. Soon thereafter an officer of Lawton's staff dashed up to me, saying, "General Lawton sends his compliments with the request that you come at once to his support." (In my official report erroneously called St. Mumma's Church.) "To arms" was instantly sounded, and quite a large number of my brave soldiers were again obliged to march to the front, leaving their uncooked rations in camp.

Still, indomitable amid every trial, they moved off by the right flank to occupy the same position we had left the night previous. As we passed, about sunrise, across the pike and through the gap in the fence just in front of Dunkard Church, General Lawton, who had been wounded, was borne to the rear upon a litter, and the only Confederate troops, left on that part of the field, were some forty men who had rallied round the gallant Harry Hays. I rode up to the latter, and, finding that his soldiers had expended all their ammunition, I suggested to him to retire, to replenish his cartridge boxes, and reassemble his command. The following extract from the official report of General Jackson will convey an idea of the bloody conflict in which my two little brigades were about to engage:

General Lawton, commanding division, and Colonel Walker, commanding brigade, were severely wounded. More than half of the brigades of Lawton and Hays were either killed or wounded, and more than a third of Trimble's, and all the regimental commanders in those brigades, except two, were killed or wounded. Thinned in their ranks, and exhausted of their ammunition, Jackson's Division and the brigades of Lawton, Trimble and Hays retired to the rear, and Hood, of Long-street's command, again took the position from which he had been before relieved." Not distant in our front were drawn up, in close array, heavy columns of Federal infantry; not less than two corps were in sight to oppose my small command, numbering, approximately, two thousand effectives. However, with the trusty Law on my right, in the edge of the wood, and the gallant Colonel Wofford in command of the Texas brigade on the left, near the pike, we moved forward to the assault. Not-withstanding the overwhelming odds of over ten to one against us. We drove the enemy from the wood and cornfield back upon his reserves, and forced him to abandon his guns on our left. This most deadly combat raged till our last round of ammunition was expended. The First Texas Regiment had lost, in the corn field, fully two-thirds of its number; and whole ranks of brave men, whose deeds were unrecorded save in the hearts of loved ones at home, were mowed down in heaps to the right and left. Never before was I so continuously troubled with fear that my horse would further injure some wounded fellow soldier, lying helpless upon the ground.

Our right flank, during this short, but seemingly long, space of time, was toward the main line of the Federals, and, after several ineffectual efforts to procure reinforcements and our last shot had been fired, I ordered my troops back to Dunkard Church, for the same reason which had previously compelled Lawton, Hays and Trimble to retire.

My command remained near the church, with empty cartridge boxes, holding aloft their colors whilst Frobel's batteries rendered most effective service in position further to the right, where nearly all the guns of the battalion were disabled.

Upon the arrival of McLaws's Division, we marched to the rear, renewed our supply of ammunition, and returned to our position in the wood, near the church, which ground we held till a late hour in the afternoon, when we moved somewhat further to the right and bivouacked for the night. With the close of this bloody day ceased the hardest fought battle of the war.

In the Military Biography of Stonewall Jackson, edited by Rev. J. Wm. Jones, D.D., occur the following passages (pp. 330–31) in reference to this engagement: "Seeing Hood in their path the enemy paused, and a Northern correspondent writes: 'While our advance rather faltered, the rebels, greatly reinforced, made a sudden and impetuous onset,* and drove our gallant fellows back over a portion of the hard won field. What we had (*The aforementioned large reinforcements were my two small brigades.) won, however, was not relinquished without a desperate struggle, and here, up the hills and down, through the woods and the standing corn, over the ploughed land and clover, the line of fire swept to and fro as one side or the other gained a temporary advantage. "Hood was now fighting with his right toward the main line of the enemy, for General Hooker had swept round so far, that, as we have said, his line was almost at right angles with its original position. Hood threw himself into the action with great gallantry, and says in his report:

Here I witnessed the most terrible clash of arms by far that has occurred during the war. The two little giant brigades of my command wrestled with the mighty force, and although they lost hundreds of their officers and men, they drove them from their position, and forced them to abandon their guns on our left. One of these brigades numbered only eight hundred and fifty-four (854) men."

The following morning I arose before dawn and rode to the front where, just after daybreak, General Jackson came pacing up on his horse, and instantly asked, "Hood, have they gone?" When I answered in the negative, he replied "I hoped they had," and then passed on to look after his brave but greatly exhausted command.

The subjoined letter, I have no doubt, obtained my promotion about this period. I had no knowledge of its existence until after the close of the war, when it was handed to me in New York by Mr. Meyer, to whom I am indebted for the favor. He was at the time of the surrender a clerk in the War Office, at Richmond, and, in consideration of the unsettled condition of affairs, placed it among his papers for preservation:

Headquarters, V. Dist. Sept. 27th, 1862

General:—I respectfully recommend that Brig. Genl. J. B. Hood be promoted to the rank of a Major General. He was under my command during the engagements along the Chickahominy, commencing on the 27th of June last, when he rendered distinguished service. Though not of my command in the recently hard fought battle near Sharpsburg, Maryland, yet for a portion of the day I had occasion to give directions respecting his operations, and it gives me pleasure to say that his duties were discharged with such ability and zeal, as to command my admiration. I regard him as one of the most promising officers of the army.

I am, General, your obedient servant, (Signed) T. J. Jackson.

Major S. Cooper,
Adjutant and Inspector General, C. 8. A.
Endorsed, New York, November 9, 1866

The enclosed letter from General Jackson to General Cooper was handed to General Hood by Mr. Meyer (a former clerk in the War Department at Richmond), at the Southern Hotel in this city. The letter is the original, and preserved by Mr. Meyer. (Signed) F. S. Stockdale.

The foregoing letter is doubly kind in its tenor, inasmuch as I was not serving in General Jackson's Corps at the time. During the 18th, the Confederate Army remained in possession of the field, buried the dead, and that night crossed near Shepherdstown to the south side of the Potomac. Soon thereafter my division marched to a point north of Winchester, and passed a pleasant month in the beautiful Valley of the Shenandoah. My arrest, which General Lee, just prior to the battle of Boonsboro' Gap, had been gracious enough to suspend, was never reconsidered; the temporary release became permanent, and, in lieu of being summoned to a Court Martial, I was shortly afterwards promoted to the rank of Major General with the command of two additional brigades.

The accession of Benning's and Anderson's brigades, which had already taken part in a number of battles, composed a division which any general might justly have felt honored to command. The former brigade had been gallantly led by General Toombs at Sharpsburg. I experienced much interest in training these troops, as I endeavored to excite emulation among them and thoroughly arouse their pride, in accordance with the system of education I had pursued with the Fourth Texas Regiment, Law's, and my original brigade. Under the unfortunate organization of brigades by States, I lost the Eighteenth Georgia Regiment and Hampton's Legion, to both of which commands, I, as well as my Texas troops, had become warmly attached. The former had served with me longer than the latter, and in every emergency had proved itself bold and trusty; it styled itself, from a feeling of brotherhood, the Third Texas.

Whilst I lost these two excellent bodies of men, I gained the Third Arkansas, a large regiment, commanded by Colonel Van Manning, a brave and accomplished soldier, who served with distinction, and, in truth, merited higher rank and a larger command. I also lost the Sixth North Carolina, Ninth and Eleventh Mississippi Regiments, which, after long and gallant service in Law's brigade, were also transferred to other commands; thus, unfortunately, were severed relations which had been engendered and strengthened by common trials and dangers.

The latter part of October McClellan's movements determined General Lee to withdraw from the Valley of the Shenandoah, leaving his cavalry in rear, and to return to the Valley of the Rappahannock. Accordingly, my division took its place, about the 26th, in the marching columns of Longstreet's Corps, which moved in the direction of the latter point. During the previous month of quiet and rest, the troops had received a supply of shoes and clothing, and had improved in drill and discipline. This splendid corps, therefore, exhibited a very different appearance from that which it presented in its ragged and bare-footed condition, a short period before in Maryland. We halted in the vicinity of Culpepper Court House, where shortly afterwards intelligence was received that McClellan had been superseded by the appointment of Burnside. This General promptly made a demonstration on the Upper Rappahannock, as he moved towards Fredericksburg. General Lee crossed to the south side of the Rapidan, and, by the latter part of November, the Federal and Confederate Armies again confronted one another at Fredericksburg, where we quietly awaited the development of events.[3]

## William T. Wofford
## June 28, 1824–May 22, 1884

William T. Wofford was born in Haversham, Georgia, on June 28, 1824. Later, he served as captain of a battalion of Georgia mounted volunteers during the Mexican War. He served in the state legislature from 1849 to 1853. He was a member of the Georgia secession convention in 1861, and voted against secession.

However, after Georgia seceded from the Union, he joined the Confederate Army as colonel of the 18th Georgia Infantry. He took part in the 1862 campaign around Richmond in Hood's Texas Brigade.

As senior colonel of the Texas Brigade, he would command the regiments at Second Bull Run (Manassas), South Mountain, and Antietam (Sharpsburg). After Antietam, the 18th Georgia would transfer to T. R. R. Cobb's Georgia Brigade, and he succeeded General Cobb when Cobb was killed at the Battle of Fredericksburg on December 13, 1862.

He was promoted to brigadier general on January 17, 1863, and was with the 1st Corps until the end of the war. He was paroled at Resaca, Georgia, on May 2, 1865.

General Wofford was elected to the United States House of Representatives; however, Republican radicals refused his seat. He was active in the Georgia railroad system and served as a trustee of several educational institutions. He died near Cass Station, Georgia, on May 22, 1884, and is buried in Cassville Cemetery.[4]

Colonel William Wofford
Commanding Officer, Texas Brigade
Headquarters Texas Brigade
September 29, 1862.
Captain W. H. Sellers

Adjutant-General

Sir: I have the honor to report the part performed by this command in the engagements on the evening of the 16th and throughout the day of the 17th instant at Sharpsburg, Md., without referring to the various positions which we occupied after halting the field.

On the morning of the 15th instant, our division being in the rear of the army from Boonsborough Mountain, this brigade was moved from in front of Sharpsburg on the evening of the 15th to the right and in front of Mumma Church, this being the left of our line and where the main and most of the fighting took place on the 17th instant. While we were moving to this position, the enemy opened a heavy fire upon us from their long-range guns, which was continued after we were in position, and resulted in the wounding of 1 lieutenant and 1 soldier in the Fourth Texas Regiment. We remained in this position the balance of the day and night of the 15th and until late in the evening of the 16th, when we were ordered by General Hood to move by the left flank through the open field in front of the church and to its left about 700 yards, to meet the enemy, who it was then ascertained, had commenced to cross Antietam Creek to our left. We then formed line of battle and moved up to acorn-field in our front, and awaited the advance of the enemy, who had, by this time, opened upon us a brisk fire of shot and shell from some pieces of artillery which they had placed in position immediately in our front and to the left of our lines, wounding 1 officers and some dozen men.

I feel it due to truth to state that the enemy were informed of our position by the firing of a half dozen shots from a little battery of ours on the left of the brigade, which hastily beat a retreat as soon as their guns opened upon us.

While our line of battle rested upon the corn-field, Captain Turner commanding the Fifth Texas, which was our right, had been moved forward into some woods, where he met a part of our skirmishers driven in by the enemy, whom he engaged and finally drove back, with the loss of 1 man. Our skirmishers, consisting of 100 men, under the command of Captain [W. H.] Martin, of the Fourth Texas, who had been moved into the woods in front and to the left of the Fifth Texas, were hotly engaged with the enemy, but held their ground until they had expended all their cartridges, and then fell into our line of battle, about 9 o'clock at night, about which time we were relieved by General Lawton's brigade, and were withdrawn from the field to the woods in rear of Mumma Church for the purpose of cooking rations, our men not having received any regular allowance in three days.

It was now evident that the enemy had effected a crossing entirely to our left, and that he would make the attack on that wing early in the morning, moving his forces over and placing them in position during the night.

At 3 o'clock in the morning of the 17th the picket firing was heavy, and at daylight the battle was opened. Our brigade was moved forward, at sunrise, to the support of General Lawton, who had relieved us the night before. Moving forward in line of battle in the regular order of regiments, the brigade proceeded through the woods into the open field toward the corn-field, where the left encountered the first line of the enemy. Seeing Hampton's Legion and Eighteenth Georgia moving slowly forward, but rapidly firing, I rode hastily to them, urging them forward, when I saw two full regiments, one in their front and the other party to their left. Perceiving at once that they were in danger of being cut off, I ordered the First Texas to move by the left flank to their relief, which they did in a rapid and gallant manner. By this time, the enemy on our left having connected falling back, the First Texas pressed them rapidly to their guns, which now poured into them a fire on their right flank, center, and left flank from three different batteries, before which their well-formed line was cut down and scattered; being 200 yards in front of our line, their situation was most critical. Riding back to the left of our line, I found the fragment of the Eighteenth Georgia Regiment in front of the extreme right battery of the enemy, located on the pike running by the church, which now opened upon our thinned ranks a most destructive fire. The men and officers were gallantly shooting down the gunners, and for a moment silenced them. At this time the enemy's fire was most terrific, their first line of infantry having been driven back to their guns, which now opened a furious fire, together with their second line of infantry, upon our thinned and almost annihilated ranks.

By this time, our brigade having suffered so greatly, I was satisfied that they could neither advance nor hold their position much long without re-enforcements. Riding back to make known to General Hood our condition, I met with you, to whom I imparted this information. By this time our line commenced giving way, when I ordered them back under cover of the woods to the left of the church, where we halted and waited for support, none arriving. After some time the enemy commenced advancing in full force. Seeing the hopelessness and folly of making a stand with our shattered brigade and a remnant from other commands, the men being greatly exhausted and many of them out of ammunition, I determined to fall back to a fence in our rear, where we met the long looked for re-enforcements, and at the same time received an order from General Hood to fall back farther to the rear to rest and collect our men. After resting a short time, we were moved back to the woods in rear of the church from where we advanced to the fight in the morning, which position we held until late in the evening, when we were moved by the right flank in the direction of Sharpsburg to a place near the center of our line, where we remained during that night and next day, and until the re-crossing of the Potomac by our army was ordered.

During the engagement of the brigade on the 17th instant I was drawn to the left of our line, as it first engaged the enemy, who succeeded in flanking us on the left, and, to escape from being surrounded, changed the direction to left-oblique, thus causing large intervals between the regiments on the left and right of the line. The Fifth Texas, under the command of Captain Turner, moved with spirit across the field and occupied the woods on our right, where it met the enemy and drove and held them back until their ammunition was exhausted, and then fell back to the woods with the balance of the brigade. The Fourth Texas Regiment, which, in our line of battle, was beaten between the Fifth and First Texas, was moved by General Hood to the extreme left of our line on the pike road, covering our flank by holding the enemy in check.

This brigade went into the action numbering 854, and lost, in killed, wounded, and missing, 560—over one-half. We have to mourn the loss of Major Dale, of the First Texas, and Dingle, of Hampton's Legion, two gallant officers, who fell in the thickest of the fight; also Captains [R. W.] Tompkins and [H. J.] Smith, and Lieutenant [James J.] Exum, of Hampton's Legion; Lieutenants [T. C.] Underwood and [J. M. D.] Cleveland, of the Eighteenth Georgia; Lieutenants [F. L.] Hoffman, [P.] Runnells, [J.] Waterhouse, [S. F.] Patton, and [G. B.] Thompson, of the First Texas. These brave deserved a better fate than to have been, as they were, sacrificed for want of proper support.

The enemy, besides being permitted to cross the creek, with scarcely any resistance, to our left, were allowed to place their artillery in position during the night, not only without annoyance but without our knowledge.

Without specially naming the officers and men who stood firmly at their post during the whole of this terrible conflict, I feel pleased to bear testimony, with few exceptions, to the gallantry of the whole brigade. They fought desperately; their conduct was never surpassed. Fragments of regiments, as they were, they moved boldly upon and drove before them the crowded lines of the enemy up to their cannon's mouth, and, with a heroism unsurpassed, fired upon their gunners, desperately struggling before yielding, which they had never been forced to do before.

I here with the transmit the reports of Captain Turner, commanding the Fifth Texas Regiment; Lieutenant-Colonel Carter, commanding the Fourth Texas; Lieutenant-Colonel Work, commanding the First Texas; Lieutenant-Colonel Ruff, commanding the Eighteenth Georgia, and Lieutenant-Colonel Gray, commanding Hampton's Legion.

Respectfully submitted,

WM. T. Wofford

Colonel, Commanding Brigade.[5]

## Jerome B. Robertson
## March 14, 1815–January 7, 1890

Jerome B. Robertson was born in Woodford County, Kentucky, on March 14, 1815. He attended medical school at Transylvania College and began practicing medicine in 1835. Dr. Robertson was elected as lieutenant in a company of Kentucky volunteers bound for Texas to join in the Texas Revolution. Arriving in Texas after the Battle of San Jacinto, he volunteered to serve in the army of the Republic of Texas for a year. In 1837, he returned to Kentucky to settle business affairs before moving to Texas permanently.

He settled at historic Washington-on-the Brazos in Washington County, Texas, and married the following year. He was the coroner of Washington County and represented the County in the Texas Legislature and Senate.

A vocal secessionist, he represented Washington County at the secession convention and after Texas seceded, he raised a company of volunteers from Washington County, which later became Company "I" of the 5th Texas Infantry Regiment. He rose rapidly in rank to colonel and commanded the 5th Texas during the summer of 1862, and was promoted to brigadier general in November, 1862. He commanded this Brigade at the crucial Battle of Gettysburg, where on July 2, 1863, was seriously wounded charging in front of his company at Little Round Top. Later, he would command the Brigade at the Battle of Chickamauga.

In the spring of 1864, after a misunderstanding with Generals Longstreet and Jenkins, he returned to Texas where he commanded the reserve forces in the state. After the war, he was active in the Masonic Lodge and the Texas Grand Lodge. He helped organize Hood's Texas Brigade Association and served as president of this veterans association eleven times. In 1879, he moved to Waco, Texas, to be near his only living son, General Felix H. Robertson. He died at his son's home in Waco on January 7, 1890, and is buried at Oakwood Cemetery in Waco, Texas.[6]

## Colonel Jerome B. Robertson
## Commanding Officer, 5th Texas Infantry

Request That the Brigade be Sent South and Praise for General Hood
Camp Near Winchester, Va., Oct 1, 1862.

Hon. W. S. Oldham, Richmond—Dear Sir, Enclose I send you and address to the President, setting forth the condition of our Brigade, and asking to have it removed to some point further south, if the army is to go into winter quarters. If active operations are to be commenced, we, of course, expect to participate in them. You are aware of the fact that the Brigade has marched from Richmond. That is one cause of our small numbers. The list of casualties in the battles we have been in shows the main cause.

I hope you will use whatever influence you have in making General Hood a major general. I ask this of you because I believe the best interest of the service will be promoted by it, and not from any motive of personal favoritism. I have seen him in camp, on the march, and on the battlefield; and confidently declare that he is one of the best officers we have. Without intending to cast blame on anyone, I have no hesitation in believing that, if Gen. Hood's urgent representations from before daybreak up to 10 a.m. on the day of the battle of Sharpsburg had been acted upon, our victory there would have been complete. At Manassas he put in every Brigade on our right, and in doing it showed superior judgment and skill. We need such officers badly, and I hope you will assist to promote him. You can show this to the President, if you think proper. I would rather you do so, as I know I speak the universal sentiment of both officers and men. Will you please write, and let me know what reception the papers I send get. Have you any news of anymore Texas troops being on the way here, or of any having been ordered here? I intend to address all our delegation. Hope you will show this to as many of them as feel disposed to join you in rendering us what service you can in the matter.

Our wounded are doing well.

Respectfully, your friend and obt. servant,

J. B. Robertson[7]

## Evander M. Law
## August 7, 1836–October 31, 1920

Evander M. Law was born in Darlington, South Carolina, on August 7, 1836. In 1856, he graduated from the South Carolina Military Academy. He taught at the Military High School in Tuskegee, Alabama, and recruited a company from the school when Alabama seceded from the Union.

He was elected lieutenant colonel of the 4th Alabama Infantry, and was severely wounded at the battle of First Bull Run (Manassas) on July 16, 1861, and was elected as colonel in November, 1861. Law led the 4th Alabama at the battles around Richmond, Second Bull Run (Manassas), and Antietam.

He was promoted to brigadier general on October 2, 1862, and led his Alabama Brigade as a part of Hood's Division, within Longstreet's Corps. At the Battle of Gettysburg on July 2, 1863, General Law led the Texas Brigade alongside his Alabama Brigade at the assault on the Devil's Den and Little Round Top. When General Hood was wounded at the Battle of Chickamauga, Law commanded Hood's Division. He was wounded at the Battle of Cold Harbor, and after recovering, he requested to be relieved of duty within the ANV.

Afterwards, he commanded a cavalry force under General Joseph E. Johnston until the war was over. After the war, General Law helped found the foundation of the educational system in Florida and was an active newspaperman. He died on October 31, 1920, and is buried at Oakwood Cemetery in Barstow, Florida.[8]

## Colonel Evander M. Law
## Commanding Officer, Alabama Brigade

Headquarters Third Brigade,
October 2, 1862.
Captain W. H. Sellers,
Assistant Adjutant-General.

SIR: I have the honor to report the part taken by my command in the engagements at Sharpsburg, Md., on September 16 and 17.

When the army arrived at the height on the south side of Antietam river on the morning of the 15th, I was ordered to take position about a mile from Sharpsburg, on the Hagerstown turnpike. The right of my brigade rested at Saint Mumma's Church (Dunkers' Chapel), and the line extended along the turnpike in the edge of a wood which bordered it on the southwest. Across the road (on the northeast) was an open field a quarter of mile in width, extending along the whole front of the line and beyond it about 600 yards. This open space was bounded on the northeast (to my front) and northwest (to my left) by woods, an opening being left at the north corner.

Late in the afternoon of the 16th, the enemy's skirmishers advanced into the woods in front of my position. They were held in check by my riflemen and the Texas skirmishers. In the mean time I was ordered by General Hood, commanding the division, to move forward and occupy the edge of the wood in which the skirmishing was going on. This was quickly accomplished, and the enemy was driven, at dark, to the farther side of the wood, toward the Antietam. My brigade was relieved during the night, and moved, with the rest of General Hood's command, to the wood in rear of Saint Mumma's Church (Dunkers' Chapel).

Soon after daylight on the 17th, the attack of the enemy commenced. The battle had lasted about an hour and a half, when I was ordered to move forward into the open field across the turnpike. On reaching the road, I found but few of our troops on the field, and these seemed to be in much confusion, but still opposing the advance of the enemy's dense masses with determination. Throwing the brigade at once into line of battle, facing northward, I gave the order to advance. The Texas Brigade, Colonel Wofford, had in the meantime come into line on my left, and the two brigades now moved forward together. The enemy, who had by this time advanced half-way across the field and had planted a heavy battery at the north end of it, began to give way before us, though in vastly superior force. The Fifth Texas Regiment (which had been sent over to my right) and the Fourth Alabama pushed into the wood in which the skirmishing had taken place the evening previous, and drove the enemy through and beyond it. The other regiments of my command continued steadily to advance in the open ground, driving the enemy in confusion from and beyond his guns. So far, we had been entirely successful and everything promised a decisive victory. It is true that strong support was needed to follow up our success, but this I expected every moment.

At this stage of the battle, a powerful Federal force (ten times our number) of fresh troops was thrown in our front. Our losses up to this time had been very heavy; the troops now confronting the enemy were insufficient to cover properly one-fourth of the line of battle; our ammunition was expended; the men had been fighting long and desperately and were exhausted from want of food and rest. Still, they held their ground, many of them using such ammunition as they could obtain from the bodies of our own and the enemy's dead and wounded. It was evident that this state of affairs could not long continue. No support was at hand. To remain stationary or advance without it would have caused a useless butchery, and I adopted the only alternative—that of falling back to the wood from which I had first advanced. The enemy followed very slowly and cautiously. Under direction of General Hood I reformed my brigade in the rear of Saint Mumma's Church (Dunkers' Chapel), and, together with the Texas Brigade, which had also retired, again confronted the enemy, who seemed to hesitate to enter the wood. During this delay re-enforcements arrived, and the brigade was relieved for the purpose of obtaining ammunition.

At 1 p. m., having been supplied with ammunition, I was again ordered to the field, and took position in the wood near the church. Here the brigade remained, under an incessant cannonade, until near nightfall, when it was moved [one] half mile nearer the town of Sharpsburg, where it lay during the night and the following day.

The good conduct of my brigade in this battle had not been surpassed by it in any previous engagement. Weak and exhausted as they were, and fighting against fearful odds, the troops accomplished and endured all that was within the limits of human capacity.

Our loss in proportion to the numbers engaged was extremely heavy. The officers suffered severely. Colonel Liddell, the gallant and beloved commander of the Eleventh Mississippi Regiment, fell, mortally wounded; Lieutenant-Colonel [S. F.] Butler, of the same regiment, received a painful wound, and Major [T. S.] Evans was killed. Colonel Stone, Lieutenant-Colonel [D. W.] Humphreys, and Major [J. A.] Blair, of the Second Mississippi, were all wounded while leading that distinguished regiment in the charge. Major Webb, commanding Sixth North Carolina, Captain [S. Made.] Tate, an acting field officer of the same, and Captain [L. H.] Scruggs, commanding Fourth Alabama, received wounds while gallantly discharging their duty.

The members of my staff-Lieutenant Terrell, assistant adjutant-general, Captain Kirkman, Lieutenant Law, of the Citadel Academy, and Private Smith, Fourth Alabama—as usual, performed every duty bravely and efficiently.

I am, Captain, very respectfully,

E. M. Law,

Colonel, Commanding Brigade.[9]


## Stephen D. Lee
## September 22, 1833–May 28, 1908

Stephen D. Lee was born in Charleston, South Carolina, on September 22, 1833, and graduated from West Point in the class of 1854. He resigned his commission in the U.S. Army on February 20, 1861, and entered the Confederate Army as captain and *aide-de-camp* to General P. G. T. Beauregard.

He served as an artillerist in the ANV through all the battles of 1861–1862, and was promoted continuously up to colonel during this time. He was promoted to brigadier general on November 6, 1862, and was assigned to the command of artillery at Vicksburg, Mississippi. He was exchanged when Vicksburg fell to Union forces on July 4, 1863, and served in the Department of Mississippi as its cavalry commander.

He was appointed lieutenant general on June 23, 1864, and assumed command of Hoods' Corps of the Army of Tennessee.

General Stephen D. Lee. (*Mississippi State University*)

He surrendered with General Joseph E. Johnston in North Carolina on April 26, 1865. After the war, General Lee resided in Mississippi as a farmer, state senator, and became the first president of Mississippi State University. He was very active in the leadership of the United Confederate Veterans and was its commander until his death on May 28, 1908. General Lee is buried at Friendship Cemetery in Columbus, Mississippi.[10]

**General Stephen D. Lee**
**Artillery Battalion Commander, Longstreet's Corps**
**Army of Northern Virginia**
*Times Dispatch*
**September 1, 1907**
**Hood's Brigade at Sharpsburg Fight**

General Stephen D. Lee's Glowing Tribute to Hood's Famous Texas Fighters
  General William R. Hamby, of Austin, Texas, writes to Comrade C. A. Richardson of this city, an interesting letter, which contains brief reference to matters of much local importance; also, a splendid tribute to a once famous command well known to ex-Confederate soldiers. The glowing tribute in question is from General Stephen D. Lee, who, it is remembered so highly complimented the Parker Battery (known as "The Boy Battery") at Sharpsburg.

General Hamby has prepared a most interesting paper entitled "Hood's Texas Brigade at Sharpsburg," which will be published in *The Confederate Veteran*.

We are permitted to quote an extract from General Hamby's manuscript descriptive of "the gamest fight of the nineteenth century." It is a very concise and truthful statement thus expressed:

The battle of Sharpsburg was fought with desperate courage by both the blue and the gray, and the 17th of September 1862, stands out conspicuously the bloodiest day in American history. More men were killed and wounded that day than on any other one day during the War Between the States, and I doubt if the dead and wounded ever lay thicker upon any field than was seen from the old Dunker church north for more than half a mile. The action commenced about daybreak, and by sunset the bloody work had ended.

## What General Lee Saw

I will not go into detail as to the criticism of your paper except to say that you could not have written a more modest paper.... I saw them pierce the Federal line at Gaines's Mill; I saw the magnificent charge at Second Manassas; I witnessed the glory the brigade won at Sharpsburg. They were under my observation all the time. I saw them go in on the evening of the 16th; I saw them come out to get their rations when they were relieved; I saw them again about daylight the 17th; I saw them sweep the enemy from their front; I saw them almost annihilated and even then I saw them contribute the greater part of the repulse first of Hooker's Corps; then of Mansfield's Corps, of the Union Army; I saw them hold off Sumner's Corps until reinforcements came; I saw them deliver volley after volley lying on the ground; I saw them broken, shattered and falling back before overwhelming numbers, the few who were left giving the rebel yell with more spirit than the hurrahs of the Union troops advancing on them.... I might go on and tell more, but it would not do justice to your grand brigade.

General Stephen D. Lee
Artillery Battalion Commander, Longstreet's Corps
Army of Northern Virginia
The *Daily Express*
February 21, 1909
Historical Reminiscences, Conducted By J. B. Polley, Floresville, Texas.

In a recent communication from our old comrade of the Fourth Texas, William R. Hamby of Austin, he says:

Complying with your request I enclose your herewith copy of the letter written to me by Gen. Stephen D. Lee in August 1907. At the request of some of our comrades I wrote my recollections of the battle of Sharpsburg, and in order that I might be historically as well as incidentally correct, I submitted them to General Lee for his criticism as our brigade was under his immediate observation during the entire battle.

I also enclose you a copy of his recollections of the interviews between General Lee and his corps and division commanders the night following the battle of Sharpsburg to which he refers in his letter to me. I do not think it has ever been published and I regard it as a most valuable contribution to history.

Sincerely,

W. R. Hamby, Your Comrade.

In his letter, above referred to, Gen. Stephen D. Lee pays a tribute to Texas and Texians that should not be suffered to remain unpublished. The glory that Hood's Texas Brigade won belongs not alone to the members of that command, but to the people of Texas and of all sections of Texas. Given the same opportunities, other Texas brigades would have fought as bravely and endured as heroically. The other paper mentioned by Mr. Hamby will appear next week. The incidents relayed have never been published and are intensely interesting.

### Columbus, Miss., Aug 6, 1907

My Dear Comrade:

I have your letter of August 3, enclosing the manuscript headed: Hood's Texas Brigade at Sharpsburg. You say this brigade was under my observation the entire day and you would like me to read what you have written and return to you with my criticism. I have read the manuscript, and I think it is remarkably a modest paper. If any brigade in the Union or Confederate Army should have its history written describing their skirmishes and battles, Hood's Texas Brigade is the one, and if no survivor of that brigade can do this, some brilliant Texian should take the record as found in the Government publications, read it carefully both sides, Union and Confederate, and then converse with the survivors and write a full and complete history of that immortal brigade.

There were very many splendid brigades in the army on the Confederate side, and while I would not say that Hood's Brigade surpassed them all, still, if I were to select a brigade to do honor to the average fighting Confederate brigade, I would select this brigade. I will not go into detail as to the criticism of your paper except to say that you couldn't have written a more modest paper. The Librarian of Congress writes to the Librarian of the State of Texas and virtually describes the brigade namely: "The known statistics of these regiments (Hood's Brigade) are so remarkable that if missing figures can be obtained it will establish a record equaled by few if any organizations in the Civil War, or indeed in modern warfare." This one quotation should emphasize my suggestion as to the full and complete history of this brigade in all its battles and skirmishes.

It was my fortune to hear the volleys of Hood's Brigade, one of the first volleys in the war, between Richmond and West Point on the York River, when McLellan tried to turn the flank of Johnson's army by getting in his rear with a corps from the West Point landing. That volley of five thousand or more muskets, answered by five or ten thousand in reply, is still ringing in my ears, and I heard no other volleys equal it. I heard it again at Second Manassas in front of Longstreet's corps in their magnificent charge on that field. I saw them pierce the Federal line at Gaines' Mill: I saw their magnificent charge at Second Manassas, and I witnessed the glory the brigade won at Sharpsburg. They were under my eyes all the time. I saw them go in on the evening of the 16th: I saw them come out to get their rations when they were relieved: I saw them go in again a little before day, 17th. I saw them sweep the enemy from their front: I saw them contribute to the greater part of the repulse, first of Hooker's Corps, then of Mansfield's corps of the Union Army. I saw them hold off Sumner's corps until reinforcements came. I saw them delivering volley after volley lying on the ground not 150 yards from the muzzle of my guns to the east of the Dunker Church. I saw them broken, shattered and falling back before overwhelming numbers; the few who were left giving the rebel yell with more spirit than the hurrahs of the Union troops.

I might go on and tell more, but it wouldn't do justice to the grand brigade. I enclose you a manuscript I wrote many years ago, which gives the incident between Hood and Lee after dark on that bloody field. I will also try and find a map of Sharpsburg and sent it to you.

With kind wishes, your comrade and friend,

Stephen D. Lee

**General Stephen D. Lee**
**Artillery Battalion Commander, Longstreet's Corps**
**Army of Northern Virginia**
**The *Daily Express***
**February 28, 1909**
**Historical Reminiscences Conducted By J. B. Polley, Floresville, Texas.**

Three personal incidents in the battle of Sharpsburg or Antietam. Fought September 17, 1862 By Gen. Stephen B. Lee.

The battle of Antietam, or Sharpsburg, was one of the bloodiest and fiercest fight in the four years' war between the States. General Lee, having defeated the Federal Army under General Pope, and driven it to the defense of Washington, the two armies of McClellan and Pope were concentrated there, and McClellan put in charge of both. General Lee determined to cross the Potomac into Maryland, capture Harper's Ferry and then concentrate his army and fight McLellan. His written plan of campaign in some way fell into McLellan's hands, who rapidly moved his army and attacked Lee, before he could concentrate at Sharpsburg on the morning of September 17, 1862.

General Lee had less than 40,000 men during the battle, while McLellan had 87,000 on the field. The losses were for the Union Army about 12,500 and in the Confederate Army 8,000 killed, wounded and missing. The same armies fought from 3 a.m. until after dark, maintaining the same relative positions they held in the beginning, and faced each other all day on the 18th of September without renewing the battle. Both armies were pretty well used up and exhausted from the terrible struggle of September 17. The battle raged fiercely near the Dunker Church on the Sharpsburg and Hagerstown Pike, on General Lee's left wing, where, with three corps, Hooker's, Mansfield's, and Sumner's, afterwards reinforced by Franklin's Corps. McClellan attempted to turn General Lee's left. This great effort was resisted by Jackson's corps and Hood's division of Longstreet's corps (mainly). By 8 o'clock in the morning two corps of the Federals back when Sumner's corps came in fresh and drove him back, and it looked like the day was lost on the Southern side, as Jackson had also been driven back with great loss. Jackson and Hood held the ground near the Dunker Church till the arrival of McLaw's division about 9 a.m., when the Federal attack was checked and the Confederate line restored and maintained.

In the fighting the Federals had forced the Confederates to form at right angles to the main line of the battle, and exposed them not only to the fire of the artillery and infantry in their front, but to the fire of twenty-pound Parrett guns across the Antietam Creek.

At the time Jackson and Hood were driven back and were with difficulty holding the ground near the Dunker Church. Hood came up to my battalion of artillery (five batteries), which had been engaged during the entire morning, and was pretty well wrecked, having lost eighty-five men and sixty horses, and ordered me to turn over my artillery to the next officer in command and to go personally and find General Lee, tell him the condition of the affairs and say to him that, unless reinforcements were sent at once, the day was lost. I protested against leaving my artillery in its wrecked condition. He insisted, however, and I went. I soon met General Lee on horseback with one orderly moving at a walk toward that part of the field and about half way between Sharpsburg and Dunker Church. I reported the condition of affairs on the left and delivered General Hood's message. He quietly said: "Don't be excited about it Colonel. Go tell General Hood to hold his ground; reinforcements are now rapidly approaching between Sharpsburg and the ford. Tell him that I am now coming to his support." I said: "General, your presence will do good, but nothing but infantry can save the day on the left." I started to return and had not gone over 100 yards when he called me and pointed to McLaw's division, then in sight and approaching at a double quick. The reinforcements arrived just in time to save the day, and this was aided by General Sumner of the Federal army halting his corps for alignment when he was driving the Confederates before him. The Confederates restored their line on the left and the Federals were content to remain in a strong line of battle the balance of the 17th and all of the 18th on their right.

The battle was renewed on General Lee's center and right, where Burnside's corps crossed the Antietam, but was finally repulsed on that part of the field before dark.

There can be little doubt that this battle was as bloody during the day (September 17, 1862) and the loss of life as great as during one day's battle during the war. Both armies were completely exhausted by the great struggle and welcomed night to stop the terrible slaughter.

General Lee's headquarters were on the pike leading from Sharpsburg to the Potomac and about one half mile from the town. An hour or more after night had set in the weird scene of the great battlefield had changed; the firing has ceased everywhere and more open work was being given to searching for the dead and carrying for the dying and wounded. General Lee summoned his corps and division commanders to meet him. For once during the day he had some of his staff and escort about him, and one by one his commanders began to arrive, generally with two or three horsemen with them. As they came up he inquired quietly: "General, how is it on your part of the line?" I too, had been summoned and was a quiet, intensely interested observer of one of the most remarkable scenes and interviews I ever witnessed. To the inquiry of Lee, Longstreet, apparently much depressed, replied to the effect that it was as bad as could be—that his division had lost terribly, his lines had been barely held and there was little better than a good skirmish line along his front, and he volunteered the advice that General Lee should cross the Potomac before daylight. D. H. Hill came next. He said that his division was cut to pieces, that his losses had been terrible and he had no troops to hold his line against the great odds against him. He too, suggested crossing the Potomac before daylight. Next came Jackson. He quietly said that he had to contend against the greatest odds he ever met. He had lost many Generals killed and several division and brigade commanders were dead and wounded, and his losses in the different commands had been terrible. He too, suggested crossing the Potomac before daylight. Next came Hood. To General Lee's inquiry he displayed great emotion, seemed completely unmanned and replied that he had no division. General Lee, with more excitement than I ever witnessed him exhibit, exclaimed: "Great God General Hood, where is the splendid division you had this morning?" Hood replied: "They are lying in the field where you sent them: but few have straggled. My division has almost been wiped out."

After the opinion of all had been given, there was an appalling stillness over the group. It seemed to last several minutes, when General Lee, apparently rising more erect in his saddle said: "Gentlemen, we will not cross the Potomac tonight. You will go to your respective commands, strengthen your lines, send two officers from each brigade toward the ford to collect your stragglers and get them up. I have had the proper steps taken to collect all the man who are in the rear. If McClellan wants to fight in the morning, I will give him battle again. Go!"

The above was in substance what occurred and what was said. The group gradually broke up, each going to his command, and if I read their countenances right, they said: "This is a rash conclusion, and we fear the Army of Northern Virginia is taking a great risk in the face of the day's battle and the great numbers opposed to us. The two armies faced each other all the next day, September 18, the guns unlimbered, the lines of battle and skirmishers in place, but everyone being careful not to let a gun go off for fear, apparently, that the terrible slaughter and scenes of the day before might be renewed. One army was afraid, the other dared not."

During the morning of September 18 a courier from General Lee's headquarters came to my battalion of artillery with a message that General Lee wanted to see me. I followed the courier, and on meeting General Lee, he said: "Colonel Lee, I wish you to go with this courier to General Jackson and say to him I sent you to report to him." I replied, "General, shall I take my artillery with me?" He said, "No, just say that I told you to report to him, and he will tell you what he wants."

I soon reached General Jackson. He was dismounted, with but few persons around him. He said to me: "Colonel Lee, I wish you to take a ride with me." We rode to the left of our lines, with but one courier, I think. It was very quiet, no one firing anywhere and everybody talking in an undertone, but intensely watching everyone else who was moving in any direction. We soon reached a considerable hill, almost similar to an Indian mound, but for its being larger. We dismounted, and General Jackson said, "Let us go on this mound or hill, and be careful not to expose yourself, for the Federal sharpshooters are not far off." The hill had evidence of fierce fighting the day before. A battery of artillery had been on it, and there were wrecks of caissons, broken wheels, dead bodies and dead horses around. General Jackson said: "Colonel I wish you to take your glasses and carefully examine the Federal line of battle." I did so, and after satisfying myself in witnessing a remarkably strong line of battle, with more troops than I knew General Lee had, and after locating the different batteries, unlimbered and ready for action, and noting the strong skirmish line in front of dense mass of infantry, I said to him: "General, that is a remarkably strong position, and there is a large force there." "Yes, Colonel Lee, I wish you to take fifty pieces of artillery and crush that force which is the Federal right. Can you do it?" I can scarcely describe my feelings as I again took my glasses and made an even more careful examination. I at once saw such an attempt must fail. More than fifty guns were unlimbered and ready for action, supported strongly by dense lines of infantry and strong skirmish lines advantageously posted. The ground was unfavorable for the location of artillery on the Confederate side, which, to be effective, should move up close to the Federal lines, and that too, under fire of the infantry and artillery. I disliked to say what I felt and knew. I said: "Yes, General, where will I get the fifty guns?" He said, "How many have you?" I replied, "About twelve out of the thirty I carried into action the day before that my losses had been great in men, horses and carriages." He said, "I can furnish you some." I replied, "Shall I go for the guns?" "No, not yet," he replied "Colonel Lee, can you crush the Federal right with fifty guns?" I said, "General, I can try. I can do it if anyone can." He replied, "That is not what I asked you, sir. If I give you fifty guns can you crush the Federal right?" I evaded the question again and again, but he pressed it home. Finally I said, "General, you seem to be more intent upon my giving you my technical opinion as an artillery officer than my going after the guns and making the attempt." "Yes, Sir," he replied, "and I want your positive opinion, yes or no." I felt a great ordeal was upon me, and I could not evade or dodge. I again took my glasses and made another examination. I waited a good while, with Jackson watching me intently.

I said, "General, it cannot be done with fifty guns and the troops you have near here." In an instant he said, "Let us ride back, Colonel." I felt that I had possibly shown a lack of nerve, and with considerable emotion begged that I might be allowed to make the attempt, saying, "General, you forced me to say what I did unwillingly. If you give the fifty guns to any other artillery officer I am ruined for life. I promise you I will fight the guns to the last extremity if you will only let me command them." Jackson was quiet, seemed sorry for me and said: "It's all right, Colonel, everybody knows you are a brave officer, and would fight the guns well," or words to that effect.

We soon reached the spot from which we started. He said: "Colonel Lee, go to General Lee and tell him what has occurred since you reported to me. Describe our ride to the hill, your examination of the Federal position, and my conversation about your crushing the Federal right with fifty guns, and my forcing you to give your opinion as to its possibility as an artillerist."

With feeling such as I never had before, nor ever expect to have again, I returned to General Lee and gave a detailed account of my visit to General Jackson, closing with the account of my being forced to give my opinion as to the possibility of success, I saw a shade come over General Lee's face, and he said: "Colonel, go and join your command." For many, many years I never fully understood my mission that day or why I was sent to General Jackson. When Jackson's report was published of the battle, I saw that he stated that in the afternoon of September 17th, General Lee had ordered him to move to the left with a view of turning the Federal's right, but he found the enemies numerous artillery so judicially posted in their front, and so near the river as to render such an attempt too hazardous to undertake. I afterwards saw General J. E. B. Stuart's report, in which he says that it was determined, the enemy not attacking, to turn the enemies right on the 18th. It appears General Lee ordered General Jackson to renew the battle on the evening of the 17th and turn the enemies right, and Jackson said that it could not be done. It also appears that from Stuart's report and the incident I relate, that General Lee reiterated the order on the 18th, and told General Jackson to take fifty guns and crush the Federal's right and make the attempt. Jackson having reported against such attempt on the 17th, no doubt said if an artillerist in whom General Lee had confidence would say the Federal right could be crushed with fifty guns, he would make the attempt.

I now have the satisfaction of knowing that the opinion which I was forced to give on the 18 of September, had already been given by Jackson on the evening of the 17th of September and that the same opinion was reiterated by him on the same day (September 18). I still believe that Jackson, Stuart and myself were right, and the attempt to turn the Federal's right on the afternoon of September 17 and also September 18 would be unwise.

The incident shows General Lee's decision and boldness in battle, and General Jackson's delicate loyalty to his commanding general in convincing him of the inadvisability of a proposed movement which he felt it would hazardous to undertake.

The three incidents as far as they relate to myself are correct to every particular. The speculation as to others may be slightly colored, but I do not think the description overdrawn.

Brigadier General Fitzhugh Lee
Brigade Commander, Army of Northern Virginia
The *Daily Express*
June 21, 1908
Historical Reminiscences Conducted by J. B. Polley, Floresville, Texas

Gen. Fitzhugh Lee, occasionally put a coloring on a story that made it seem strange to a listener. In 1899, we think it was, the following was published in the *Galveston News*:

Gen. Fitzhugh Lee tells this story of his experience with Hood's Texas Brigade. The battle of Sharpsburg had begun, but the brigade had not yet gone in and was lying on the left of the Confederate line waiting for orders. From a commanding position in its rear General Fitz discovered that a division of Federal cavalry was advancing to attack it, and, much concerned, rode hurriedly down to the brigade. The Texians were lying and sitting down, half of them asleep, and several squads playing poker. Approaching the nearest regiment he asked, "Where is General Robertson?"

"Don't know, General," lazily replied a Texan, looking up, but not saluting: "he was 'round here a little while ago, but I don't see him nowhere just now."

Riding to the next regiment General Fitz made the same inquiry and received the same answer, and at the third and fourth his inquiries were equally fruitless.

"Well," said he, speaking directly to a party of four who were engaged in a game of poker, "General Robertson must be found at once and you men get into line. A division of Federal cavalry will be here on you in three minutes, and unless you are fixed for them they will capture the last one of you."

More for the purpose, apparently, of acknowledging that he heard this intelligence than for any other, one of the men looked over his shoulder at the excited officer and asked: "Do you really think so, General?" Then facing his companions inquired, "Whose deal is it, boys?"

General Fitz turned away in wrath and scarcely gone two hundred yards when a long line of blue-coated cavalry engaged from the woods in front, and, with ringing huzza, charged straight upon the Texians. There was no stir among the latter, though, until the Federals were within a hundred and fifty yards. Then the roar and flash of minie and Enfield rifles burst from the ranks of the Texas Brigade, and emptied so many saddles that in dismay the surviving Federals retreated as fast as they had come. "Two minutes afterwards," says General Fitz, "the party of four men were again playing poker, and most of their comrades lay flat on their backs asleep."

## General George B. McClellan
## Commanding General, Army of the Potomac
## *New York Times*
## November 15, 1908

In the same sale is a letter of General George B. McClellan to W. H. Aspinwall, dated Headquarters, Army of the Potomac, in Camp.[11] Oct. 5, 1862, and relating to the battle of Antietam (Sept. 16–17, 1862,) in which Gen. McClellan commanded the Union Army. It reads in part:

Will you allow me to present to you the accompanying piece of the color staff of a flag of a Texas regiment of Hood's Brigade? The colors and staff were captured by the United States Army of the Potomac at the battle of Antietam. The staff was broken by a ball—the colors are deposited in Washington. Please accept this staff as a memento of our trip over the field of Antietam today.

# Other Texans, a Louisianan, a North Carolinian, and a few Yankees who fought at Antietam

Many of the Texans who fought at Antietam were not in Hood's Texas Brigade, but were from other Confederate regiments located throughout the South. After the war, the soldiers wrote and were interviewed about being in the Battle of Antietam. A soldier from Louisiana that was interviewed in Mamie Yeary's *Reminiscences of the Boys in Gray* is also included, as well as a soldier from North Carolina, who saw Hood's Texas Brigade in action at Antietam.

Two Union soldiers, one from the 12th Massachusetts Infantry and one from the 9th Pennsylvania Infantry, wrote about fighting Hood's Texas Brigade at Antietam. Their stories are also included.

### William B. Abernathy
### 17th Mississippi Infantry Regiment
### McKinney, Texas
### Hardest Fought Battle

An unfortunate controversy scarcely creditable to those who participated in it, has arisen over the finding of Lee's lost order. It seems that when Lee issued orders to his troops to concentrate around Harper's Ferry that a copy of this order fell into McClellan's hands. Seeing the position of the troops Lee, McClellan rushed his men to the fighting before Lee could concentrate. This controversy has been participated in by some of the general officers. I am, by however, talking of the boys who carried the muskets, and it was theirs to do and theirs to die.

After the capture of Harper's Ferry, and the pushing of Lee by McClellan, the troops engaged at Harper's Ferry started on the run for Sharpsburg. Jackson, being south of the Potomac, left first reaching Sharpsburg on the night of the 16th day of September. The Federal troops having gotten between McLaw's division and Lee's command, McLaw's had to cross the Potomac and follow in Jackson's footsteps. All the same he went on a run, too, halting some miles from Sharpsburg, resuming

Battle of Antietam—Army of the Potomac: Gen. Geo. B. McClellan, commanding. September 17, 1862, by Kurz & Allison, *c.* 1880. (*Library of Congress*)

his run the next morning. As the regiment passed a little hamlet the Maryland side, an old lady gave the boys this kind of a blessing: "YOU dear dirty ragged souls you." And there wasn't a word amiss in the blessing.

Before dawn the carnage had begun. Heavy masses of Federal troops before daylight were thrown in fiercely upon Hood and his Grand Division. Back and forth the lines wavered until Jackson threw his troops into the lead, and again the Confederates gave ground. Nearly sixty thousand Federal soldiers had been thrown upon less than ten thousand Confederates, and John Sedgwick crossed the Antietam and hurried to the support of the Federals. Soon after they came on the battle field around the old Dunker Church. McLaw's troops came at a double-quick upon the scene, and around the peaceful old church the storm of battle in terrible earnestness raged with fearful force, and Hood's, Jackson's, and McLaw's troops rallying again to the call of Jackson swept the entire Federal force from the field. And there was not upon that part of the ground an organized Federal Command capable of assuming the offense. And before nine o'clock there had been a fearful battle fought on the left wing. But Richardson, Trench and other General Officers had come and were assailing the Confederate center.

The Confederate line in the center extended a mile or more along a sunken road and in that sunken road was Longstreet and D. H. Hill that stern old Presbyterian fatalist. Here with renewed vigor the conflict raged. Longstreet himself, the gunners of one of his batteries having been disabled, manned a gun and fought the battle through.

Colonel Cocke, commanding a North Carolina Regiment held his troops in line taking the fire of the enemy without a shot, holding his troops to meet the advancing enemy with the bayonets. The slaughter of the Confederates among this portion of the lines, held in position by the stern presence of Longstreet, was such that blood ran along the lane, and it retains to this day the surname won by the gallant Confederates, "Bloody Lane."

And now on the right of the Confederate army came in the afternoon another blow, all day long the Federals had attempted to cross the stream at Burnsides bridge and Bob Toombs, who could fight as well as talk, had valiantly held Burnsides advance back; late in the afternoon the Federals managed to cross, steadily drove the Confederates back, step by step, until they reached of the little town, Sharpsburg, when A. P. Hill, at the head of his troops, in his picturesque red shirt, leading his division, putting them into line as they ran, appeared upon the scene and with the bayonet, charged, drove the Federals back again and then there was quiet, for there was none able to fight.

## Two of Our Mess Fell

In this fateful struggle two of the mess went down, Jesse D. Franklin and Jesse H. Franklin. Jesse D. Franklin, always lively, always full of life, fun and energy, his was the lips on whom was always a Jest. Life to him was a comedy, and every sunbeam brought a smile; every moment was a tinkle of joy. The wounds received that day carried him finally to his grave—not, however, until disabled as an infantry soldier, he was transferred to the 18th Mississippi Cavalry and did his service as one of Forrest Troopers.

Jesse H. Franklin, a sedate member of the Methodist Church, quiet and composed in all he did, scarcely ready to smile, though Nestor swore in jests were laughable, ever ready to duty, never missing a roll call, nor faltering in battle. His injuries were not so severe, but after a weary time at point Look-Out he rejoined the Command, only to go down with more severe injuries in the Campaign of 1864 in the Wilderness.

The Master has sounded the last Roll Call for him, and there was none fitter to go and none readier to answer.

It was here one of the Mess went down in the battle around the old church that men were want to preach "Glory to God in the Highest, and on Earth Peace, Good Will Towards Men."

The army remained around Sharpsburg another day and then back across the Potomac River. This time they were not singing "Maryland, My Maryland," but it was to the refrain of "Carry Me Back to Old Virginia."

## In Hostile Territory

Western Maryland was no sympathizer for the Southerners. It was in this same battle of Sharpsburg that there was engaged on the Confederate side thirty thousand troops, while McClellan, having united his army with that of Pope had over one hundred and thirty thousand, you will see that there was some disparity in number, but then we had Lee.[1]

**J. A. Bonnett
26th Georgia Infantry
Eagle Pass, Texas
The *Daily Express*
April 25, 1909
Historical Reminiscences
Conducted by J B Polley, Floresville, Texas.**

J. A. Bonnett of the Twenty-Sixth Georgia Infantry writes from Eagle Pass, March 8, 1909 the following:

I have been reading your "Reminiscences," especially as I am quite familiar with the campaign of Lee's army and its movements in Virginia from the battle "Around Richmond," when we drove General McClellan back to the banks of the James River after fighting him at Cold Harbor, Gaines Mill and Malvern Hill, at all of which place part of my corps took part in the fight. Having been a private in the ranks, I know very little, of course, of the movements outside my immediate brigade or corps, for you know that a private in the ranks has little opportunity to see what is going on in other parts of the field. I have met privates who seem to know all about the positions and doings of both armies—how they became informed and at the same time were able to handle their muskets, I am at a loss to understand, unless their war records were clipped from history. I am satisfied that a soldier, unless, he was a courier or field officer, knew very little of what was going on outside his immediate brigade, and I frankly admit that the Yankees in the front of me kept me just as busy as I could be attending to them, and I had no spare time to reconnoiter.

But what I am trying to get at is: In your reminiscences of the battle of Sharpsburg (Antietam) you omit any mention of Stonewall Jackson's Corps and the part it played in that battle. Belonging to it as I did, I have a vivid recollection of what happened namely:

Our corps was detached and sent to capture Harper's Ferry, where we arrived during the night. Early the next morning, about daylight, we were ordered into line of battle; in this position we remained until about sunrise, facing the breastworks and entrenchments of the fort there, and were then ordered to fix bayonets and march toward the trenches, being then about 600 yards from the enemy's double line of entrenchments, and onward we marched with fixed bayonets. Just then a battery composed of about thirty-five pieces of Confederate artillery opened such a terrific fire on the enemy's artillery, which was still parked, and at such close range, that the Federals were unable to man their guns; our batteries threw something like ninety shells per minute into them. This vicious firing kept up for about five minutes, while we were still moving toward the breastworks, and when we were within a short distance of their firing line a courier came dashing in front of our lines and ordered a halt. As soon as we halted, and looking to our right toward the hills, we saw the most beautiful sight I ever witnessed, namely, a large white flag hoisted over the fort at Harper's Ferry, showing that the fort had surrendered. Presently I saw a horseman in Yankee uniform, with a flag; when they met both flags were dipped. It was not until then that we understood what it was all about. I never shall forget that beautiful white flag, or table-cloth, whatever it was; it lifted a heavy weight off my breast. We cheered, and this ended the capture and surrender of Harper's Ferry.

But Jackson's Corps, although having captured something between 11,000 and 15,000 men, with all their "fixings" was not through with its task, for as soon as we could snatch a mouthful of something to eat, we were force-marched back to Sharpsburg, where we were thrown into line of battle as soon as we arrived, in front of the enemy at a place since named Dead Man's Lane, on the account of the heavy slaughter that took place there the next day. At daylight the next morning the enemy advanced in double column, and one of the bloodiest encounter of the war was precipitated. My regiment went in with 196 men and that evening only twenty-eight were accounted for, the others having been numbered with the killed, wounded, captured, missing and demoralized. Thus ended Stonewall Jackson's part of the Battle of Sharpsburg.

James Boyd
Early's Brigade (unknown regiment)
Belton, Texas
*Temple Daily Telegram*
September 18, 1914
Confederate Anniversaries

Belton, Sept 17.—Today marks the fifty-second anniversary of the last day of the battle of Sharpsburg, Maryland. In this battle the first Texas suffered a loss of 82 percent of its men. This regiment was fighting in Hood's brigade. General Early's brigade of Jackson's command was sixteen miles away and hastened to reinforce the Confederate forces, reaching the battlefield just in time to be sent to the relief of the First Texas. Fighting with Early's brigade was Capt. Jas Boyd of this city.

C. C. Cummings
17th Mississippi Regiment
Fort Worth, Texas
*Fort Worth Gazette*
October 21, 1894
A Grand Sight
Storming of Maryland Heights and Capture of Harpers Ferry

The year 1862 was the high tide of the Southern Confederacy. In it was concentered all the most potent energies of the stormy little nation. The spring opened with Jackson's valley victories. The summer ushered in the seven days' battles and victories before Richmond. Mid-summer was crowned by the signal defeat of the braggart, Pope, at Second Manassas, who boasted that he was the young Lochinvar, come out from the West, where he had seen only the backs of his enemies and that henceforth his headquarters were only to be found in the saddle till he had swallowed up all the opposition and victory should perch on his helm. But she didn't perch for him. His headquarters didn't show up when the gray boys went gunning for them, but his hindquarters did, badly lacerated by Jackson and his men. He violated the biblical injunction by boasting when putting on his armor instead of waiting till he put it off.

On the 6th of September, 1862, we crossed the Potomac under Lee, in force, at Leesburg, on the Maryland campaign, which ended after two weeks fighting about in brigades and divisions, by a full array of forces on both sides, at the drawn battle of Antietam, on Sharpsburg, on the 17th of September, 1862. We sang "Maryland, My Maryland" to those prosy old farmers over there, and called on them to rise and shine and shake the despot's heel from off their shore. But they were not afflicted with the shakes to any visible extent. The fact is, the drowsy old drones thought more of preserving apples and making apple butter and hiding it from the gray jackets, than they did about rising and shining and shaking their heels at despots. On Saturday, the 12th of September, we—the Mississippi brigade and Kershaw's South Carolina brigade—began to climb Maryland Heights overlooking Harper's Ferry, to capture a fort up there, manned by an Ohio command. We labored all Saturday night, drawing the artillery up by hand, climbing about a mile up in the clouds. Sunday morning found us on the top—a backbone ridge about wide enough to allow a regiment to form across it. On either side were rocks—huge boulders—piled on each other, covered by timber, from base to summit. One of the boys thought this must be Mount Ararat. Another thought there wasn't any rat there. A third said if so, it was sure enough an airy rat. Presently we have in sight of the fort, at the end of the ridge, overhanging the ferry. Then there was music in the air. Zip! Bang! Ping! Pang! Whe-e-ew! went the leaden billet doux about us and into us, like hornets out of a hornets nest. The poor boys quit their foolishness and began to pray and "promise God a heap of good things," as one of them said about it afterwards. Kershaw was given the post of honor to charge the fort in front through the *chiveaux du frieze*, which made one's blood freeze to look at it. It was a poor business well followed, and the Mississippians lifted not up their voices against it, nor did they weep that it was so ordered. We were assigned a job that looked equally dangerous—but was not so because they over-shot us. We climbed up the rocky heights by the left flank, while Kershaw and his men assailed in front, struggling through sharpened sticks, falling at every step under the brisk fire of the blue boys. I fell for the little rice birds and can see them now in about the sorriest job I ever hope to witness again. Kershaw was a trim little cock, all dressed up in gray with buff trimmings and seemed to me the gamest bird that ever fluttered, as he led his men right into the jaws of death and over into the fort. A last lunge on the side brought us right up to his angle. As we reached the fort the Yanks skedaddled in haste to the ferry below where they were bagged with the rest. I was detailed with a squad to follow after and see them safely in their little bed. Walker was on Loudon Heights on the Virginia side. Old Jack drew up his men and gave them fifteen minutes to surrender or he would charge. They surrendered—10,000 men in blue. I climbed one of the tallest pines overhanging the canon and saw one of the grandest scenes mid the grandest scenery on the continent.

C. C. Cummings
Seventeenth Mississippi Regiment.


## G. B. Ford
## 16th Mississippi Infantry
## Bangs, Texas

I was promoted to Corporal in 1862, to Sergeant in 1863, and to Chief of Corps Observation in 1864, and served in that capacity till the close of the war. Was in the battles of Fort Royal and Winchester under Stonewall Jackson, in the Valley Campaign of 1862, Gaines' Mill and Malvern Hill under Lee, Antietam and Second Fredericksburg, Chancellorsville, Gettysburg, Wilderness, Spotsylvania Court House, Turkey Creek, Siege of Vicksburg to the end.

Just after the battle of Manassas we were ordered to Richmond and put into a brigade composed of the Fifteen Alabama. Twenty-First Georgia, Twenty-First North Carolina, and Sixteenth Mississippi, commanded by I. N. Trimble. Here we did a little outpost duty and had only one little scrap with the Yankees. Winter coming on we dropped back to Manassas and went into winter quarters where we fared quite sumptuously with little or nothing to do.

While in winter quarters the Confederate Congress passed an order offering all who would enlist for the war a thirty day furlough. With others I accepted the offer and received my pay, sixty dollars commutation money. We were soon off for home where we had a fine time with homefolks and sweethearts. Furlough being out we were sent back by way of Mobile and thence by steamer to Montgomery, Ala. On returning we found our Division, Ewell's, left to watch Gen. Seigle at Fredericksburg, while Johnston's main army had gone to the Peninsula to meet Gen. McClellan. In a few days we were ordered to the valley to reinforce Jackson. We raced Banks down the valley nearly to Harper's Ferry, when Seigle tried to get behind us. They "skedaddled" back up the valley at a rate of thirty miles a day, winning the sobriquet of "Jackson's Foot Cavalry," On the 8th of June 1862, we fought the battle of Cross Keys, on the 9th that of Port Republic, defeating Milroy, after which we went into camp and rested a week.

Just before the battles of Cross Keys, Seigle tried to get in Jackson's rear and as the Yankees were marching by Gen. Lewis' home they were singing "Shackson in a Shug, Boys, Shackson in a shug." (They were Dutch). A few days later they came back, minus hat and gun when the young ladies hailed: "Hey, thought Shackson was in a shug." "Och! De stopper flew out."

After about six days rest Jackson moved toward Richmond in rush time. Crossed the Blue Ridge, striking the railroad near Charlottesville. The trains picking up the hindmost brigades and carrying them about forty miles, put them down and returned for others.

So we got on McClellan's right flank by the 27th, and fought the sanguinary battle of Gaines' Mill, crushing his right wing about sundown, thus gaining the day for Gen. Lee. We were not in any more fights till we reached Malvern Hill. After this fight we followed the Yanks to Harrison's Landing.

The day after the battle of Gaines' Mill Jackson succeeded to taking the York River railroad, cutting off several of McClellan's trains. The enemy, finding they could not get them out, put a lighted fuse to an ordnance train and sent it down amongst us. The rush and roar sounded like a cavalry charge. We were lying on the roadside resting when Gen. Ewell came dashing down the line. "Attention!" We soon found out it was no cavalry charge. The car exploded doing no harm. An Irishman in our regiment looked wildly about and said: "Be Jasus! You had as well kill a man as to skeer him to death."

After the fighting below Richmond, Lee's army went into camp and was somewhat reorganized. The troops from each state were put in brigades and commanded by officers of their own State. Here we were transferred from the Immortal Stonewall to the corps of Gen. Longstreet. Our new brigade was composed of the Twelfth, Sixteenth, Nineteenth and Forty-eighth Mississippi Regimens commanded by Genl. Featherstone. We did no more fighting till the Second Manassas, when Longstreet arrived just in the nick of time to save Jackson.

After the unpleasantness at Manassas was over we cut across to Maryland and after remaining there until the 17th of September, and capturing Harper's Ferry, fought the bloody battle of Antietam and recrossed into Virginia. My only brother was wounded here and died from his wounds at Lynchburg. On the way to Maryland many of us were without shoes and our feet blistered so that we could not keep up.[2]

The *Daily Express*
March 22, 1908
Historical Reminiscences
A Review of Times That are Past but Live in History—Prepared
By J. B. Polley, Floresville, Texas

The letter of General Lee to Senator Wigfall, which is referred to by Major Stiles, was written a few weeks after the battle of Sharpsburg, or Antietam. What effort was made to comply with the request has never been disclosed. Whatever it was it was unavailing. Kirby Smith was then in command of the Trans-Mississippi Department, and he and all the troops in Texas under his command had an idea that to win the independence of the South it was absolutely necessary to hold Texas free of invasion. At any rate, enlisted from first to last not over 15,000 did serve east of the Mississippi. We are making no assertion, understand—only a suggestion—but perhaps quite a good many of those who neglected to appear on the firing line hold the view of the ambulance driver up in Virginia.

An officer whom this driver had carried as near to the battle then in progress as he dared to go asked: "Why don't you tie your mules, Grover, get a gun and go with me into the fight? You are better able to handle a musket than I am."

"That's so Captain," assented Grover, looking scornfully at the slim form of his questioner, obviously comparing it with his own big bulk and muscle; "that's edxackly so suh. But there's a differ yer know."

"A differ," said the officer, no little surprised, "Well, what is the differ?"

"Why," replied Grover, "it's this er way, Captain, You listed ter git killed er shot all ter pieces, an' all I listed fer war ter drive this here old avalanche."

James T. Hall
6th South Carolina Infantry
Farmhill, Louisiana

Was in the battles of Seven Pines, Second Manassas, South Mountain, Fredericksburg, Chickamauga, Wilderness, Spotsylvania, Cold Harbor, Knoxville, Fort Harrison and various battles from Richmond to Appomattox Court House, at the surrender of Lee's Army.

Early in the Spring of 1862, the forces in camp at Centerville and the surrounding country under the command of Joseph E. Johnston, were ordered to break camp and march with all haste to Richmond, to join in the organization then going on, they were forming to meet the forces then advancing on our Capitol under the leadership of General George B. McClellan. Johnston, with a small army, of which our brigade formed part, was ordered to Yorktown, Va., where McClellan was fortified and making preparation for an advance on Richmond. After many demonstrations and bluffs on Johnston's part to Hold McClellan at that point while we were fortifying the Capitol for the grand campaign which now seemed inevitable.

Johnston, like a sly old fox, broke camp and slipped away on his famous retreat to Richmond, just that night McClellan planned an attack on our little army. So quick was McClellan to perceive the mistake of his delay that he pressed on after Johnston with such vigor we were compelled to make a stand at Williamsburg in order that our wagon train and heavy artillery could be gotten ahead. We engaged the enemy all day against great odds, and when hostilities ceased we still held our original position. Jenkin's Brigade was stationed in the flank of Fort McGruder (the P. S. S. holding the fort proper) commanding the key of opposition to McClellan's progress, with orders to hold it at all hazards, which we did until ordered to take up the line of march for Richmond. Here Robert Hemphill, my friend and classmate, was killed by the enemy. On the night of the 30th day of May a terrible rainstorm broke forth over that portion of the country lying along the James River. Our scouts who had been for sometime watching closely the enemy's movements. Our General thought this might be an opportune time to strike the enemy in detail. Our troops failing to move the enemy, save Jenkin's Brigade, who succeeded in penetrating the line some three times, driving the enemy before them, making our last charge some half hour before sun set. It was in this last charge on the Williamsburg Road, near an old log cabin, that I received a wound in my right hip, the ball passing through my ammunition box, just glazing the hip joint, lodging near the spine. I made my way back to our field hospital, narrowly escaping capture several times as I was really in the enemy's lines. The ball was taken out by Dr. Post, our brigade surgeon, and I lay down on some blankets to sleep and rest. When I awoke in the morning I was somewhat surprised to see one of my company by my side, J. P. Barron, with a wound in the left cheek. Barron expired on a cot in the hospital and in my father's arms. Being disabled on account of my wounds, I was not in the fight (Seven Days) around Richmond. But when Gen. Lee made his campaign I was again in my place and with my regiment made the campaign.

I was in the battle of South Mountains and also at the battle of Sharpsburg, at the last named battle, our brigade was placed in a position on the right of the town looking towards the enemy near the apple orchard, Capt. Smith's Company, to which I belonged, was ordered on the skirmish line and to occupy a rock fence to our front. While occupying this position, we were charged on by a line of the enemy's skirmishers whom we repulsed and again by two lines with like results, then a solid line of battle which we drove back in disorder, and again by three regiments, but continued to hold our position until the enemy was near us and then Capt. Smith seeing the position of line on our right gave way, giving the command to fall back to the main line. The advance of the enemy now became general all along the line but were soon driven back with heavy loss, thus ended Lee's first campaign into Maryland. We again crossed the Potomac River into the state of Virginia. Longstreet's Corps, Field's Division, to which my brigade belonged, was placed in position near Staunton, where we spent the greater part of winter. I forgot to state that on our way into Maryland the second battle of Manassas was fought almost on the same ground as the former Bull Run battle. Jenkin's Brigade, with a part of Stuart's Cavalry, turned the Federals' left flank from Manassas Heights with terrible slaughter.[3]

## Jasper N. Haney
## 13th Alabama Infantry
## Canyon City, Texas

Born on the 16th day of December, 1844, in Alabama, and very early in 1861 I became a member of Company D, Thirteenth Alabama Regiment. James Aiken, Captain, and B. D. Fry, Colonel. After being mustered into service at Montgomery, Ala., we were transported direct to Richmond, Va., thence to the historic town of Yorktown, where we remained for the winter, during which time we had many alarms, forced marches and several skirmishes with the "boys in blue," as they were landing and attempting to land from Federal gunboats. We evacuated Yorktown and marched towards Richmond, experiencing quite a warm time at Williamsburg with the enemy in our rear. Halting and skirmishing, we continued our march to within a few miles of Richmond. After the battles around Richmond and McClellan had given up his intention of marching into Richmond, we went on forced march towards Washington City: crossed the Potomac River, and had a spirited interview on South Mountain, in Maryland, in plain view of the city. After we decided to put off the visit to the Yankee capital, we fell back, intending to re-cross the Potomac, but we were forced to contest our right to do so. On the night of the 16th of September, we slept in line of battle within a few hundred yards of a similar line of "blue jackets." About sun-up, on the 17th of September, 1862, opened the historic battle of Antietam (or Sharpsburg) by a fixed bayonet charge on the enemy's lines. These successive charges and repulses were kept up with stubborn persistence until near 4 o'clock in the afternoon, when the flag of the old Thirteenth was shot out of my hands by a minie ball, passing through my left elbow. I have and ever will be a cripple. This ended my active participation in battle as Ensign Sergeant of the regiment.

Gen. D. H. Hill, the Brigade commander, was within ten feet of my side when the old flag fell, and several months later wrote a very complimentary indorsement on my assignment to light duty, where I served under Gen. Wilson in the commissary department at No. 316 Broadway, Richmond, for the remainder of the "unpleasantness."

The Confederate Congress had passed a law prohibiting any permanently disabled soldier, who was qualified for light duty in any of the departments of the government, from being discharged; but instead, should be assigned to light duty.

I will now give you my opinion of war, based upon actual observation and experience "of the real thing?" War is livid hell; it is a relic of barbarism and heathenism. The saying that "the pen is mightier than the sword" is not only inspired, but is divine. When a people become civilized and intelligent, there will be no more internecine war. I am anxious to contribute to a monument to be erected to the heroes and heroines of peace. I want my posterity to regard war as a crime and politicians as criminals. True chivalry is not bloody; true statesmanship is not murder. "Let us have "peace" is an echo from the throne of God.[4]

John W. Hanks
3rd North Carolina Infantry
Columbia, Texas
*Houston Post*
April 13, 1903
The Lone, Starry Hours

I am indebted to the kindness of Mrs. W. T. Berry of Houston, J. D. Rudd of Warkom, Texas, and J. W. Hands of Columbia, Texas for the words of the old song, which I asked for some time since. The letter from my old friend J. W. Hanks is so interesting that I am going to publish it. The song was published yesterday:

Dear Friend: Reading your column in *The Post* last night, which I do every night, as regular as I say my prayers, I noted your "search your memory" request, and I am glad I am able to comply therewith. This, however, is an act of recollection rather than memory, as I had to "think back" about fifty years—which will prove to you that the "registering ganglia" of my old brain is yet in working order. The last time I sang this old melody (and where I buried it) was on the night before the great battle of Sharpsburg, September 17, 1862. There was a group of young officers of the regiment—Third North Carolina—gathered in a little knot, talking of the fearful struggle they knew would commence with the day—of homes and about friends—when one asked me to sing "Lone, Starry Hours." They were William Quince, Tom Cowan, Willie Gillespie, Captain Rhodes and Swift Galloway. Before the rising sun, the battle was on in all its red fury, and when the sun went down, only one in that circle was among the living.

I have never sung that song since that night. When I read your request I began to work my "recollection" and succeeded in reviewing two versus; if there was another, I have totally forgotten it. The song was very popular with the old soldiers.

Your true friend,

J. W. Hanks

John W. Hanks
3rd North Carolina Infantry
Columbia, Texas
*Houston Post*
June 13, 1909
Story of Reunion
MAJ. Hanks Met Man Who Saw Him Killed.
First Meeting Since Battle of Sharpsburg—Hanks was Taken Prisoner During Battle

Major John F. Hanks of Columbia, justice of the peace of his precinct and who is commander of Clinton Terry camp 423, United Confederate Veterans, spent yesterday in Houston *en route* home from attending the Memphis reunion. "It was a most delightful encampment," he stated, "and the only thing that tended to mar it was the fact that Houston did not land the next one."

Major Hanks came to life in Memphis after being dead more than forty years. He was killed at the battle of Sharpsburg. At least it was reported that he was dead, his boon companion John Riggs, member of his company, having seen him die on the field and having reported the death to the company officials. Hanks was mourned for dead by his parents for several months.

Riggs and Hanks were in a corn field during the battle. They had just taken a drink from a cup when a bullet pierced Hanks' both legs. He was knocked down within a foot or so of Riggs. Almost simultaneously with this shot a shell burst over their heads. Riggs, seeing Hanks lying on the ground went to him and turned him over. He thought Hanks had been killed by the shell not knowing that the wound in the legs had knocked him down.

Hanks, however, was not dead, but unconscious. Riggs reported him as dead and he was so listed. Meantime a couple of Yankees picked Hanks up and took him to their hospital and he was held as prisoner of war for several months. After the exchange his wounds having healed he returned to his own company. Riggs by that time was in the hospital. When Riggs was able to go back to his company again Hanks was once again in the hospital. Hanks was in the hospital three times. The two men kept passing each other back and forth to the hospital and never met after the incident in the corn field in Sharpsburg.

Riggs left the war thinking that Hanks was dead. Last Wednesday Major Hanks was seated at headquarters in Memphis when an aged soldier tottered in. Hanks asked him what company and command he was with during the war. Riggs told him. Neither of the men recognized each other. Hanks told him that he could give the roster of the company and to the surprise of the men did so. When Riggs asked his name and he replied that it was Hanks. Riggs disputed this very vehemently, stating that he knew that Hanks was dead. Hanks recited the incident of drinking from the same water cup in the corn field and then it slowly dawned upon Riggs that the boon companion he had so long mourned as dead was still in the flesh.

Oh we had a fine time together after the recognition, stated Major Hanks. We never separated until I left for home and we lived the old trying days over again.

They always ask us how many Yanks we killed. No one knows anything about that. I always tell them that I put two out of the battle at Sharpsburg. The two men who carried me to the rear did not go back to the front, and they were to for all intent purposes so far as fighting was concerned dead.

Major Hanks won his star at the battle of Gettysburg.

## James Madison Hubbard
## 2nd Mississippi Infantry
## Clarksville, Texas

The regiment was never sent out of Virginia, except to Goldsboro, N. C., the winter of 1862, for detached service on Black Water. Was wounded at the first battle of Manassas, shot through right cheek. Seven Days' Fight around Richmond, flesh wound in right side and lost left leg below the knee at the battle of Sharpsburg. I was assisted off the field by two comrades to the old Dunkard Church, where the regiment was formed for action in the first charge against the enemy, in which our company lost five killed and seventeen wounded. At the reorganization in 1862, I was appointed Second Sergeant, and was acting Orderly at the time I was wounded. Our brigade and Hood's Texas Brigade formed Hood's Division, which did such a heroic service in that memorable engagement. I was in the battles of First Manassas, Seven Pines, on June 25, 1862, Whiting's Division, and Hood's Division, was attached to Jackson's command and fought the battle of Gaines; Mill. After the battle of the Seven Days around Richmond, our troops were turned north to meet and demolish the great Pope. So, Aug. 30 found Hood's and Whiting's Brigades going over the mountains by a foot-path to turn the enemy. On the following day found Hood's Brigade deployed across turnpike getting in position for the battle of Second Manassas. Our next engagement was South Mountain, and then Sharpsburg, where I lost my leg, which put me out of commission for the remainder of the war.[5]

J. S. Johnston
11th Mississippi Infantry
San Antonio, Texas
The *Daily Express*
October 31, 1909
Historical Reminiscences
Conducted by J. B. Polley, Floresville, Texas

It is mighty hard for the young folks of the present day to believe that almost all of the sober-faced and dignified old Southern gentlemen they meet were once heedless, audacious and reckless boys and daringly brave Confederate soldiers, ragged and dirty, and often hatless and shoeless, and risking their lives on the skirmish and battle line and on scouts. Who would suspect, when talking with Capt. Dan Oppenheimer at his bank that in his youth he aced the grim monster. Death, on hundreds of occasions, and thought no more of the risk he ran than he does nowadays of that he takes when he insists, on having gilt edge security for the cash he loans? Who would think, when chatting with Sam Maverick about everyday happenings, that as a member of that noted command, the Terry Rangers, he hunted for Yankee gore before breakfast, after breakfast and all day long, and perhaps risked his life to capture a haversack of provisions?

What is there in the manner and general appearance of Mr. Monserrate to remind one that he was a member of Kemper's Confederate brigade, the color-bearer of his regiment, and never failed to keep his flag well to the front, and that hunger once drove him to catch on his morsel of bread the drippings from confiscated pork? And who, when listening to the eloquence and solid good sense of Bishop J. S. Johnston, as robed in his sacred calling, he stands in the pulpit and calls on the people to serve God and live righteous lives, that he too, was once a wild, rattling and irresponsible Confederate soldier, and yelled as loud if not louder than the next man when charging the enemy? Still, that was what the bishop once was and once did, and, to prove it on him, we take the liberty of republishing a contribution from his pen that appears in volume 8 of *Southern Historical Society Papers*, page 526. The article is copied verbatim, and is as follows:

The following incident, which came under the observation of the writer, who was a courier on the staff of Colonel Law of the Fourth Alabama Regiment, commanding the Third (Bee's) Brigade of Hood's Division, Army Northern Virginia, has never to his knowledge been published, and is recorded here at the suggestion of a friend as an interesting reminiscence of the late war between the States, and as illustrative of the character of the beloved chieftain, the least incident of whose grand life is cherished by those brave men who for three years followed him on fields of glory, but to final defeat.

In the early morning of September 16, 1862, McClellan opened the battle of Sharpsburg (Antietam) by an attack in force of our center, just at the junction of

Jackson and Longstreet's corps. Hood's division was the left of Longstreet's corps; the commander of Jackson's right is not known to the writer. At 11 o'clock on the previous night Hood, who had covered the retreat from South Mountain, was relieved by a brigade which had just joined the army and had seen but little real service. The attack was so heavy that these troops soon began to waver, and couriers were sent in quick succession to Hood, who was a few hundred yards in the rear, resting his weary and hungry men, to hold himself in readiness to move to the front in the support of heavily pressed lines.

Soon the order to fall in was given, and the division, nine regiments front, with no supports or reserves, and nothing between them and the Potomac, moved forward in splendid style. Up to that day that division had never known defeat. A part of it had made a glorious record at the First Manassas. The whole of it had taken part in the battle of Seven Pines; it was the first to successfully charge and carry the strong-works at Gaines' Mill; it had made a splendid record at the Second Manassas, and demolished the Duryee Zouaves, who had requested that they might be pitted against the Texans to recover the honor lost at Gaines Mill; it had held Fox Gap, on South Mountain against every attempt to carry it by Burnside's division; and on that day they moved forward in gallant style, making the air ring with the well-known rebel yell, and soon met the on-coming tide of Federals, flushed with victory, and rolled it back like a wave is shattered and beat back when it strikes a rock. Soon the field was strewn with the flying fragments of the attacking force, and the ground covered thick with the wounded and dead.

The pursuit was continued for about a quarter of a mile, when the victorious Southrons were in turn met by a fresh corps of Federals. The regiments had become scattered by the long charge, and were now in a cornfield where a new alignment was impossible. Retreat became necessary, and the order was given to fall back. There was no rout, no frantic rushing to the rear, though the fire of musketry and cannon was fearful. The men fell back in squads—often stopping to replenish their empty cartridge boxes from those of the dead and wounded and then turning and returning the deadly fire of overwhelming numbers before whom they were slowly and doggedly retiring. When they reached the woods, from which they had debouched about two hours before, 4000 strong, only 700 could be mustered to form a new line to hold the Northern hordes in check until McLaws could come up from Harper's Ferry.

Out of the nine regiments, but one field officer besides Colonel Law, who bore a charmed life that day, reported for duty; he was a major of a Texas regiment. The following fatalities are known to the present writer: Colonel Liddell of the Eleventh Mississippi had been killed the night before in a heavy skirmish on this same ground. The lieutenant colonel, Butler, and the major (name forgotten), both mortally wounded and left on the field. Colonel Stone of the Second Mississippi, upper lip shot away, unable to talk, and yet only going to the rear under the positive orders of Colonel Law. Lieutenant Colonel (name forgotten), left arm shattered, yet insisting on staying until ordered to the rear. Major Blair, shot in the throat, with a buckshot against the windpipe, unable to talk, yet wanted to remain, but ordered to the rear.

These 700 were formed into two regiments, one of which was deployed as skirmishers, behind a breastwork of rails made the morning before, along the Hagerstown Pike; the other was held in reserve about 100 yards in rear. After the Federals had shelled the woods furiously they moved up in force, slowly and timidly, on the little handful of men holding them, supposing of course, they were encountering fresh troops, when they were met by the brisk fire of this skirmish line of lion-hearted men. It was fully a half hour before they were compelled to leave their position. They then fell back on the supporting line, and here the same progress was repeated; the Federals evidently afraid to make a decisive charge, which must certainly have resulted in cutting the Southern army in two, and in the complete destruction of it before it could cross the Potomac. When finally driven from their second position, and entirely out of the woods, which alone concealed the utter desperation of our situation, they were met by McLaws, who soon succeeded in restoring the line to its original position.

Shortly after this repulse Hood was accosted by General Evans of South Carolina, who asked him, "Where is your division?" Hood replied, "Dead on the field."

After being relieved by McLaws, Hood marched the remnant of his division some distance to the rear, where it was deployed as skirmishers in the shape of a V, with orders to pass all stragglers, regardless of regiment or division, down to the point of the V. In the course of two or three hours 5000 men had been collected at this point. They were then formed into companies, regiments and a brigade. It was, perhaps an anomalous organization in warfare. No man knew any officer over him, nor even his file leader, or the man to the right or left of him. And thus was taken away every influence which gives men confidence and conduces to their greatest efficiency as soldiers. It was about 4 o'clock in the evening when this strangely constructed brigade was ordered to fall in to march to the front. A little after they had begun marching in column of fours by the right flank the men at the lead of the column saw General Lee standing with bared head and calm, but anxious expression, under the shade of an apple tree close beside their line of march. As they passed he said loud enough to be heard by several companies at the time: "Men, I want you to go back on the line and show that the stragglers of the Army of Northern Virginia are better than the best troops of the enemy." The effect, was magnetic. "The Stragglers' Brigade," as it was afterwards called, was thrilled with enthusiasm, and had they been called into action, that day would have fully realized the expectations of their noble chief. But the battle had changed from our left and center to the right, and nothing was required of this brigade but to remain as a reserve to General Pryor, who occupied the line in their immediate front.

When night began to fall these men, all strangers to each other, began to long for their comrades, and so to become restive and uneasy among the strange faces which surrounded them; so by 9 o'clock there was scarcely one of them to be found in the line, excepting those who belonged to the division.

This speech of General Lee, which I have never seen recorded, and which this reminiscence was written to preserve is, I think fully equal to that of Napoleon at the Pyramids of Egypt: "Soldiers, from those pyramids forty centuries contemplate your actions!" The two speeches are eminently characteristic of the two men— the watchword and guiding principle of the Frenchmen being "glory"; that of Lee, "duty."

## M. I. Jones
## 1st Louisiana Infantry
## Dallas, Texas

Harper's Ferry surrendered with 1,200 prisoners early in the morning of the 17th. My regiment went into the fight at Sharpsburg about daylight and was engaged till noon. At Sunken Road the enemy enfiladed our regiment and we were forced to fall back under a terrible artillery fire. Here we had four Color Bearers killed and our division commander, Gen. Starke. Our line fell back to the position occupied early in the morning. Gen. McLaw was in line, lying down on the battlefield, in the edge of the woods, awaiting the enemy's line. He gave them a volley at close range and charging them, drove them back.[6]

## George Kimball
## 12th Massachusetts Infantry
## *Boston Globe*
## March 17, 1898
## Twelfth Massachusetts at Antietam

At the reunion of the survivors of the Twelfth Massachusetts in this city Wednesday, Secretary Kimball made the following statement:

I am aware that it is a startling statement to make that the loss of the Twelfth Massachusetts at Antietam was the highest in percentage of any organization in the entire world, in modern times, in civilized warfare, under normal conditions, but is there not good reason to believe it to be true?

The fighting was terrific, as everyone knows. Let me simply say that a letter which I wrote a friend on the 30th of September, 1862, says my company (A) had twenty-two men killed and wounded out of thirty, and of the eight who escaped unhurt five had missiles strike either their clothing or equipment. Only thirty-two marched off the field under the flag of the regiment when relieved by the Twelfth Corps. One of the Confederate regiments, the First Texas, Hood's division, which we encountered in our advance through the cornfield, and which afterwards occupied a position a little to our right, had 186 killed and wounded out of 226 taken into action—a percentage of loss 82.3.

## E. J. Lake
## Bonham's Brigade, Army of Northern Virginia
## Lindale, Texas

Enlisted in the Confederate Army in March, 1861, near Pomaria, S. C. as a private in Company E, Bonham's Brigade, McLaw's Division, Longstreet's Corps, Army of Northern Virginia. J. D. Nance first Captain and James Williams first Colonel. Was wounded at the battle of Seven Pines; also at the battle of Gettysburg. I fell into the hands of the enemy when Gen. Lee retired from Gettysburg on the 5th of July, 1863, and not being able to be moved, was sent to David's Island, N. Y., and exchanged the latter part of October 1863. Was in the battles of Bull Run, Williamsburg, Seven Pines, Seven Days Battle near Richmond, Second Manassas, Harper's Ferry, Sharpsburg, Fredericksburg, Chancellorsville and Gettysburg.

Our brigade was the first at Fairfax Courthouse, Va. We remained there until the Federals advanced, then retreated back to Bull Run. The weather was very warm, and we were closely pursued by the enemy until the 21st of July, when the enemy attacked us. The next night we marched all night to Vienna, where we picketed within six miles of Washington.

In the spring of 1862, Gen. McClellan attacked Gen. Magruder at Yorktown, and Gen. Johnston moved us to meet them. The Peninsula is a low flat country. After the passing of the wagon train, artillery and army, the road was about knee-deep in mud. We left at night and the next day we reached Williamsburg. Here a squad of the enemy's cavalry attacked us, and we repulsed them, with a heavy loss to them. On our retreat to Chickahominy we were without a morsel of food. After the battle of Seven Pines, where Gen. Johnston was wounded, Gen. Lee took command. He attacked Gen. McClellan, and for seven days we had continual fighting. He drove the enemy under cover of his gunboats at Harrison's Landing. Language would fail to describe the hardships we endured during these seven days. Gen. John Pope had a large force in Northern Virginia and Gen. Lee moved our army to meet him and attacked him at Manassas. Then we fought the battle of Sharpsburg and then back to Virginia. During this campaign we had little to eat, yet with hard marching and fighting and very short rations, there was scarcely any murmuring.[7]

R. H. Little
1st Georgia Infantry
Belton, Texas
The *Temple Daily Telegraph*
June 27, 1913
R. H. Little

Mr. Little was born in Newman, Coweta county, Georgia, December 10, 1837. Was raised on a farm. On March 18, 1861, he joined Co. A. 1st Georgia volunteer infantry. Went to Pensacola, Florida; in June went to West Virginia, under Gen. Garnett who was killed at Carrick's Ford. Was in a picket and artillery fight at Laurel Hill in West Virginia. Was assigned to the army of Gen. Henry R. Jackson and was in a victorious fight at Rich Mountain. Was transferred to the army of Stonewall Jackson and made a raid on the Yankees in the northeastern part of Virginia, the enemy always retreating. In March, 1862, the regiment was disbanded at Augusta. In thirty-six days he reenlisted in the 44th Alabama, Law's brigade. Besieged Suffolk for 22 days, was in the Second Battle of Manassas in which he went into action about the middle of the morning and fought until 9 o'clock at night, pursued the enemy for three miles and won a victory. Besieged Harper's Ferry, captured it with 11,000 men, guns and munitions. Had a hot time at Sharpsburg— when he took notice of the surroundings he was the only living man in a space of fourteen steps to the right; when he kneeled to load his gun he could touch five dead men without getting off his knees, and could have walked on dead men in any direction until he could reach the living; saw two comrades about thirty steps away, went to them and they were killed after he got to them. He was shocked by an exploding shell but was able to fall into line again next morning. Was captured with forty others between Lookout and Raccoon mountain by General Hooker's army and confined for 17 months at Camp Morton prison, Indianapolis. Mr. Little farmed in Alabama for a year following the war, was ten years in Arkansas, came to Texas in 1877, now lives in Belton, where he has been for twenty years.


T. J. Marshall
9th Pennsylvania Reserve Infantry
West Middlesex, Pennsylvania
*National Tribune*
April 11, 1907
The Pennsylvania Reserves at Antietam
There were only 5,000 of them, which Hood mistook for 20,000

Editor: *National Tribune*: Hood says he was confronted by 20,000 Federals at the battle of Antietam. I wish to state that it was the Pennsylvania Reserves with less than 5000. My regiment, the 9th, was in the immediate front of the Texas Brigade as it came thru the cornfield. We held our fire until we could see their knees, and then let them have it. After firing two or three times, we advanced and found three Texas flags lying where they fell, which were carried back to Gen. Meade, and if not returned with the other rebel flags are now in the War Department at Washington. The Texans were not in line of battle, but the other regiments were massed closely, and I think we could have stepped from on end of a regiment to another on dead men without touching the ground. On the night of July 2, at Gettysburg, in front of the "Devil's Den," I was the Sergeant on the picket line in front of the 9th. The ground was covered with dead and wounded Confeds, and in passing along I assisted some to easier positions. One poor fellow, who was shot thru the lung, asked me to what troops I belonged, and when I told him the 9th Pa. Reserves, he said, "Oh, we met you at the cornfield at Antietam." He said he belonged to the 5th Texas, and was one of 12 of his regiment, who got out of that field alive; "but," he added, "this is my last battle, and I'm glad of it." We had him carried to our field hospital. The wounded Confeds were crying for water, and on the morning of the 3d our pickets asked the Arkansans in the Devil's Den to allow us to give their wounded water, to which they agreed. Serg't McMunn, Co. G., and some others filled canteens and came out. When McMunn was in the act of placing the canteen to the mouth of a badly wounded man, one of the Arkansans shot him thru the head, taking the roof of his mouth away. He was sent to the hospital with a silver plate fitted in his mouth, which enabled him to talk, and he returned to his regiment with a Lieutenant's commission, serving out his time. Our regiment meets Dec. 20 each year at Pittsburgh, to commemorate the anniversary of the battle of Dranesville, Va., which was the first battle won by any portion of the Army of the Potomac. It was fought by the Third Brigade (Ord's), and a proud lot of boys we were.—T. J. Marshall, Co. H., 9th P. R., West Middlesex, Pa.


## J. C. Meares
## 3rd North Carolina Infantry
## Chilton, Texas

When we first enlisted our regiment was not in any brigade or division that I know of but in 1862 we were placed as above stated. I was color bearer at the battle of Sharpsburg and when the color bearer was killed I picked up the flag and carried through the battle and was promoted to Second Sergeant and was attached to Corps of Sharpshooters were I remained till the close of the war.[8]


## W. E. Moore
## 1st Louisiana Infantry
## Blossom, Texas

On April 19 at Williamsburg, Va., I was elected Captain of the Grays. That evening we had a skirmish with Gen. McClellan's cavalry and artillery in the first siege of

Richmond. Was in the battle of Seven Pines, and at Malvern Hill. The next after that was Second Manassas—three days. On the last day I was promoted to Lieutenant Colonel. The next was Harper's Ferry, and the next and last was at Sharpsburg, Md., called by some "Bloody Lane," where I was promoted on the field to Colonel of the First Louisiana Regiment. Just as we reached the fence on our side of the lane our Colonel was wounded, we being on the extreme left of Gen. Lee's line of battle. We were engaged with the Federal infantry across the lane and were flanked, the enemy having crossed the lane and were advancing from our left and rear. Retreating to the timber, our brigade of five Louisiana regiments was formed, and I found myself in command. We charged the brigade which was pressing us and drove them back with heavy loss.[9]

## Henry A. Morehead
## 11th Mississippi Infantry
## McGregor, Texas

At Sharpsburg, on Sept. 17, 1862, we fought nearly all night, here we lost our Colonel, P. F. Lidell, one of the best men I ever knew, and as brave as the bravest. We also lost Lieut. Col. Evans and Major Butler, both good men. We also lost heavily in the ranks. His battle was fought in a cornfield and as the corn was just in roasting ear, the boys at the whole ate it raw. I don't think there was a stalk standing and the dead and dying men could be seen everywhere. Next morning they attacked us again, and we drove them back and held them while our army started back to Virginia, skirmishing nearly all the way. When we got to the Potomac, it was up, and we had to wait for our men to put in a pontoon bridge. We were then ordered to Richmond, and from there to Suffolk, where we stayed a month or two, and then went to Goldsboro, N. C.[10]

## John "Finey" Oden
## 10th Alabama Infantry
## Galveston, Texas

Among other things you give prominence to their many intellectual, physical and social graces, together with their political prominence. Now it may be that you reckoned better than you know, and that you did not know that there were some ex-Confederates who were constant readers of your valuable and in your immediate vicinity who have special cause to know and remember the illustrious and patriotic family. I allude particularly to Capt. John 'Piney' Oden, Company K, Tenth Alabama Regiment, Confederate Volunteers, who was severely wounded, on Wednesday, September 17th, 1862, at Sharpsburg, receiving a wound fourteen inches long, reaching the whole length of the thigh, from which he has been a permanent cripple and great sufferer ever since. Besides he received at the same time a painful wound in the left side from a piece of bomb-shell.

He lay upon the battlefield in that helpless condition for twenty-six hours. When all other efforts for removal failed, he made some Masonic characters upon a piece of paper and requested that they be carried to the general in command of the Federal army, he being then within the Federal lines. Very soon six men came for him with an improvised litter, an old army blanket. They made a slip in the fence, near which he lay, and ran across the hill to a field hospital with him upon the litter, which was more than one punctured with balls from his friends' guns, they not understand what was going on. He was finally removed to the Hagerstown, Md., courthouse, which had been converted into a Federal hospital.

Here he first met and learned to love and honor the name of Magill and the members of the family, for the daughters that were then at home came to the hospital and inquired especially if there were any Confederate soldiers among the wounded there. Capt. Oden being pointed out, they began immediately to beseech, in the view of his condition, that he be paroled and they be allowed to carry him into their private dwelling, which request, at their earnest and importunate solicitation, was granted.

For six months the members of the family, including Dr. Chas. Macgill, J., who was then at home, continued their ministrations. At one time the femoral artery sloughed in two and Capt. Oden's said that he was especially indebted to Miss Mollie Macgill, now Mrs. Rosenberg of Galveston, and named a daughter Mollie Macgill Oden in honor and grateful remembrance of her. The intimacy and friendship between the Macgill and Oden families has been kept up ever since the war by correspondence and interchange of visits.

Capt. Oden died in Ondena, Talledge County, Ala., May 25, 1895.[11]


James G. Ramsey
Palmetto Light Artillery Battery
Army of Northern Virginia
*Atlanta Constitution*
July 11, 1909
Brave Old Soldier Gone to His Rest
Sketch of Colonel John Cheves Haskell who Died in South Carolina


Now I will revert to another great piece of hard service performed by his (Haskell) battalion of artillery. Gen McClellan was pouring his legions of troops through South Mountain, on the Frederick City road, through Boonsboro Gap, a narrow winding pass from Hagerstown. Gen. Lee ordered Gen. Hood to report to him to repel this attack on his retreat to Antietam. Hood being under arrest, Gen. Lee said, 'I will suspend your arrest until this impending battle is fought.' Hooker's corps had swung around on our right on the Pike, and Hood was ordered to deploy the Texas brigade on left and Law's Alabama brigade on right of Pike, and the eighteen guns composing our battalion were placed to hold this vast army of federal troops. We planted our guns from hill to hill, and ploughed deep furrows through the federal masses as they advanced on our thin and decimated lines. The Texas brigade was nearly demolished in corn fields near Dunker church. We fought them 15th, 16th and 17th of September, where the bloody battle of Sharpsburg was fought. Our rations were awful slim here, green apples and corn about all we had. Here Gen. Hood and Haskell displayed some of the hardest fighting on record under very trying circumstances. After the battle of 17th Gen. Hood was promoted to major-general for gallantry and his arrest was never brought up. Col. Haskell had two brothers, one Alex Cheeves, brigadier general of cavalry, and Joseph Cheeves, adjutant general to E. P. Alexander, commanding artillery Longstreet's corps.

"Peace to the memory of these two brave men who fought side by side for four years, General J. B. Hood and Col. John Cheeves Haskell."

A Color bearer of One of His Batteries.

## J. H. Robertson
## 5th Florida Infantry
## Marlin, Texas

J. H. Robertson, Marlin, Texas (in reply to the inquiry of Cleve Rowan, Campbellsville, Miss, for any incidents in connection with the hoisting of a white flag by the Federals at the battle of Antietam.)

I was in Roger A. Pryor's Brigade, and was in the road in line of battle. Gen. Pryor passed in twenty steps of me in going to and coming back from the white flag. I saw him when he rode up to the Federals that had the white flag, about half a mile from me. They met in an open field. In a few minutes Gen. Pryor came back and, as he passed us, he said: "They will be firing in fifteen minutes," but in about two minutes they opened fire. I heard at the time that the white flag was hoisted by the Federals to give them a chance to get their wounded out of the apple orchard. I belonged to Company H, 5th Florida Regiment, Pryor's Brigade. After the Sharpsburg fight, we were commanded by Gen. Perry.

I was captured at Gettysburg on the second day of the battle, in Longstreet's charge, taken to Fort Delaware and kept a prisoner till the 11th of June, 1865, and I got to my home in Florida on the 28th day of June '65. Should be glad to hear of any of my old friends who were with me in that prison.[12]

James Thomas Rosborough
6th North Carolina Infantry
Texarkana, Texas

Was first wounded at Malvern Hill, the last of the Seven Days' Fight around Richmond, next was at Sharpsburg, Md., which was a very severe wound in the head and came near being fatal. Was never taken prisoner. Was in the battles of Bull Run, Winchester, Hanover Court House, Seven Pines, Seven Days' Fight around Richmond, Second Manassas, Culpepper Court House, Harper's Ferry, Boonsboro, Sharpsburg, Fredericksburg, Chancellorsville, Gettysburg, and almost daily skirmishing, besides many other battles not mentioned; something over twenty battles.[13]

A. T. Tannar
18th Mississippi Infantry Regiment
Normangee, Texas

Was in the battles of Bull Run, Seven Days' Battle around Richmond, Harpers Ferry and Sharpsburg. On last campaign we left Richmond with perhaps sixty rank and file, crossed the Potomac near Leesburg, Loudon County, went by the way of Frederick City, and invested Harpers Ferry on the north, while Stonewall Jackson had it invested on the south; captured it on the 16th of September; crossed over the Potomac on pontoon bridge, marched all night and crossed back on north side just at daylight. The water was up to our armpits, and we had to hold our ammunition above our heads. The battle was on in a short time after daylight. About 10 a.m. I fell victim to one of their bullets. I lay on the field until under cover of darkness I was removed. My company after the battle numbered only thirteen.[14]

"T. D. B."
1st North Carolina Infantry
*Murfreesboro Index*
February 8, 1895

After we had been engaged more than two hours an order came for us to retire, and we feel back in admirable order to a skirt of woods where Hood's Texas Brigade had reformed. It was here I saw J. B. Hood the first and only time. He had reformed his brigade—what was left of it—for it was a skeleton only, and we took position with him to meet the advance of the enemy. They came on very slowly for we had given them a lesson they would not soon forget. If we had suffered severely they had undergone greater loss, for ours was only a regimental line while they had brought into action not less than three lines of battle. Hon. J. C. Scarborough, who visited the field a few years back, has told me that in our front there was one grave marked with the names of more than thirty Federal soldiers and that was only one of many. When Gen. Robert Ransom's brigade came upon the field, we were withdrawn to procure ammunition and were not actively engaged during the remainder of the day. Impressions made at such times are very lasting. I have never forgotten that Gen. Ransom was putting his Brigade into action Gen. Hood rode up to Ransom and asked permission to accompany him into the fight. Having obtained Ransom's consent, Hood rode back to the remnant of the Texas Brigade and turning over to the senior officer his command, remarked that he was going with Ransom to see that fun. His men cried out, "Come back General, don't go— you will be killed!" but his blood was on fire with the spirit of battle and he would not yield to their wishes.[15]

S. F. Tenney
3rd Georgia Infantry
Crockett, Texas
The *Houston Post*
March 24, 1912
The Battle of Sharpsburg
A Letter Written Fifty Years Ago Just After the Famous Engagement

The following letter was written by Rev. S. F. Tenney of Crockett nearly fifty years ago, when he was a soldier of the Third Georgia Regiment. There is a bit of romance about it, as Mr. Tenney had forgotten writing such a letter and did not know that it was still in existence until a few weeks ago, when a Virginia paper was sent to him with this article marked.

"When I wrote you last, I believe we were near Leesburg. The next day we crossed the Potomac and for the first time, as soldiers, stood on Maryland soil. The event was hailed with cheers and "My Maryland" from the bass bands attending our army. The scene of the army fording the Potomac was most interesting and would have afforded a fine occasion for the employment of an artist's skill in forming a picture of the surrounding beauty of nature, and the interesting movements of men.

"We marched directly on, advancing towards Frederick City. In some places as we passed along ladies greeted us with Confederate flags and waved their handkerchiefs. The advance of our army arrived in Frederick on the 8th instead and by their sudden appearance surprised both our friends and foes. The Federals in their haste left some army stores, burned a large quantity of hospital bedding and were obliged to leave behind some of their sick.

"We were encamped near the city three days. During that time we found some friends for our cause, but the city is strongly Union in its sympathies. Many of our troops purchased articles at very low prices, but a number of the merchants refused to take Confederate money and closed their stores. As we marched through the place, however, a number of Confederate flags was displayed through windows and many a white handkerchief cheered us on our way. But I think the larger portion of the population have little sympathy for the "rebels," as they called us. I have heard that two companies were made up in and around the city, which joined our army. The splendid railroad bridge of the Baltimore and Ohio railroad at that place was blown up by order of our general. From Frederick we marched contrary to the expectation of everyone toward Harpers Ferry. A portion of our army went to Hagerstown. We then laid siege to Harpers Ferry, and in three days occupied the town and received the surrender of spoils and prisoners. Our forces in front took Maryland Heights without much fighting, while Jackson crossed the river above and got in the rear of the enemy, and on the morning after the 15th the instant had his artillery posted on hills commanding Bolivar's Heights, and completely surrounding it. The post was surrendered early in the day, the general commanding surrendering his entire command, consisting of about 12,000 men, and all his artillery, about fifty pieces, and his army supplies. A large number of stolen negroes were recovered at this place. The captured batteries are all supplied with splendid artillery horses. The prisoners general were a good looking set of men, and seemed very cheerful over their fate, and at the prospect of a long furlough.

"In the meantime other portions of our army were fighting the Federal army, which had followed in our rear from Frederick City,

"Our division was marched nearly all night and arrived near Sharpsburg, Md., early in the morning of the 17th, having forded the Potomac at daylight. At Sharpsburg the battle commenced early, and we hurried up to reinforce the portion of our army already engaged. Our brigade went into the fight about 10 a.m. and for three hours fought hard with the enemy until our ammunition was exhausted. Failing to receive reinforcements in proper time, our brigade was compelled to fall back from their position. Reinforcements finally came up and relieved us and saved us from losing much ground, though we were compelled to leave a number of dead and wounded in the possession of the enemy. In the fight General Wright was severely wounded and brought off the field; also our Major General Anderson. The colonel next in command of our brigade was shot down, also the captain commanding our regiment and our adjutant. In our regiment the total loss was seventy of 115 taken into battle. The loss in many other regiments was much greater.

"Throughout the while day the battle raged, both parties obstinately contested the field. In some parts of the field we pressed the enemy back, and in other portions our forces were forced to retire and leave the enemy in possession of our dead and wounded. I think it must have been the hardest fought battle of the war.

"The Federals stood up in fine line of battle with their colors constantly flying and were directly facing us in an open field and within easy musket range. I think their loss was great than ours, but we lost heavily.

"The next day was occupied in getting of the dead and wounded, and on Thursday night (the 18th) our army recrossed the Potomac, making a successful retreat to this side. The whole army was brought over under cover of darkness, and such a time as we had in fording the river in the dark and marching over rough and slippery roads, you cannot imagine and it is not in my power to describe. The next night we fell back eight or ten miles further, and again on Saturday night marched to this place.

"The enemy attempted to cross the river and pursue us but they were repulsed with heavy loss. I have no doubt that the Federals will claim a great victory at the battle of Sharpsburg. The fruits of victory, however, will be few to them. Except that we left them the battleground—I don't think there is any other evidence of victory for them.

"I have learned that General Lee expresses himself at being satisfied with the result. His design in crossing the Potomac with the while army was to extricate General Longstreet's corps, which had become tightly pressed while drawing off the attention of the enemy from Harper's Ferry.

"Taking the series of battles together, we have been highly successful. For the capture of Harpers Ferry, with its immense results, we are indebted to the mercy of God and the skill of our generals. Let the whole nation give thanks to God for so great a victory.

"The portion of Maryland that we have been through has suffered little from the war. It is a rich country and abounds with picturesque and beautiful scenery. It is well watered with cool, bold springs, and its rolling hillsides and valleys team with abundant growing crops.

"The people through the country have been generally kind to us, even when they did not sympathize with our cause. I have met many too, who gave us their best wishes and offered their best hospitality to our men. But on the whole our men are generally dissatisfied with our reception in Maryland. I think, though, that we have been in a portion of the state where we could not expect an exhibition of much sympathy with us."

## Stephen D. Thruston
## 3rd North Carolina Infantry
## Dallas, Texas

Dr. Stephen D. Thruston practiced his profession in Wilmington, North Carolina, until April 13, 1861, when he enlisted as a private in the Wilmington Light Infantry. After serving one month, he was made Captain of Company "B," Third Regiment of

North Carolina State troops, enlisted for the war and was early made colonel of the regiment. His regiment was in the Third Brigade, Stonewall Jackson's division, from the first until the close of the war. The Doctor was well acquainted with General Jackson and a great admirer of his military genius and Christian and gentlemanly qualities. He (Col. Thruston) took part in all the battles and hardships of that division and corps through Virginia, Maryland and Pennsylvania.

At Antietam, or Sharpsburg, September 17, 1862, while in the front of the Dunker Church, his jacket was punctured with forty-seven bullet holes. One of the balls, entering his right lung, the others doing him no injury.[16]

Colonel Stephen D. Thruston
3rd North Carolina Infantry
*Daily Review*
March 10, 1879
Honors to a Former Wilmingtonian

A friend has handed us a Dallas (Texas) paper from which we learn that a former citizen of this city, but now a resident of the above named place, has been promoted from the Captaincy of the Dallas Stonewall Greys, a volunteer military organization, to the Colonelcy of the First Texas Regiment—a compliment not undeserved when we consider that the former citizen and gentleman in question is none other than the gallant Thruston, late Colonel of the Third N. C. Infantry—though it is just possible that the Texans did not know their new Colonel as well as we know him here; we who started out in the war with him, and served with him in camp and on the march, in bivouac and on the battlefield, or his promotion would not have stopped at a colonelcy. Col. S. D. Thruston entered the Wilmington Light Infantry in April 1861 as a private and at the conclusion of the war had reached the Colonelcy of the Regiment named above; and had reward moved space with merit, the brave commander of this N. C. Regiment would have had his three stars encircled with a wreath. As it was, however, he was infrequently acting as brigade commander.

Thrice wounded, once on the bloody field of Sharpsburg, again at Chancellorsville, and lastly at Winchester in the valley of Virginia during Early's last campaign there, Col. Thruston has a war record that he may be proud of. In his report of the battle of Sharpsburg Gen'l D. H. Hill, after paying a handsome and well deserved compliment to Col. Wm. L. De Rosset, when it was thought at the time had received a mortal wound, compliments Col. Thruston also, who was then only a Major, and mentions the fact that though wounded, Major Thruston still remained on the field in command of his regiment.

When D. H. Hill complimented an officer or soldier there is one thing the public would feel well assured of, and that was, that the one thus complimented was no laggard in a fight.

# Endnotes

## Introduction

1. Wood, C., *(1842–1914): A Memoir Recollections of his Life, Family History and Military Service*. Manuscript (Atlanta, Georgia: Emory University Library Archives, 1907–1908)
2. Simpson, H., *Hood's Texas Brigade: A Compendium* (Hillsboro, TX: Hill Jr. College Press, 1970), p. 101.
3. Williams, E. B., *Hood's Texas Brigade in the Civil War* (Jefferson, NC: McFarland and Company, 2012), p. 303.
4. *Ibid.*, p. 103.
5. Priest, J. M., *Antietam, The Soldiers' Battle* (New York, NY: Oxford University Press, 1989), p. 343.
6. history.stackexchange.com/questions/25/how-many-troops-died-on-d-day.
7. en.wikipedia.org/wiki/Casualties_of_the_September_11_attacks.
8. Simpson, *op. cit.*, p.176.
9. Simpson, *Hood's Texas Brigade, Lee's Grenadier Guard* (Waco, TX: Texian Press, 1970), p. 169.
10. *Ibid.*, Map Section, p. 337.
11. *Ibid.*, p. 178.
12. *Ibid.*, p. 285.
13. *Ibid.*, p. 327.
14. *Ibid.*, p. 468.

## Chapter 1

1. Otott, G., *Antietam the Maryland Campaign of 1862* (Campbell, CA: Savas Publishing Company, 1997), p. 73.
2. First Texas Infantry, *Handbook of Texas Online*, www.tsaonline.org/handbook/online/articles/qkf13.
3. Simpson, H., *Hood's Texas Brigade: Lee's Grenadier Guard* (Waco, TX: Texian Press, 1970), p. 144.
4. *Ibid.*, p. 169.
5. *Ibid.*, p. 169.
6. Otott, *op. cit.*, p. 89.

7. Simpson, *op. cit.*, pp. 172–173.

8. *Ibid.*, p. 174.

9. *Ibid.*, p. 174.

10. *Ibid.*, p. 174.

11. P. A. Work to Colonel William Wofford, September 23, 1862, in *The War of the Rebellion: A Compilation of the Official Records of the Union and Confederate Armies*, 128 vols. (Washington, D.C., 1880–1901), Series 1, Vol. 19, pt. 1, pp. 253–254. Hereafter cited as OR. All references are to Series 1 unless otherwise noted.

12. Simpson, *op. cit.*, p. 177.

13. Philip Alexander Work, *Handbook of Texas Online*, www.tshaonline.org/handbook/online/articles/fwo25.

14. *Ibid.*

15. Hooks H. A., *Lt. Col. Phillip A. Work: General Without a Star* (TX: Texian Press, 1984), pp. 1–2.

16. Reagan, C. K., Work, Philip Alexander, Handbook of Texas Online: www.tshaonline.org/handbook/online/articles/fwo25.

17. OR 19, pt. 1, pp. 931–934.

18. Hooks, *op. cit.*, pp. 26–34. The second account of the Battle of Sharpsburg written by Lt. Col. Work was written to Private Tom Langley of the 1st Texas Infantry in May 1908.

19. Vivian, J., Todd, George T., Handbook of Texas Online: www.tshaonline.org/handbook/online/articles/fto07.

20. Todd, G., *First Texas Regiment* (Waco, TX: Texian Press, 1964), p. 17.

21. Simpson, *Hood's Texas Brigade: A Compendium* (TX: Hill Jr. College Press, 1970), p. 57.

22. Gaston, William, Henry, Handbook of Texas Online: www.tshaonline.org/handbook/online/articles/fga63.

23. *Dallas Morning News*, January 25, 1927.

24. Glover, R., (ed.), *"Tyler To Sharpsburg" The War Letters of Robert H. and William H. Gaston Company H, First Texas Infantry Regiment, Hood's Texas Brigade* (Waco, TX: W. M. Morrison, 1960), p. 2. Lieutenant Robert Gaston, Company "H," 1st Texas Infantry was killed at Antietam (Sharpsburg) on September 17, 1862. His body was found farther within Union lines than any other solder at Miller's Cornfield, and marked the point of deepest Confederate penetration. The Union soldiers who found his body recognized his bravery by giving him a decent, separate burial and marking his grave.

25. *Ibid.*, p. 21.

26. Graham, L., (ed.), "Anderson County in the Civil War, Anderson County Genealogical Society", *The Tracings*, Vol. 5, No. 1 (Winter, 1986), pp. 5–6.

27. Simpson, *op. cit.* (1970), p. 25.

28. Allport, J., *The Story of Captain Sam Willson, Company F, Woodville Rifles 1st Texas Regiment Confederate States Army* (personal papers, 2001), pp. 1–4.

29. Cherokee County Historical Commission, *Cherokee County History* (Rusk, TX: 2001), p. 599.

30. Senator F. B. Sexton to President Jefferson Davis, September 30, 1862, Personal papers of Joe Allport.

31. Confederate Congressman from the 4th District of Texas.

32. Pre-war Texas Attorney General, Confederate Congressman.

33. *Austin American Statesman,* February 10, 2010.

34. Hamilton, D. H., *History of Company M: First Texas Volunteer Infantry, Hood's Brigade, Longstreet's Corps, Army of Northern Virginia* (Waco, TX: W. M. Morrison, 1962), p. 2.

35. Lasswell, M., (ed.), *Rags and Hope, The Recollection of Val C. Giles, Four Years with Hood's Texas Brigade, Fourth Texas Infantry 1861-1865* (New York, NY: Coward McCann Inc., 1961), p. 7.

36. *Ibid.*, p. 215.

37. *Dallas Morning News,* February 5, 1915.

38. Giles, V., "The Flag of First Texas, A. N. Virginia" in *Confederate Veteran*, Vol. 15 (September, 1907), p. 417.

39. Owen, J., and Drais, R., *Texans at Gettysburg: Blood and Glory with Hood's Texas Brigade* (Charleston, SC: Fonthill Media LLC, 2016), p. 34.

40. *Dallas Morning News,* October 3, 1897.

41. Owen and Drais, *op. cit.*, pp. 34–35.

42. Stiles Gen, A Family History Website: www.stilesgen.com/getperson. php?personID=I11793&tree=SG2012.

43. Simpson, *op. cit.* (1970), p. 46.

44. Smith, W., Malachiah Reeves, Find a Grave: findagrave.com.

45. Eads, L. R., (ed.), *Malachiah Reeves—Memoirs of the mercies of a covenant God, while traveling through the Wilderness of this world of life: being the autobiography of Malachiah Reeves, originally of many places, from middle Alabama and through much of East Texas, and now of Ranger, middle West Texas* (Hillsboro, TX: Unpublished manuscript, *circa* 1910, Texas Heritage Museum–Historical Research Center), Appendix A.

46. OR 19, pt. 1, p. 933.

47. *Brotherhood of Locomotive Firemen and Engineer's Magazine,* Vols. 46–47 (Knoxville, TN: University of Tennessee Press, 1909), p. 116. Polley and McCaslin, *A Soldier's Letters to Charming Nellie* (1908), p. 268n. The article about Corporal Day being killed at the Battle of Antietam is in error. Corporal Day, though badly wounded, survived the battle of Antietam, and died in 1910.

48. Lewis Publishing Company, *Memorial and Biographical History of Dallas County, Texas* (New York, NY: Lewis Publishing Company, 1892), pp. 533–534.

49. Carter, B. F., Handbook of Texas Online: www.tshaonline.org/handbook/online/ articles/fbe52.

50. Hanks, O. T., *History of Captain B.F. Benton's Company, Hood's Texas Brigade, 1861–1865* (Austin, TX: Morrison Books, 1984), pp. 15–17.

51. Berryman, H. W., to Berryman, M., September 22, 1862, Hood's Texas Brigade Letters (Texas Heritage Museum–Historical Research Center).

52. Palmquist, P., and Kailbourn, T., *Pioneer Photographers From the Mississippi to the Continental Divide: A Biographical Dictionary, 1839-1865* (Stanford, CA: Stanford University Press, 2005), p. 116.

53. *Ibid.*, p. 117.

54. Yeary, M., *Reminiscences of the Boys in Gray* (Dallas, TX: Smith and Lamar, 1912), pp. 60–61.

55. Simpson, *The Marshall Guards: Harrison County's Contribution to Hood's Texas Brigade* (Marshall, TX: Port Caddo Press, 1967), p. 7.

56. Simpson, *op. cit.* (1970), p. 34.

57. "Sheriffs of Navarro County" in *Navarro County Scroll*, Vol. XXI (Corsicana, TX: Navarro County Historical Society, 1976), p. 420.

58. Gillihan, B., John C. Robinson, Find a Grave: www.findagrave.com/cgi-bin/ fg.cgi?page=gr&GRid=9723810.

59. Yeary, *op. cit.*, pp. 647–648.

60. Excerpt of speech given by S. O. Young at the Hood's Texas Brigade reunion in Galveston, Texas on June 23, 1896. Chilton, *Unveiling and dedication of Monument*

to Hood's Texas brigade on the capital grounds at Austin, Texas, Thursday, October Twenty-Seven, nineteen hundred and ten, and minutes of the thirty-ninth annual reunion of Hood's Texas brigade association held in Senate chamber at Austin, Texas, October twenty six and twenty seven, nineteen hundred and ten, together with a short monument and brigade association history and Confederate scrap book (1911), p. 199.

## Chapter 2

1. Fourth Texas Infantry, Handbook of Texas Online: tshaonline.org/handbook/online/articles/qkf0.
2. Simpson, H., *Hood's Texas Brigade: Lee's Grenadier Guard* (Waco, TX: Texian Press, 1970), p. 12.
3. John Bell Hood, Handbook of Texas Online: tshaonline.org/handbook/online/articles/fho49.
4. Simpson, H., *Gaines' Mill to Appomattox, Waco & McLennan County In Hood's Texas Brigade* (Waco, TX: Texian Press, 1963), pp. 85–89.
5. Farber, J., *Texas CSA: A Spotlight on Disaster* (San Antonio, TX: The Jackson Company, 1947), p. 150.
6. Simpson, *op. cit.* (1963), pp. 106–107.
7. Simpson, *op. cit.* (1970), p. 179.
8. Carter, B. F., Handbook of Texas Online: tshaonline.org/handbook/online/articles/fcafe.
9. Simpson, *op. cit.*, pp. 148, 178.
10. Carter, B. F., Handbook of Texas Online: tshaonline.org/handbook/online/articles/fcafe.
11. *OR*, 19, Pt. 1, pp. 934–936.
12. Winkler, C. M., to Winkler, M. C., *The Navarro County Scroll* (1959, reprinted with permission of the Navarro County Historical Society).
13. *Memorial and Biographical History of Navarro, Henderson, Anderson, Limestone, Freestone, and Leon Counties* (Chicago, IL: Lewis, 1893), p. 483, *The New Texas Handbook* (Austin, TX: Texas State Historical Association, 1996), p. 3296.
14. Winkler, C. M., to Loughridge, J. R., November 18, 1862, Hood's Texas Brigade files, (Texas Heritage Museum–Historical Research Center).
15. *Biographical Encyclopedia of Texas* (New York, NY: Southern Publishing Book Company, 1880), p. 45.
16. Davis, N. A., The Handbook of Texas: tshaonline.org/handbook/online/articles/fda46.
17. Everett, D. E., (ed.), *Chaplain Davis and Hood's Texas Brigade* (Louisiana State University Press, 1999), preface xi.
18. Davis, N., *The Campaign From Texas to Maryland With The Battle of Fredericksburg* (Richmond, VA: The Office Of The Presbyterian Committee of Publication of The Confederate States, 1863), pp. 88–93.
19. Polley, J. B., and McCaslin, R. B., *Hood's Texas Brigade: Its Marches, Its Battles, Its Achievements* (The Neale Publishing Company, 1910), Introduction. For over twenty years, Quarter Master Polley collected reminiscences about the Civil War from other soldiers in Hood's Texas Brigade and different Texas regiments and published them in weekly articles in the San Antonio *Daily Express*.
20. Davis, *op. cit.*, pp. 159–167.
21. Polk, J. M., *The North and South American Review* (Austin, TX: J. M. Polk, 1912), pp. 15–16.
22. Murray, J. C., to parents and sister (September 22–October 11, 1862) (2-23/882), Original letters written by James C. Murray, a member of Hood's Texas Brigade (4th

Texas Infantry) to his family in Texas (Archives and Information Services Division, Texas State Library and Archives Commission).

23. Daffan, K., *My father as I remember him* (Houston, TX: Gray and Dillaye, 1907), pp. 44–47.

24. Spencer, J., *From Corsicana to Appomattox* (Corsicana, TX: The Corsicana Press, 1984), pp. 44–45.

25. Anonymous, "The Texans at Sharpsburg, By a member of the 4th Texas" in *Confederate Veteran*, Vol. 23 (December, 1914), p. 555.

26. Hamby, W. R., Handbook of Texas Online: tshaonline.org/handbook/online/articles/fha31.

27. Hamby, W. R., "The Tom Green Rifles" in *Confederate Veteran*, Vol. 26 (1918), pp. 20–23.

28. Hamby, W. R., Handbook of Texas Online: tshaonline.org/handbook/online/articles/fha31.

29. Hamby, W., "Hood's Texas Brigade at Sharpsburg" in *Confederate Veteran*, Vol. 16 (January, 1908), pp. 19–22.

## Chapter 3

1. Schmutz, J., *"The Bloody Fifth" The 5th Texas Infantry Regiment, Hood's Texas Brigade, Army of Northern Virginia, Vol. 1: Secession to the Suffolk Campaign* (El Dorado Hills, CA: Savas Beatie, 2016), p. 118.

2. Williams, E. B., *Hood's Texas Brigade in the Civil War* (Jefferson, NC: McFarland and Company, 2012), p. 303.

3. Schmutz, *op. cit.*, p. 182.

4. *Ibid.*, p. 182.

5. Simpson, H., *Hood's Texas Brigade: Lee's Grenadier Guard* (Waco, TX: Texian Press, 1970), p. 178.

6. Simpson, *Hood's Texas Brigade: A Compendium* (Hillsboro, TX: Hill Jr. College Press, 1970), p. 230.

7. *OR*, 19, pt. 1, pp. 936–937.

8. Simpson, *Hood's Texas Brigade: A Compendium*, p. 182.

9. Simpson, H., *Hood's Texas Brigade in Reunion and Memory* (Hillsboro, TX: Hill Jr. College Press, 1977), p. 118.

10. Schmutz, *op cit.*, p. 321.

11. Williams, W. D., to Wilson, L., October 2, 1862, Hood's Texas Brigade files (Texas Heritage Museum–Historical Research Center).

12. Schmutz, *op. cit.*, p. 322.

13. *Ibid.*, p. 317.

14. Simpson, *Hood's Texas Brigade: A Compendium*, p. 92.

15. Stevens, J., *Reminiscences of the Civil War* (Hillsboro, TX: Hillsboro Mirror Print, 1902), p. 188.

16. Schmutz, *op. cit.*, p. 305.

17. Yeary, M., *Reminiscences of the Boys in Gray* (Dallas, TX: Smith and Lamar, 1912), p. 336-337

18. Simpson, *Hood's Texas Brigade: A Compendium*, p. 207.

19. Barnes Campbell, W. L., to Barnes, E. A., September 20, 1862, Wood & Tobert Families Ancestors, collaterals and other associates of William Boyd Wood Jr.

20. Barnes Campbell, W. L., to Barnes, E. A., February 26, 1863, Wood & Tobert Families, Ancestors, collaterals and other associates William Boyd Wood Jr.

21. Simpson, *Hood's Texas Brigade: A Compendium*, p 222.

22. *Ibid.*, p. 232.

23. Schmutz, *op. cit.*, p. 294.

24. Simpson, *Hood's Texas Brigade: A Compendium*, p. 95.

25. Schmutz, *op. cit.*, p. 306.

26. *Ibid.*, p. 300.

27. Felder, R. K., to Felder, C. B., September 23, 1862, Hood's Texas Brigade files (Texas Heritage Museum–Historical Research Center).

28. Felder, R. K., to Felder, E., October 1, 1862, Hood's Texas Brigade files (Texas Heritage Museum–Historical Research Center).

29. Chicoine, S. (ed.), Felder, R. K., (ed.), "Willing to Never go into Another Fight": The Civil War Correspondence of Rufus King Felder of Chappel Hill" in *The Southwestern Historical Quarterly*, Vol. 6, No. 4 (Texas State Historical Association, April, 2003), pp. 582–583.

30. Simpson, *Hood's Texas Brigade: A Compendium*, p. 24.

31. *Ibid.*, p. 209.

32. *Ibid.*, p. 179.

33. Pomeroy, N., *The Memoirs of Nicholas Pomeroy* (Unpublished manuscript, *circa* 1909, Texas Heritage Museum–Historical Research Center).

34. Simpson, *Hood's Texas Brigade: A Compendium*, p. 224.

## Chapter 4

1. Folsom, J., *Heroes and Martyrs of Georgia. Georgia's record in the revolution of 1861* (Macon, GA: Burke, Boykin and Company, 1864), p. 13.

2. Simpson, H., *Hood's Texas Brigade: A Compendium* (Hillsboro, TX: Hill Jr. College Press, 1970), p. 323.

3. *Ibid.*, pp. 323–324.

4. *Richmond Campaign*, June 27, 1862.

5. Krick, R. A., *Lee's Colonels: A Biographical Register of the Field Officers of the Army of Northern Virginia, Third Edition, Revised* (Dayton, OH: Morningside House Inc., 1991), p. 328.

6. OR 19, pt. 1, pp. 929–930.

7. Lemon, M., *Feed Them the Steel! Being, the Wartime Recollections of Capt. James Lile Lemon, Co A, 18th Georgia Infantry, CSA* (Mark Lemon: 2013), pp. 8, 12.

8. Simpson, *op. cit.*, p. 328.

9. Lemon, *op. cit.*, pp. 34–35.

10. *Ibid.*, p. 84

11. *Ibid.*, p. 85.

12. Excerpt is taken from the larger article of the history of the 18th Georgia during the Civil War, titled, "Georgia Heroism, The Battles of the Eighteenth Regiment, 1861–1865."

13. Captain James Lile Lemon, Company A, 18th Georgia Commanding Officer.

14. *Journal House of Representatives* (1862), p. 372.

## Chapter 5

1. Sturkey, O. L., *Hampton Legion Infantry C. S. A.* (Wilmington, NC: Broadfoot Publishing Company, 2008), p. 1.

2. *Ibid.*, p. 5.

3. *Ibid.*, p. 38.
4. *Ibid.*, p. 38.
5. Simpson, H., *Hood's Texas Brigade: A Compendium* (Hillsboro, TX: Hill Jr. College Press, 1970), p. 397.
6. Warmer, E. J., *Generals in Gray: Lives of the Confederate Commanders* (Baton Rouge, LA: Louisiana State University Press, 1959), p. 102.
7. OR 19, pt. 1, pp. 930–931.
8. Excerpt is from Col. Martin's eulogy read by a soldier in Hampton's Legion.
9. Krick, R. A., *Lee's Colonels: A Biographical Register of the Field Officers of the Army of Northern Virginia, Third Edition, Revised* (Dayton, OH: Morningside House Inc., 1991), p. 120.
10. Sturkey, *op. cit.*, pp. 326–327.
11. Priest, J. M., (ed.), *Stephen Elliott Welch of the Hampton Legion* (Shippensburg, PA: Burd Street Press, 1994), p. 1.
12. *Ibid.*, p. 15
13. Simpson, *Hood's Texas Brigade: A Compendium*, p. 448.
14. Priest, *op. cit.*, p. 93.
15. *Ibid.*, pp. 5–11.
16. Sturkey, *op. cit.*, pp. 408–409.
17. Carson, "Hampton's Legion and Hood's Brigade" in *Confederate Veteran* (July, 1908), pp. 342–343.
18. Simpson, *Hood's Texas Brigade: A Compendium*, p. 430.
19. The names of the soldiers of Hampton's Legion is taken from a larger list of soldiers that were buried near Frederick City, Maryland, during the Maryland campaign.
20. The Hampton Legion and the 18th Georgia Infantry Regiment were always considered an integral part of Hood's Texas Brigade. They fought together from the battle of Eltham's Landing to Sharpsburg. After the war, Hood's Texas Brigade would invite them to attend their yearly reunions throughout Texas.

## Chapter 6

1. Warmer, E. J., *Generals in Gray: Lives of the Confederate Commanders* (Baton Rouge, LA: Louisiana State University Press, 1959), p. 143.
2. OR 19, pt. 1. pp. 922–924.
3. Hood, J. B., *Advance and Retreat: Personal Experiences in the United States and Confederate Armies* (New Orleans, LA: Beauregard, 1880), pp. 41–48.
4. Warmer, *op. cit.*, pp. 343–344.
5. OR 19, pt. 1, pp. 927–929.
6. Wright, M., and Simpson, H., *Texas in the War 1861–1865* (Hillsboro, TX: Hill Jr. College Press, 1965), pp. 90–91.
7. Simpson, H., (ed.), *Touched With Valor: Civil War Papers and Casualty Reports of Hood's Texas Brigade, Written and Collected by General Jerome B. Robertson Commander Hood's Texas Brigade* (Hillsboro, TX: Hill Jr. College Press, 1964), pp. 28–30.
8. Warner, *op. cit.*, pp. 174–175.
9. OR Series 1 19, pt. 1, pp. 937–938.
10. Warner, *op cit.*, pp. 183–184.
11. The letter was owned by John Davies of Brooklyn, New York and was sold at an auction the week of November 8, 1908.

Chapter 7

1. Hoopes, J., "The Confederate Memoir of William M. Abernathy" in *Confederate Veteran*, Vol. 2 (2003), pp. 15–16.
2. Yeary, M., *Reminiscences of the Boys in Gray* (Dallas, TX: Smith and Lamar, 1912), pp. 232–234.
3. *Ibid.*, pp. 295–297.
4. *Ibid.*, pp. 305–306.
5. *Ibid.*, pp. 359–360.
6. *Ibid.*, p. 392.
7. *Ibid.*, pp. 415–416.
8. *Ibid.*, pp. 508–509.
9. *Ibid.*, p. 537.
10. *Ibid.*, pp. 538–539.
11. Brown, J. H., (ed.), *Indian Wars and pioneers of Texas* (Austin, TX: Book, 1880), p. 147.
12. *Confederate Veteran Magazine*, Volume IV, November, 1896, p. 389.
13. Yeary, *op. cit.*, p. 652.
14. *Ibid.*, p. 738.
15. Excerpt of the actions of General Hood and the Texas Brigade, taken from an article of the 1st North Carolina Infantry Regiment at Antietam, written by T. D. B.
16. Lewis Publishing Company, *Memorial and Biographical History of Dallas County, Texas* (New York, NY: Lewis Publishing Company, 1892), p. 475.

# Bibliography

Books

*Biographical Encyclopedia of Texas* (New York, NY: Southern Publishing Book Company, 1880)

Brown, J. H., (ed.), *Indian Wars and pioneers of Texas* (Austin, TX: Book, 1880)

*Chaplain Davis and Hood's Texas Brigade* (Baton Rouge, LA: Louisiana State University Press, 1999)

Cherokee County Historical Commission, *Cherokee County History* (Rusk, TX: 2001)

Chilton, F., *Unveiling and dedication of Monument to Hood's Texas Brigade on the Capital Grounds at Austin, Texas, Thursday, October Twenty-Seven, nineteen hundred and ten, and minutes of the thirty-ninth annual reunion of Hood's Texas brigade association held in Senate chamber at Austin, Texas, October twenty six and twenty seven, nineteen hundred and ten, together with a short monument and brigade association history and Confederate scrap book* (Houston, TX: F. B. Chilton, 1911)

Daffan, K., *My father as I remember him* (Houston, TX: Gray and Dillaye, 1907)

Davis, N., *The Campaign From Texas to Maryland With The Battle of Fredericksburg* (Richmond, VA: The Office Of The Presbyterian Committee of Publication of The Confederate States, 1863)

Everett, D. E., (ed.), *Chaplain Davis and Hood's Texas Brigade* (Louisiana State University Press, 1999)

Farber, J., *Texas CSA: A Spotlight on Disaster* (San Antonio, TX: The Jackson Company, 1947)

Folsom, J., *Heroes and Martyrs of Georgia. Georgia's record in the revolution of 1861* (Macon, GA: Burke, Boykin and Company, 1864)

Glover, R., (ed.), *"Tyler To Sharpsburg" The War Letters of Robert H. and William H. Gaston Company H, First Texas Infantry Regiment, Hood's Texas Brigade* (Waco, TX: W. M. Morrison, 1960)

Hamilton, D. H., *History of Company M: First Texas Volunteer Infantry, Hood's Brigade, Longstreet's Corps, Army of Northern Virginia* (Waco, TX: W. M. Morrison, 1962)

Hanks, O. T., *History of Captain B. F. Benton's Company, Hood's Texas Brigade, 1861-1865* (Austin, TX: Morrison Books, 1984)

Hood, J. B., *Advance and Retreat: Personal Experiences in the United States and Confederate Armies* (New Orleans, LA: Beauregard, 1880)

Hooks, H. A., *Lt. Col. Phillip A. Work: General Without a Star* (Waco, TX: Texian Press, 1984)

*Journal House of Representatives of the state of Georgia at the annual session of the state assembly commenced at Milledgeville, November 6, 1862* (Milledgeville, GA: Boughton, Nisbet & Barnes, State Printers, 1862)

Krick, R. A., *Lee's Colonels: A Biographical Register of the Field Officers of the Army of Northern Virginia, Third Edition, Revised* (Dayton, OH: Morningside House Inc., 1991)

Lasswell, M., (ed.), *Rags and Hope, The Recollection of Val C. Giles, Four Years with Hood's Texas Brigade, Fourth Texas Infantry 1861-1865* (New York, NY: Coward McCann Inc., 1961)

Lemon, M., *Feed Them the Steel! Being, the Wartime Recollections of Capt. James Lile Lemon, Co A, 18th Georgia Infantry, CSA* (Mark Lemon: 2013)

Lewis Publishing Company, *Memorial and Biographical History of Dallas County, Texas* (New York, NY: Lewis Publishing Company, 1892)

*Memorial and Biographical History of Navarro, Henderson, Anderson, Limestone, Freestone, and Leon Counties* (Chicago, IL: Lewis, 1893)

Otott, G., "Clash in the Cornfield: The 1st Texas Volunteer Infantry in the Maryland Campaign" *Antietam the Maryland Campaign of 1862* (Campbell, CA: Savas Publishing Company, 1997)

Owen, J., and Drais, R., *Texans at Gettysburg: Blood and Glory with Hood's Texas Brigade* (Charleston, SC: Fonthill Media LLC, 2016)

Palmquist, P., and Kailbourn, T., *Pioneer Photographers From the Mississippi to the Continental Divide: A Biographical Dictionary, 1839-1865* (Stanford, CA: Stanford University Press, 2005)

Polk, J. M., *The North and South American Review* (Austin, TX: J. M. Polk, 1912)

Polley, J. B., *A Soldiers Letters to Charming Nellie* (New York, NY: The Neale Publishing Company, 1908)

Polley, J. B., and McCaslin, R. B., *Hood's Texas Brigade: Its Marches, Its Battles, Its Achievements* (The Neale Publishing Company, 1910)

Priest, J. M., (ed.), *Stephen Elliott Welch of the Hampton Legion* (Shippensburg, PA: Burd Street Press, 1994); *Antietam, The Soldiers' Battle* (New York, NY: Oxford University Press, 1989)

Robertson, J., and Simpson, H., (ed.), *Touched With Valor: Civil War Papers and Casualty Reports of Hood's Texas Brigade, Written and Collected by General Jerome B. Robertson Commander Hood's Texas Brigade* (Hillsboro, TX: Hill Jr. College Press, 1964)

Schmutz, J., *"The Bloody Fifth" The 5th Texas Infantry Regiment, Hood's Texas Brigade, Army of Northern Virginia, Vol. 1: Secession to the Suffolk Campaign* (El Dorado Hills, CA: Savas Beatie, 2016)

Simpson, H., *Gaines' Mill to Appomattox, Waco & McLennan County In Hood's Texas Brigade* (Waco, TX: Texian Press, 1963); *Hood's Texas Brigade: A Compendium* (Hillsboro, TX: Hill Jr. College Press, 1970); *Hood's Texas Brigade: Lee's Grenadier Guard* (Waco, TX: Texian Press, 1970); *The Marshall Guards: Harrison County's Contribution to Hood's Texas Brigade* (Marshall, TX: Port Caddo Press, 1967); *Hood's Texas Brigade in Reunion and Memory* (Hillsboro, TX: Hill Jr. College Press, 1977); (ed.), *Touched With Valor: Civil War Papers and Casualty Reports of Hood's Texas Brigade, Written and Collected by General Jerome B. Robertson Commander Hood's Texas Brigade* (Hillsboro, TX: Hill Jr. College Press, 1964)

Spencer, J., *From Corsicana to Appomattox* (Corsicana, TX: The Corsicana Press, 1984)

Stevens, J., *Reminiscences of the Civil War* (Hillsboro, TX: Hillsboro Mirror Print, 1902)

Sturkey, O. L., *Hampton Legion Infantry C. S. A.* (Wilmington, NC: Broadfoot Publishing Company, 2008)

*The New Texas Handbook* (Austin, TX: Texas State Historical Association, 1996)

Thrall, H., *History of Methodism in Texas* (Houston, TX: E. H. Cushing, 1872)

Todd, G., *First Texas Regiment* (Waco, TX: Texian Press, 1964)

Warmer, E. J., *Generals in Gray: Lives of the Confederate Commanders* (Baton Rouge, LA: Louisiana State University Press, 1959)

Williams, E. B., *Hood's Texas Brigade in the Civil War* (Jefferson, NC: McFarland and Company, 2012)

Wright, M., and Simpson, H., *Texas in the War 1861–1865* (Hillsboro, TX: Hill Jr. College Press, 1965)

Yeary, M., *Reminiscences of the Boys in Gray* (Dallas, TX: Smith and Lamar, 1912)


## Websites

Carter, B. F., Handbook of Texas Online: www.tshaonline.org/handbook/online/articles/fbe52; www.tshaonline.org/handbook/online/articles/fcafe

Cutrer, T., Stephen Heard Darden, Handbook of Texas Online

Davis, N. A., The Handbook of Texas: tshaonline.org/handbook/online/articles/fda46

en.wikipedia.org/wiki/Casualties_of_the_September_11_attacks

Fourth Texas Infantry, Handbook of Texas Online: tshaonline.org/handbook/online/articles/qkf0

Gaston, William, Henry, Handbook of Texas Online: www.tshaonline.org/handbook/online/articles/fga63

Gillihan, B., John C. Robinson, Find a Grave: www.findagrave.com/cgi-bin/fg.cgi?page=gr&GRid=9723810

Hamby, W. R., Handbook of Texas Online: tshaonline.org/handbook/online/articles/fha31

Hathcock, J., First Texas Infantry, Handbook of Texas Online: www.tshaonline.org/handbook/online/articles/qkf13

history.stackexchange.com/questions/25/how-many-troops-died-on-d-day

John Bell Hood, Handbook of Texas Online: tshaonline.org/handbook/online/articles/fho49

Martin, M., Benton, Benjamin Franklin, Handbook of Texas Online: www.tshaonline.org/handbook/online/articles/fbe52

Miller, A. S., Benjamin F. Carter, Handbook of Texas Online: www.tshaonline.org/handbook/online/articles/fcafe

Reagan, C. K., Work, Philip Alexander, Handbook of Texas Online: www.tshaonline.org/handbook/online/articles/fwo25

Smith, W., Malachiah Reeves, Find a Grave: findagrave.com

Stiles Gen, A Family History Website: www.stilesgen.com/getperson.php?personID=I11793&tree=SG2012 (accessed July 28, 2016)


## Newspapers, Articles, and Magazines

"Sheriffs of Navarro County" in *Navarro County Scroll*, Vol. XXI (Corsicana, TX: Navarro County Historical Society, 1976)

*Alto (TX) Cherokeean Herald*

*Alto (TX) Herald*

*Anderson (SC) The Intelligencer*

Anonymous, "The Texans at Sharpsburg, By a member of the 4th Texas" in *Confederate Veteran*, Vol. 23 (December, 1914)

*Armies, 128 vols.* (Washington, D.C., 1880–1901)

*Atlanta (GA) Constitution*

*Augusta (GA) Chronicle*

*Bellville (TX) Countryman*

*Boston (MA) Globe*

*Brotherhood of Locomotive Firemen and Engineer's Magazine,* Vols. 46–47 (Knoxville, TN: University of Tennessee Press, 1909)

*Brownsville (TX) Daily Herald*

Carson, "Hampton's Legion and Hood's Brigade" in *Confederate Veteran* (July, 1908)

Chicoine, S., (ed.), and Felder, R. K., "Willing Never to go in Another Fight": The Civil War Correspondence of Rufus King Felder of Chappel Hill" in *The Southwestern Historical Quarterly,* Vol. 6, No. 4 (Texas State Historical Association, April 2003)

*Colorado (TX) Citizen*

*Columbia (SC) Daily Phoenix*

*Dallas (TX) Morning News*

*Edgefield (SC) Advertiser*

*El Paso (TX) Herald*

*Fairmont (IN) News*

Felder, C. (ed.), "Willing to Never go into Another Fight": The Civil War Correspondence of Rufus King Felder of Chappel Hill" in *The Southwestern Historical Quarterly,* Vol. 6, No. 4 (Texas State Historical Association, April, 2003)

*Fort Worth (TX) Daily Gazette*

*Fort Worth (TX) Morning Register*

*Gaffney (SC) Cherokee Times*

*Galveston (TX) Daily News*

*Galveston (TX) Texas Almanac*

Giles, V., "The Flag of First Texas, A. N. Virginia" in *Confederate Veteran,* Vol. 15 (September, 1907)

Graham, L., (ed.), "Anderson County In The Civil War, Anderson County Genealogical

*Hagerstown (MD) Morning Herald*

Hamby, W., "Hood's Texas Brigade at Sharpsburg" in *Confederate Veteran,* Vol. 16 (January, 1908); "The Tom Green Rifles" in *Confederate Veteran,* Vol. 26 (1918)

*Harlingen (TX) Valley Morning Star*

Hoopes, J., "The Confederate Memoir of William M. Abernathy" in *Confederate Veteran,* Vol. 2 (2003)

*Houston (TX) Weekly Telegraph*

*Houston, (TX) Tri-Weekly Telegraph*

*Jasper (TX) Weekly Newsboy*

*Livingston (TX) Polk County Enterprise*

*Logansport (IN) Pharos-Tribune*

*Manning (SC) Times*

*Marietta (GA) Journal*

*Morrisville (VT) News and Citizen*

*Murfreesboro (NC) Index*

*New York (NY) Times*

*North Platte (NE) Semi-Weekly Tribune*

*Richmond (VA) Campaign*

*Richmond (VA) Times Dispatch*

*Rusk (TX) Cherokeean*

*San Antonio (TX) Daily Express*

Smith, F., "Heroes and Heroines of Virginia" in *Confederate Veteran,* Vol. 2 (September, 1894)

Society", *The Tracings*, Vol. 5, No. 1 (Winter, 1986)

*Temple (TX) Daily Telegram*

*The War of the Rebellion: A Compilation of the Official Records of the Union and Confederate*

*Waco (TX) Evening News*

*Washington (D. C.) National Tribune*

*West (TX) Weekly News and Times*

Winkler, C. M., to Loughridge, J. R., November 18, 1862, Hood's Texas Brigade files, (Texas Heritage Museum–Historical Research Center)

Winkler, C. M., to Winkler, M. C., *The Navarro County Scroll* (1959, reprinted with permission of the Navarro County Historical Society)

## Letters and Manuscripts

Allport, J., *The Story of Captain Sam Willson, Company F, Woodville Rifles 1st Texas Regiment Confederate States Army* (personal papers, 2001)

Barnes Campbell, W. L., to Barnes, E. A., February 26, 1863, Wood & Tobert Families, Ancestors, collaterals and other associates William Boyd Wood Jr.

Barnes Campbell, W. L., to Barnes, E. A., September 20, 1862, Wood & Tobert Families Ancestors, collaterals and other associates of William Boyd Wood Jr.

Berryman, H. W., to Berryman, M., September 22, 1862, Hood's Texas Brigade Letters (Texas Heritage Museum–Historical Research Center)

Eads, L. R., (ed.), *Malachiah Reeves—Memoirs of the mercies of a covenant God, while traveling through the Wilderness of this world of life: being the autobiography of Malachiah Reeves, originally of many places, from middle Alabama and through much of East Texas, and now of Ranger, middle West Texas* (Hillsboro, TX: Unpublished manuscript, *circa* 1910, Texas Heritage Museum–Historical Research Center)

Felder, R. K., to Felder, C. B., September 23, 1862, Hood's Texas Brigade files (Texas Heritage Museum–Historical Research Center)

Felder, R. K., to Felder, E., October 1, 1862, Hood's Texas Brigade files (Texas Heritage Museum–Historical Research Center)

King, R. S., to Felder, E., October 1, 1862, Hood's Texas Brigade files (Texas Heritage Museum–Historical Research Center)

Murray, J. C., to parents and sister (September 22–October 11, 1862) (2-23/882), Original letters written by James C. Murray, a member of Hood's Texas Brigade (4th Texas Infantry) to his family in Texas (Archives and Information Services Division, Texas State Library and Archives Commission)

Pomeroy, N., *The Memoirs of Nicholas Pomeroy* (Unpublished manuscript, *circa* 1909, Texas Heritage Museum–Historical Research Center)

Ross, M., to Wilson, I. R., December 20, 1920, Wilson Family Papers, Personal Collection of Wilson Family

Williams, W. D., to Wilson, L., October 2, 1862, Hood's Texas Brigade files (Texas Heritage Museum–Historical Research Center)

Wood, C., *1842–1914: A Memoir Recollections of his Life, Family History and Military Service* (Atlanta, Georgia: Emory University Library Archives, 1907–1908)

# Index